Accession

Where in the World Have I Been?

By

Paul A. Hays

To Jack + Linda Bissinger,
Our great neighbors.
Paul + Margaret Hays
15 Aug 06

ISBN 0-7414-3476-8

Published by:

INFINITY
PUBLISHING.COM

1094 New Dehaven Street, Suite 100
West Conshohocken, PA 19428-2713
Info@buybooksontheweb.com
www.buybooksontheweb.com
Toll-free (877) BUY BOOK
Local Phone (610) 941-9999
Fax (610) 941-9959

Printed in the United States of America
Printed on Recycled Paper
Published July 2006

Preface

"Chen Chu Pei, Calcutta, India, Jan 14, 1946, on the way to the States," was hand printed on the first free endpaper of *Maxim Litvinoff*, DK268.L5P61943a. What is this book doing in the Salmon Library, The University of Alabama in Huntsville, and how did it get there? This is just one of many intriguing questions about books in the Salmon Library for which I will *not* provide answers, but allow you to imagine your own answers.

Books have great longevity in our dynamic world. The greatest books, whether measured by content or age, are infrequent travelers because they are mostly priceless. They reside in ancient monasteries and very old libraries. Occasionally those books come to auction at extremely high prices and winning bidders tend to keep those books in their safekeeping for a long time. Those long times might be measured by a generation, but more likely multiple generations because the buyers were institutions with past or future longevity of centuries.

Public libraries are driven by keeping books that the general public wants to read, and not necessarily for research purposes. Public libraries maintain aggressive discard procedures to keep within their physical limits and circulation demands. The number of potential books to be accessed in the current era is significant, as there are approximately 160,000 new titles in the United States each year. Public libraries use friends-of-the-library bookstores as the principal method of cycling books out of the library to obtain some financial return that can be used to purchase new materials.

University libraries generally keep all of their accessions because the university is rated by the number of volumes in its library, which is matter of accreditation and bragging rights in writing about the virtues of each university. The students have access to loads of material from which to research their papers.

The development of the Academy for Lifetime Learning at The University of Alabama in Huntsville (UAH) in 1993 provided an opportunity to learn by presenting and moderating courses at the Academy. The organization, led by Jean Foster Herron, encouraged its members to be all they can be, to borrow the phrase from the U.S. Army of some years ago. One of the benefits of the Academy is the right to use and check out books from the UAH library. In a continuous search for new material, I developed and presented 24 hours about various aspects of books. I also wrote *Harem of Books*, which is primarily about the books in my library, but includes several books in the Salmon Library at UAH, including Special Collections.

The above knowledge led me to this effort. My thanks to Gary Glover, Document Delivery Coordinator, whose office is in the basement of the Salmon Library, for telling me the story about the accession initiative by Dr. Delmus Williams, Dean of the Library, which started me on this project.

The University started modestly in 1950 as The University of Alabama's Huntsville Center. Redstone Arsenal started graduate studies in 1951. Gradually the Army and the university increased cooperation in science and engineering to support the growing rocket, missile, and space programs. Other normal college programs, such as education, were also increasing. All programs continued to increase and finally in 1966 the Huntsville campus received recognition as a branch of the University of Alabama and became officially known as The University of Alabama in Huntsville. An adequate library was a lagging facility as the classroom activities grew. The library did not have a separate building until 1969. The previous discussion is necessary to understand that the library was surviving on hand-me-downs from the mother school in Tuscaloosa and had to struggle to increase volumes to keep up with the growing student population.

Dr. Williams, during his tenure as library dean from 1985 to 1991, took the bull by the horns and aggressively pursued the gathering of books for the library from multiple sources on a negligible budget. He personally went to the Library of Congress (LC) under its Gift and Exchange Office whereby an accredited institutional representative could select individual titles from a collection that had been culled or not added to federal libraries in a region. There were two basic categories of shelves, one that required bids and another that could be had for free. He collected many books and utilized Alabama congressmen's franking privileges to ship the boxes to Huntsville. The many military base and unit books also came from the Library of Congress collection. He remembers one especially good cache when the Department of State closed a reading room.

Dr. Williams also aggressively sought books being discarded by libraries where he had contacts. There were many volumes from Mississippi State University (MSU), of which I only cited one or two. MSU used to send out a circular of books it wanted to dispose of. He drove a university station wagon to MSU and other Alabama, Georgia and Mississippi universities and loaded up as much as it would hold. He used other sources and techniques to obtain books at the least possible cost to the university. Dr. Williams estimated that he increased the approximate 180,000 volumes by 35-40% during his tenure at an average cost of $0-2.00 per book, a bargain by any standards.

The volumes gathered by Dr. Williams became the principal targets of my research to find where the books had been by their bookplates, stamps and inscriptions. I had no clue to what I might find.

My methodology was to systematically screen the bookshelves for books that might provide information on their travels before they ended up on the shelves of the Salmon Library at UAH. I started with the beginning of the Library of Congress alpha-numeric cataloguing system and organized the material with the catalog number at the beginning of each description. Each shelf was scanned for candidate books using several visual criteria. The spine was the easiest, as I looked for age of the cover in terms of wear and readability of the title. The second item was the degree of wear or destruction of the top of the spine where the index finger is placed to pull and rotate the book from its shelf. I pulled the books above eye level for inspection if I could not see the tops of the pages. An additional judgment was made if I could see the tops of the pages. I looked for yellowed or dirty paper on the tops, as well as a blacked-out previous-ownership stamp on the top of the leaves.

With the book leaning on my right hand, I left-thumbed open the front cover where 90 percent of the desired information was available. A library stamp is frequently on the front cover verso. Sometimes it might be on the first free endpaper, but that leaf is easily removed. Much of the previous ownership data I was hunting for was blacked out. The thoroughness of the UAH accession personnel made it difficult to look through the blacked-out, previous owner's stamp. It appears that sometimes the entire first free endpaper was sliced off. Regardless of whether I found a gem or not, the book leaned into my left hand and the right thumb sprang into action. The inside of the back cover was seldom productive because the UAH accession personnel placed a sign-out card pocket, which would cover any previous-owner information. The book was then leaned to the right again so the left thumb and left index finger could search for the title page. The title page sometimes had new information, so I always hoped there was something new or perhaps a sloppy job of blacking out the previous owner's stamp. Occasionally there was previous owner stamp on the top or bottom of the compressed pages, but the blackening needed to be only slight to destroy the ability to read the words. The sign-out pocket frequently carried the stamp, "Huntsville Campus Library" and the circle of the University of Alabama, 1831, which indicated an accession early in the life of UAH. This information was not helpful as I was only seeking ownership that fit the criteria cited above about gathering volumes from whatever source.

When I started this project I did not realize the extent to which the UAH library accession censors were determined to destroy the provenance of the books. They completed their mission successfully, for the most part. They left very few scraps of information for my purposes. The censors' mission was the age-old practice by invading tribes, nations and other groups for millennia. Books, art works, and other cultural symbols were destroyed or eradicated to wipe out the old culture and establish the supremacy of the new regime. I was faced with a daunting archeological task of trying to uncover what was buried. Unfortunately, the censors buried the information under a nasty black mark, which could not be removed. I stood on a chair to get closer to the ceiling lights to try to emulate Superman's x-ray vision to discern hidden treasures. The book was twisted every imaginable angle to try to see through the black marking to the underlying stamped letters. Some success was achieved, and sometimes at least a minute of effort led to miserable failure. I tried a flashlight and magnifying glass to penetrate the blackness, but that produced no more success that standing on the chair. I wonder if there is a handheld spectroscope that could do the job such as I see on forensic television programs. After a dozen or so research trips to the library, my efforts took on a more personalized determination to capture what I wanted and defeat the censors' efforts as much as possible. How dare they deface those wonderful and creative bookplates designed by proud readers and owners! You will see many of them, because they deserve to be documented, even if partially disfigured.

I arbitrarily placed the blame on the UAH censors. Perhaps previous library owners exercised censorship before the book left their possession. Susan McCreless, Head, Technical Services, with over twenty years service in the UAH library, suggested that the black-outs were to avoid confusion as to the real owner if the book was loaned to another library. I reviewed the approximately 320 bookplate figures in this book. I categorized the applicable ones, not considering inscriptions, into four groups: institutional – defaced (48); institutional – not defaced (64); individual – defaced (54); and individual – not defaced (104). Individual – defaced outnumbered the institutional – defaced. The individual – defaced books must have had another reason for the havoc placed upon those wonderful bookplates. There does not appear to be any logic about what was or was not defaced. There is one caveat to the above numbers. I eye-balled nearly every book, however quickly. I documented slightly over 1,000 entries in this effort, but probably opened the cover of at least 10,000 books. The 320 bookplates, stamps and inscriptions do not count the blacked-out items that I was unable to discern the underneath bookplates and stamps. As an aside, there are 19 bookplates with sailing ships, but I am unable to explain the popularity of ships with books.

There were many books rebound with new covers. The binderies, therefore, had removed covers that may have yielded more entries for my research effort. I also believe that many first free endpapers were removed in the process so even more evidence was lost to posterity. Such a shame.

At any rate, not all was lost. I received some leg exercise going up and down the chair, as well as standing on the little, round, spring-loaded, circular stool to reach the top shelf of books. I used a cloth-covered, sponge rubber pad to mitigate the hard rubber ridges of the circular stool. I worked in stocking feet since I spent much time standing on the padded stool. I changed my movements to create the most efficient time-motion procedures. I used a 1 x 2 foot board as a lap desk as I sat in the chair to write my findings. Soon I put the board on the arms of the chair and sat on the padded stool to write. The board had bubble-wrap on the underside to protect the furniture. The chair, writing board and stool moved in unison in front of each stack column.

The material is organized by the Library of Congress alpha-numeric cataloguing system. Each item contains the catalog designation, book title, author, publisher, city of publication and date published. Two slash marks delineate the start of the descriptions of the various marks that identify previous ownership.

The Library of Congress's cataloguing system will be briefly explained so the reader can better appreciate the alpha-numeric system. The Library was established in 1800 with 740 volumes. Most of the books were burned by the British when they burned parts of Washington, D.C. in 1814 during the War of 1812. Thomas Jefferson offered his personal library to restart the Library of Congress. Eventually his 6,487 volumes were purchased for $23,950. Jefferson also established a classification system of 44 categories based on an earlier system by Francis Bacon of England a century and a half earlier. Jefferson's system became the basis for the current Library of Congress system.

The publisher assigns the catalog number when it processes the book. My first book was self-published and I contracted with a company which prepared the cataloging-in-publication data, to include key search words and the call number. My call number is not in the Library of Congress data base because I did not send the data to it. The Library of Congress publishes every year thick volumes which identify books by ISBN and author and provide the catalog number to libraries so they can properly label their holdings.

It takes 32 pages to provide the subjects associated with the alpha of 1, 2 or 3 letters which form the first part of the classification and up to 4 numbers which follow the letters to further breakdown subjects. That part of the alpha-numeric designation ends with a period.

The alpha-numeric characters which follow the period are called "cutters" and provide more details about the subject and author so each of the millions of books have different catalog numbers. If there is one set of alpha-numeric cutters, it refers to the author's last name. The letter identifies the first letter of the author's last name. The numbers following help identify more letters of the author's last name according to a published code. There are different codes which apply, depending whether the author's last name begins with a consonant or a vowel.

If there are two sets of cutters, the author's are the second set. The first set is a further amplification of the subject matter as a continuation of the first alpha-numeric categorization before the period. As the old saying goes, "Do not try this at home, leave it for the professionals."

There was considerable duplication of book sources, so the decision was made to include only one book per source, with some exceptions. Sometimes there were other markings in the book that were deserving of visibility. Sometimes I forgot that the source was already identified and I did not want to throw away my recording effort. There was no attempt to quantify the number of items from a single source. The majority of the bookplates are shown at original size. Some of the smallest were enlarged enough to write the figure identification below in one line. Many inscriptions and some bookplates were reduced so they did not totally dominate the adjacent words.

The majority of the explanatory details were obtained via Google.com from a variety of other secondary sources and it became an unnecessary burden to document them for this effort. I tried to add enough information to provide the reader with an understanding of the location of the previous owners, and in some cases expanded on military abbreviations. Although tempted at times, I tried to refrain from making inferences about the books' travels to the Salmon Library. Each book has its individual story, unknown to this author, so the reader is encouraged to use his/her imagination to make up a possible story to your own satisfaction.

I credit the accession staff over the years with developing complete sets of volumes on a subject when a volume was missing by mixing and matching a volume from a second source. This was easily identified by the different covers, bindings and ages of the added volumes.

This project was officially started on 17 August 2005. I maintained a log of the dates and times spent inside the library building, the number of items recorded each visit and the last item of that day's search. The research was finished on 31 May 2006. I made 70 trips to the library and spent 166 hours and 45 minutes on the job in the stacks. I wish I had known that before I started, but then that would have taken away the challenge and fun of browsing through so many books, which I understand is about 400,000. My real enjoyment came from the handling of so many books, opening them to discover the bookplates, inscriptions, other markings and the publication dates, particularly in old and rare books. Another benefit was to discover books on subjects that I would not have guessed were in the UAH library, such as the Nürnberg Trials and the Pearl Harbor Investigation. My time in retirement is largely spent researching books in order to present courses at the Academy at UAH or to write books on subjects of interest. During my search I discovered pockets of books that will support possible future efforts, such as universities, writing history, religion and The South. I am now set up to go in several directions, the only problem is to make a decision on which path to commit myself.

I wish to acknowledge the assistance and helpfulness of the Salmon Library staff, especially Gary Glover for planting the seed of this effort, Anne Coleman for guiding me through the library organization, and Susan McCreless for her efforts to help me partially understand the Library of Congress cataloguing system and for explaining the Salmon Library accession process.

My special thanks to Dr. Delmus Williams, who provided the material for this book through his persistent efforts to improve the UAH library by increasing the number of volumes, and the insights into his efforts to achieve significant results for the library's enhancement.

This book is dedicated to Margaret, my wife and soul mate, who was my constant mentor and support for Adobe Photoshop graphics and other computer issues.

Globalization of economics is now a favorite characterization of our world today. Western civilization was expanded by world exploration in the late 15th and early 16th centuries. Books followed the Western European nations as they sought riches, religious converts or trade. The development of the American empire starting with the Spanish-American War in 1898 accelerated the globalization of many facets of life. Globalization is not new as many people would like to believe, particularly those folks who see it in a negative manner. As you read this book, let your imagination wander through the global movement of books as a critical element in diffusing knowledge and culture throughout the world community.

Let the geography lesson begin.

AC5, B54, *Some of My Very Best*, Jim Bishop, All Saints Press, NY, 1960 // Dedication page stamp, "Bolling Air Force Base Library, Wash. D.C." Bolling Air Force Base is on the east side of the Potomac River directly across from Ronald Reagan Washington National Airport. It was a primary airport in the propeller-driven aircraft days for Washington very-important-persons (VIPs) to fly out of the city in Air Force aircraft. That role has long been moved to Andrews Air Force Base about seven miles further to the southeast from Bolling, but Bolling still provides the housing for top Air Force officials.

Figure AC 8.B73

AC8.B73, *University and Historical Addresses*, James Bryce, Macmillan, NY, 1913 // Front cover verso and first free endpaper stamps, "Mount Saint Mary's College, Sisters of St. Joseph." Back cover recto bookplate, "The Charles Willard Coe Memorial Library Fund, Mount Saint Mary's College, Los Angeles, California." Figure AC8.B73.

AC8.B732, *Execution Eve*, William F. Buckley, Jr., Putnam's, NY, 1972 // Front cover verso stamp, "Gunter Base Library, Gunter Air Force Base, Alabama, USAF."

AC8.D54, *A Budget of Paradoxes*, Augustus De Morgan, Dover, NY, 1954 // Bookplate, "Library of Willy Ley." Willy Ley was probably the most effective writer to popularize space flight. He was born in Berlin, Germany on 2 October 1906 and died 24 May 1969 in Queens, New York. Ley studied astronomy, physics, zoology and paleontology at the University of Berlin. He was fluent in German, English, Italian, French and Russian. Ley received his degree in journalism at the University of Koenigsberg, Germany. He was a founding member of the German Society for Spaceship Travel (VfR) in 1927. Ley published several books promoting manned space travel and edited the journal of the VfR, *Die Rakete*. He left Germany for the United States in 1935 as he did not like the Nazi regime and the government had taken over all rocket development projects for military applications. He continued to write articles about space in the United States, but discovered that most Americans believed it was all science fiction. Ley became an American citizen in 1944. Ley continued to be the most prolific writer about space and a variety of other subjects. He died just weeks before the first moon landing. Most of his extensive personal library is housed in the Archives Special Collections Section of the Salmon Library, although many books from his library are in the open shelves.

AC8.G98, *The League of Nations*, William D. Guthrie, Columbia University Press, NY, 1923 // "Mount St. Mary' College, Los Angeles California" (back cover bookplate) $3.50, 95 cents.

AC8.H7317, *Before the Sabbath*, Eric Hoffer, Harper & Row, NY, 1979 // Front cover verso stamp, "Foreign Service Institute Library, Department of State."

AC8.R68, *A Pride of Prejudices*, Vermont Royster, Alfred A. Knopf, NY, 1967 // "Surplus Duplicate, Library of Congress" stamped on first free endpaper. The Library of Congress executes the copyright law in the United States. Authors send two copies of their work to the Library of Congress and about six months later a certificate is returned to the author. The LOC does not keep copies of the over 160,000 books published every year. It throws them away or otherwise disposes of them with the stamp cited above. Further information is available at www.loc.gov.

AC8.W3, *Glimpses of the Cosmos*, Lester F. Ward, 6 volumes, Putnam's Sons, NY, 1913 // First free endpaper stamp, "From the Library of Morris Gilmore Caldwell" Caldwell, 1893-1972, was a sociologist and I found many of his stamped books during my search.

AG5.S84, *A Book About a Thousand Things*, George Simpson, Harper, NY, 1946 // First free endpaper stamp, "C.G. Mourraille"; Front cover verso UAH bookplate "From the Library of Willy Ley"; in pencil "WS 50 cents".

AG27.D15, *DBG-Handlexicon*, Deutsch Buch-Gemeinschaft, 1964 // Second free endpaper verso, "Gift of Goethe Institute, Atlanta, Georgia for Hertha Heller Retirement Fund."

AG243.B3, *Curiosities of Olden Times*, S. Baring-Gould, John Grant, Edinburgh, 32 George IV Bridge, 1896 // UAH bookplate "From the Library of Willy Ley"; small plate on bottom right of front cover verso "Floeser & Co. Brooklyn Book Store' top of pages roughly cut through p.176, pgs. 177-196 uncut at top (8-page groups). In the era of 100 years ago the publishers cheaply bound their books and did not cut the three outer edges as they bound the spine. Other printers would cut the edges and bind them with more expensive material such as morocco, a handsome, hard-wearing leather made of goat-skin, thereby increasing the price of the book for the upper class folks who could afford it and wanted prestigious items sitting on their book shelves.

Figure AG243.M3

AG243.M3, *Hoaxes*, Curtis D. MacDougall, Macmillan, NY, 1941 // Bookplate on front cover verso, "Ex Libris Willy Ley." Figure AG243.M3.

AG243.S84, *Strange Stories, Amazing Facts*, Readers Digest, 1976 // Embossed stamp on title page "Western Illinois Library System, Monmouth, Illinois". The Western Illinois Library was one of twenty-one regional library systems across the state. Several of them, including Western, combined into Alliance Library System. Monmouth, Illinois is also the birthplace of the legendary sheriff, Wyatt Earp. As I investigated more books, I found many items from this source, the Western Illinois Library System, and so stopped citing them. I noticed that books from this system always had a ½ x 2-inch sticker about three inches from the top of the first free endpaper. It would have 8-12 digits on it, usually well blacked out by the UAH accession censor. This was a solid clue that on the title page, on the right side and midway vertically, there would be the embossed stamp as identified above. The routine by the accession personnel at both Illinois and UAH never failed, so I stopped pursuing those books immediately upon sighting that blacked out sticker on the endpaper. Dr. Williams came to UAH from Western Illinois University where he was familiar with the Illinois public libraries' rotating system and that had collected many volumes that they wished to dispose of. He was a willing recipient, paying only the postage.

AM7.R5, *The Sacred Grove*, Dillon Ripley, Simon & Schuster, NY, 1969 // Back cover recto stamp, "Surplus Duplicate, Library of Congress;" page 69 stamped in red, "U.S. Atomic Energy Commission, AEC Library, Washington, D.C. 20545."

AM101.K5192R36, *A History of the Kaffrarian Museum*, Brian Raudles, The Kaffrarian Museum, King William's Town, South Africa Lovedale Press, Ciskei, South Africa, 1984 // Title page verso stamp, "Library of Congress, August 6, 1986, Exchange & Gift Division." The Library of Congress accepts books printed in other countries, as those countries do with ours. The Library of Congress website, www.loc.org, contains a list of countries.

AM101.K756, *Kristiansund Museum*, 6 Copy, 9512M, 25 Jy 66, O.H. Voleknar, 1894-1904-1964 // Apparently in Norwegian language.

AM305.L36, *The Passionate Collector*, Ellen Land-Weber, Simon & Schuster, NY, 1980 // Title page stamp, "Illinois Valley Library System Rotating Collection, Galesburg, Illinois." This is another one of the multiple regional library systems in Illinois. See AG243.S84.

AO31.M3945, *Making News*, Martin Mayer, Doubleday, NY, 1987 // Title page verso stamp, "Library of Congress, Copyright Office, April 27, 1987."

AP2.44.B63A3, *The Americanization of Edward Bok, An Autobiography*, Schribner's Sons, NY, 1920 // Front cover verso stamp, "Gift of the People of the United States Through the Victory Book Campaign (A.L.A.,-A.R.C.-U.S.O.) To the Armed Forces and Merchant Marine, Enlisted Men's Service Club, Library No. 2, Fort McClellan, Alabama." ALA = American Library Association, ARC = American Red Cross and USO = United Services Organization.

AP2.44H4W5, *W.R. Hearst, An American Phenomenon*, John K. Winkler, Simon & Schuster, NY, 1928 // "Library U.S. Army War College", on defaced bookplate on front cover verso and punched holes in title page; "E. Steiger, $3.72" (in pencil). The U.S. Army War College is in Carlisle, Pennsylvania.

AP2.44M365, *The Best of McDermott*, William F. McDermott, World Publishing Co., Cleveland, Ohio, 1959 // First free endpaper stamp, "Property USAF, Bolling Base Library, Bolling Air Force Base, 25 D.C.;" also Library of Congress stamp.

AP2.44.M47A3, *Forty Years in News-Paperdom*, Milton A. McRae, Bretano's Publishers, NY, 1924 // Front cover verso stamp, "Presented to Library, National War College" (bookplate with crest), From the Library of Frederk William Wile 1941; Title page has holes punched "Library Army War College"; also "Library of Congress Duplicate."

AP2.44S43A3, *Not So Wild a Dream*, Eric Severeid, A.A. Knopf, NY, 1946 // Bookplate on cover verso, "Library of the University of Illinois" with three stone arches on top of the words.

AP2.69.N32S88, *Afternoon Story*, John Wilds, Louisiana University Press, Baton Rouge, LA, 1976 // Back cover recto bookplate, "Louisiana State University at Alexandria Library" and "Gift" stamped.

AP2.69P58O73, *Making the Day Begin*, Robert C. Notson, Oregonian Publishing Co., 1976 // UAH bookplate on front cover verso, "From the Library of Leroy Alanson Simms." Notson's book was the story of his 50 years with *The Oregonian*, Portland, Oregon. Simms was a lifelong journalist, so it makes sense that he had some books about journalism. Simms was the Alabama correspondent for The Associated Press during the period 1933-58 and was the publisher of *The Huntsville Times* from 1964 until 1985. He was also president of *The Huntsville News* 1968-85. He donated his collection of almost 1,000 books on the Civil War to the library at The University of Alabama in Huntsville.

AP3.G6F5, *The Lady of Godey's*, Ruth E. Finley, J.B. Lippencott Co., Philadelphia & London, 1931 // Title page stamp, "Carroll College Library, Helena, Montana, Discarded from Carroll College Library."

AP3.23.S8A33, *The River of Life*, John St. Joe Strachey, G.P. Putnam's Sons, NY, 1924 // Front cover verso and first free endpaper stamps, "Compliments of Conrad Library, Bernard(?) Baruch Institute of New York, 25 South Street"; "$1.50" in pencil.

AP63.15B83P55, *Defense of Freedom*, by the Editors of LaPrensa, The John Day Co., NY, 1952 // Title page stamp, "Salvaged from Library Acct. LI 24.2, Library, The Armored School, Fort Knox, Kentucky, Property of U.S. Army." Military libraries tend to have the most multiple marking in their books. "Salvaged from Library Acct. LI 24.2" was frequently stamped in large letters in a 1 x 3inch rectangle diagonally across the page on many of the accessions from the Fort Knox, Kentucky library.

AZ108.H44, *Signs and Symbols Around the World*, Elizabeth S. Helfman, Lothrop, Lee & Shepard Co. NY, 1967 // First free endpaper stamp, "Naval Station Library 6 _? _? _ ? FPO 90630 San Francisco, California."

AZ341.H3, *The Christian Scholar in the Age of the Reformation*, Elmore Harris Harbison, Charles Scribner's Sons, NY, 1956 // Cursive on front cover verso, "Milton Otto Winkler, 677 So. Gerhart Avenue, Los Angeles 22, California" // Stamped on first free endpaper "John G. Binkley."

AZ361.B48, *A Defence of Free Learning*, Lord Beveridge, Oxford University Press, London, 1959 // Front cover verso and first free endpaper stamp, "Library, US Armor School, Property of US Army."

AZ361.D38 1970, *The One Culture*, William Henry Davenport, Pergamon Press, Elmsford, NY, 1970 // "Surplus Library of Congress" // First free endpaper stamp, "AFSC HQ Library US Air Force" The Headquarters, Air Force Systems Command is at Wright-Patterson Air Force Base, Dayton, Ohio.

AZ999.E8, *The Natural History of Nonsense*, Bergen Evans, Alfred A. Knopf, NY, 1946 // Bookplate on front cover verso, "Ex Libris, Dorothy and Harry Andersen", with a tall "torch of learning" on the left side and handwritten on upper left corner of front cover verso "Xmas '46" // first free endpaper "$2.50."

AZ999.E82, *The Spoor of Spooks*, Bergan Evans, Alfred A. Knopf, NY, 1954 // Front cover verso, "UAH bookplate From the Library of Willy Ley."

B72.C62v.1, *History of Philosophy*, Frederick Copleston, S.J., The Newman Press, Westminister, Maryland, 1950 // Front cover verso bookplate, "Ex Libris, Jean Michel Perreault" which is black with white organ pipes and two small white circles and one large black circle. Figure B72.C62v.1. There are numerous ink underlines and handwritten marginal notes. Marking up a book in ink? Isn't that a terrible thing to do to a book? Well, let us reflect on some thoughts on the subject by Mortimer J. Adler, 1902-91, American philosopher and educator. "I contend, quite bluntly, that marking up a book is not an act of mutilation but of love. ...Why is marking up a book indispensable to reading it? First, it keeps you awake. (And I don't mean merely conscious; I mean wide awake.) In the second place, reading, if it is active, is thinking, and thinking tends to express itself in words, spoken or written. The marked book is usually the thought-through book. Finally, writing helps you remember the thoughts you had, or the thoughts the author expressed. ...a book should be a conversation between you and the author. ...Or. You may say that this business of marking books is going to slow up your reading. It probably will. That's one of the reasons for doing it." [Archer, Jerome & Schwartz, Joseph, *A Reader*

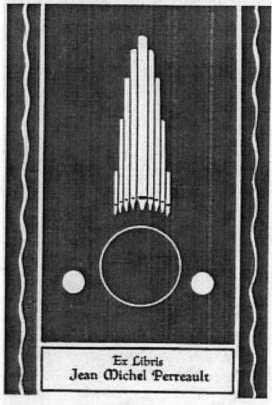

Figure B72.C62v1

for Writers, pgs. 150-4, McGraw-Hill Book Company, 1962.]. Jean Michel Perreault was a former director of the archives and special collections in the UAH Library and provided numerous other books.

B74.C85v.1, *A Beginner's History of Philosophy*, Herbert Ernest Cushman, L.L.D., Ph.D., Houghton Mifflin Co., The Riverside Press Cambridge, 1910 // Front cover verso and first free endpaper stamps, "From the Library of Morris G. Caldwell."

B108.N3 1922, *Die Vorsokratiker in Auswahl Ubersetzt und Herausgegeben* [loose translation] (The contemporary Greek philosophers to Socrates, selected translations and publication), Wilhelm Nestle, Verlegt bei Eugen Diederichs, Jena (Germany), 1922 // UAH bookplate, "From the Library of Willy Ley", penciled on front cover verso, "$3.50."

B171.B78, *The Philosophers of Greece*, Robert S. Brumbaugh, Thomas Y. Crowell Co., NY, 1964 // Title page stamp, **"WITHDRAWN"** over stamp, "The Library Indiana State University Evansville Campus."

B824.6v613 1951, *Positivism*, Richard von Mises, Harvard University Press, Cambridge, MA, 1951 // Front cover verso stamp, "Air University Library, Maxwell Air Force Base, Alabama."

B2430.T374L836, *Teilhard*, Mary and Ellen Lukas, Doubleday & Co., Garden City, NY, 1977 // Unconfirmed crest of Society of Jesus (Jesuits) imprinted on front cover verso and first endpaper, consisting of complex figures and the circular words "Igneus Estollis Vigor Et Celestis Orico." // Stamped on bottom of closed pages **"USS Missouri BB 63 Library."** This was obviously overlooked by UAH accession personnel because probably the same words were well blacked out on top of the closed pages and inside the front and back covers. I appreciate their oversight. Teilhard was a well known Jesuit geological and paleontology scientist. The USS Missouri is probably the best known ship name in American because it was the site of the Japanese surrender at the close of World War II.

B2799.M5.H42, 1951, A philosophy book about Heidegger and Kant, which is in German, and from the library of Jean Michel Perreault in which he wrote marginal notes in English. Obviously he was very fluent in German to understand the text and respond in English.

BC50.S8, *Introduction to Logic Theory*, P.F. Strawson, Methuen & Co., London, 1952 // Library of Congress duplicate surplus // "Property of United States Army" on front cover verso, "Property of E.R.D.L., Technical Reference Library, Fort Belvoir, VA." ERDL = Engineering Research and Development Laboratory.

BC71.T51860, *Outline of the Laws of Thought*, William Thomson, D.D, Provost of the Queen's College, Oxford, Sheldon & Company, NY, 1860 // UAH bookplate on front cover verso, "Gift of Lloyd S. Johnson in Memory of Wayne L. Johnson, Former Professor Mathematics" // first free endpaper in beautiful cursive "Cara J. Carter, March 1861", on second free endpaper in same cursive, "Cara J. Carter, Prof Agarsiz(?) School, Cambridge, Mass. Mr. Wrights, Instructor" // on back of foldout between pages 218-19, in cursive pencil "April 2 – 1861, very stormy – snowing , April 15th – Went to orchestral Concert, One of the loveliest days of the season", // inside back cover in cursive "Cara J. Carter, March 25, 1862, Conely(?) & Nochats"

BC71.W41957, *An Introduction to Critical Thinking*, W.W. Werkmeister, Johnson Publishing Company, Lincoln, Nebraska, 1948/1957 // Handwritten in ink on the first free endpaper, "Albert E. Morris, Jr. 11418 Louise Ave. Granada Hills, Calif, $5.50, Sept 1958.

BC108.J51890, *Logic*, W.S. Jevons, American Book Company, NY, 1980 // First free endpaper in pencil cursive, "Lucy A. Sheehan," in ink cursive "Edna M. Kennedy L IV" in ink cursive "Halfmoon Oct 1902."

BD32.M31962, *An Introduction to Philosophy*, Jacques Maritain, Sheed & Ward, NY, 1937 // Front cover verso had a second different bookplate from Jean Michel Perreault. It had a black holy cross in the middle with white radiating lines emanating from the center. On the left side, top, and rights side was "DOMINUS ILLUMINATIO MEA ET SAIUS MEA QUEM TIMEBO." On the first free endpaper was handwritten "Jean Michel Perreault" at the top and above the standard UAH gift bookplate with Perreault's name as the donor. Figure 32.M31962.

Figure BD32.M31962

BD331.M88, *Encounter with Reality*, Gardner Murphy, Houghton Mifflin Co., Boston, 1968 // Library of Congress surplus duplicate stamp // First free endpaper stamp, "Property of the Laboratory of Socio-Environmental Studies. Return to: Bldg 10. Room 39D-45." No other location information.

BD431.B74, *Life and I*, Gamaliel Bradford, Houghton Mifflin Company, Boston, 1928 // Bookplate on front cover verso, a drawing of two men drinking wine in a library and the following across the top "Old Friends, Old Wine, Old Books. "Ex Libris" across the bottom of drawing. Names on the left and right sided of the bookplate were not decipherable because the blacking out was too effective.

BD444.D46, *The Way We Die*, David Dempsey, Macmillan Publishing Co., NY, 1975 // "Property of US Navy" stamped in many places // Gray cover well stained from water and pages warped. Maybe someone was reading it on a ship deck and a wave hit the book, and reader?

BD450.R48, *The Triumph of the Therapeutic*, Philip Rieff, Harper & Row, NY, 1966 // Stamped "NASA MSC Technology Library," stamped "Library, Oct 27, 1966, Manned Spacecraft Center, Houston Texas."

BJ1402.S54, *The Philosophy of Evil*, Paul Siwek, The Ronald Press Company, NY, 1951 // Bookplate on front cover verso, "Library of the Catholic Foreign Mission Society of America," Sticker on front cover verso "Jan Leeman Brooks, ACSW, PO Box 313, University of Alabama 35486," and another stamp on first free endpaper "Maryknoll Library."

Figure BJ1461.F31960 *1961*

BJ1461.F31960, *The Freedom of the Will*, Austin Farrer, Charles Scribner's Sons, NY, 1958 / 1960 // Front cover verso bookplate, "Ex Libris" and handwritten "Materjan(?) Czarneck(?), Schenectady, NY, 1961" with drawing of a cat standing on three books and looking at the leaves of the top book. Figure BJ1461.F31960. Quite a distinctive bookplate.

BJ2193.M31954, *Manners in Business*, Elizabeth Gregg MacGibbon, The Macmillan Company, NY, 1954 // Front and back endpapers, "US Naval Base, Portsmouth, N.J., Library, Bldg. No. 22."

BL80.2R66, *New Gods in America*, Peter Rowley, David McKay Company, Inc., NY, 1971 // On title page, "Station Library, US Navy Radio Station, Sugar Grove, VA 26815."

BL460.B7, *Sex Worship and Symbolism of Primitive Races*, Sanger Brown, Richard Badger, Boston, 1916 // Front cover verso plate, "Ex Libris, Huntington Cairns" with a drawing of Don Quixote charging a windmill. Figure BL460.B7. Huntington Cairns, 1904-1985, was a

Figure BL460.B7

lawyer in Baltimore by profession. He was also a prolific writer on law, art, philosophy, literature and criticism through his professional associations, writings, and friendships with prominent writers and scholars. He served in a variety of positions during his career: Special legal advisor to the Customs Bureau of the Treasury Department; Member of the Maryland Tax Revision Commission; Secretary and member, American Commission for Protection and Salvage of Artistic and Historic Monuments in War Areas; Secretary-treasurer and general counsel, National Gallery of Art; and Chairman, Presidential Inaugural Concert Committee. The Library of Congress contains 58, 450 items from Huntington Cairns. I presume that the book in the Salmon Library was discarded by the Library of Congress when it catalogued his papers, which are contained in 166 containers plus 17 oversized, and taking 73.1 linear feet of shelf space.

BL805.L3, *Survivals of Roman Religion*, Gordon Laing, Longmans, Green & C0., NY, 1931 // Brown bookplate on first free endpaper, "Ex Libris" with an open window, an open book and a shelf of books in front, name not identified. There is writing on both sides: left "A GOOD IS LIKE A BOOK" and right side "I WOULD FOREVER KEEP." Through the open window can be seen a tree and a fountain. Figure BL805.L3.

BM176.B41920, *Hellenism*, Norman Bentwich, The Jewish Publication Society of America, Philadelphia, 1919 // First free endpaper, UAH bookplate, "Gift of Dr. Delmus Williams" This is the same Dr. Williams who was the library director and took the actions which became the basis for this research.

B3329.S483S31923, *Moralia*, Max Scheler, Der Neue Geist-Verlag, Leipzig, Germany, 1923, Text in German // Bookplate on front cover verso, "Library, Michigan State University, Gift of Professor Paul Honigsheim." Dr. Paul Honigsheim, 1885-1963, was a distinguished

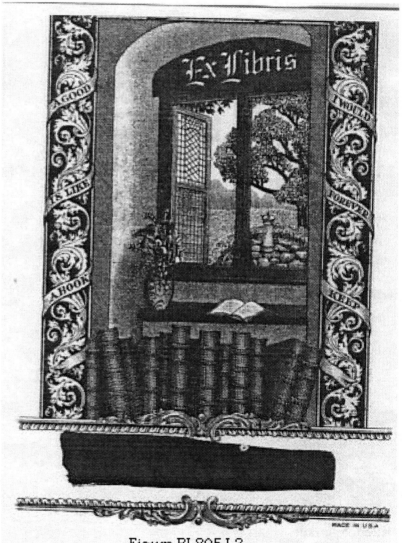

Figure BL805.L3

sociologist in Germany and the United States. He was a student of the famous German sociologist and political economist, Max Weber, 1864-1920. Honigsheim is best known for his book, *The Unknown Max Weber,* but also wrote other works about Weber. Several of Honigsheim's research projects were published after his death. In 1988, the Department of Sociology at Michigan State University distributed *From Rhineland to Michigan, The Sociologist and Pedagogue Paul Honigsheim, Migrant and Mediator Between Two Cultures.* Honigsheim in English is 'honey home.' Verlag is the German word for publishing firm and appears frequently in this book.

BT75.07190?, *The Christian View of God and the World*, James Orr, Andrew Elliot, Edinburgh, Scotland, 1893 // Library of Congress surplus duplicate // Front cover verso at the bottom left is a paste-on sticker of a book fanned open with the spine toward the viewer. "Foyles" is on the spine, on the back cover is the address, "121 Charring Cross Rd, London. On the front cover is "Book sellers, Catalogues Free." Across the bottom of the book encompassing the entire width is, "We allow more for books bearing this label." The sticker is also bottom left of the first free endpaper verso. Figure BT75.07190.

Figure BT75.O7190_

BT380.L56v2, *Studies in the Sermon on the Mount*, D. Martyn Lloyd-Jones, Minister, Westminister Chapel, London , Wm. B. Eerdmans Publishing Company, Grand Rapids, Michigan, 1960 // Front cover verso had a mailing address sticker, "Rev. Clifford H. Sleeth, 1141 East Normal, Springfield, Missouri." // There was also a Grissom High School 1990 course schedule for a not-to-be-named student left in the pages.

BV3400.D4, *The Democratic Movement in Asia*, Tyler Bennett, Association Press, New York, 1918 // Front cover verso had the following mailing address sticker, "Rev. James S. Watson, Spuyten Duyvil, New York City."

BV5072.M8, *Mystiche Texte aus dem Mittelalter*, Verlag Benno Schwabe & Co., Klosterberg, Basel, Switzerland, Text in German, 1943 // Front cover verso has a UAH Willy Ley bookplate // Bottom of first free endpaper has a small sticker, "Schoenhof's Foreign Books, Inc., 1280 Massachusetts Avenue, Cambridge, 38, MASS" and $1.50 in pencil. I assume Willy Ley bought this book in Cambridge, perhaps while browsing local bookstores in between speaking engagements in the Boston area. Schoenhof's is now located one block away from its earlier location. It is the fourth oldest bookstore in the United States and the oldest foreign language book dealer. Reference to Ley's brief biography in AC8.D54 of being fluent in five languages, he must have gone crazy with the buying opportunities in Schoenhof's. It should be considered a must-stop for any book lover in the area.

BX8301962.A3G3, *The Documents of Vatican II*, Walter Abbott, Herder and Herder, Association Press, 1966 // "Frank Russel?, Box 421A, R.F.D., Bradford, R.I., 36 East Beach Road, Quonochontaug, R.I., Wed., May 25, 1966" all in cursive.

BX8301962.A45L523, *Religious Liberty*, A.F Carrillo De Albornoz, Sheed and Ward, NY, 1967 // Embossed on the title and following page, "Western Illinois Library System, Monmouth, Illinois." There are numerous books from this library system in the Salmon Library. Further citations will not be identified unless there is new material associated with it.

BX841.C25, *The Catholic Encyclopedia*, numerous editors and contributors, 15 volumes and an index volume, Robert Appleton Company, NY, 1907 // Front cover verso, which is marbled, has a bookplate (Figure BX841.C25) in the form of a religious building, with a steeple in each top corner and a cross in the center. Below the cross is the word "PAX." The center of the building is hollowed out and contains the words, "Library, Saint Bernard Abbey, ALA, Class 203, Auth. C363, Acc. 14116, and v...." Class and Auth. pertain to the cataloguing process, while Acc. is the accession sequence number. Brother Leo, archivist and librarian at Saint Bernard's Abbey, per my phone conversation, 30

September 2005, said that St. Bernard's had a college which closed in 1979. Books excess to its future needs were sold to several organizations, but he has no records of the specifics. A two-inch circumference embossed circle is on the 2nd free endpaper and 2 title pages, "St. Bernard Abbey, St. Bernard ALA."

BX850.A48, *Principles for Peace*, Rev. Harry Koenig, National Catholic Welfare Conference, Washington, 1943 // Bookplate on front cover verso, "Ex Libris," pile of books, cardinals hat over crest, and at bottom "Quaerite Regnum Dei. Joseph Gilmore." Figure BX850.A48.

BX890.N451963, *The Heart of Newman*, Erich Przywara, Templegate, Springfield, Illinois, 1930 // Title page verso, "USAF, FL 4609, Kincheloe AFB, MI 49788; U.S. Air Force Base, Whiteman AFB, MO; Library of Congress Surplus & Duplicate."

BX891.B471966, *They Call Us Dead Men*, Daniel Berigan, S.J., The Macmillan Company, NY, 1962, // First free endpaper, "NAS Branch, Norfolk, VA, 23511-5117 // "John L. FitzGerald." hand printed.

Figure BX841.C25

BX955.C66, *The Papacy*, James A. Corbett, D. Van Nostrand Company, Princeton, New Jersey, 1956 // Front cover verso bookplate from "Columbia University in the City of New York, Libraries, Burgess Library." Figure BX955.C66.

BX1462.K4, *Catholicism, Nationalism, and Democracy in Argentina*, John J. Kennedy, University of Notre Dame Press, 1958, // First free endpaper in cursive, "Property of Latin America Bureau, NCWC, 1312 Massachusetts Ave., N.W., Washington 5, D.C."

Figure BX850.A4B

BX1490.5.S7413, *Eastern Politics of the Vatican*, Hansjakab Stehle, originally published by R. Piper & Co., Verlag, Muenchen, Zurich, 1975 // This book has a little mystery to it. There is a UAH bookplate in the front, "Gift of Dr. Henry Lane Hull." The checkout pocket in the rear has the following due dates as it was signed out to "H.L. Hull: Sep 26 '84, May 11, 1985; Sep 2, '85; Mar 16, '86; and Sep 26, '86." Loose between the front cover and the first free endpaper was an 8 x 2 inch bookmark paper with the words, "Harry M. Hull, Counsellor at Law, 3211 Quesada Street, N.W. Washington, D.C. 20014, Telephone E.M. 2-8464." This appears to be father and son, as they have different middle initials. It seems strange that H.L. Hull would sign out the book five times during 1984-86, and then be the donator of the book to the library. The bookmark with Henry M. Hull seems to be of an older vintage paper.

BX1519.C331949, *Cardinal Mindszenty Speaks,* by himself, Longmans, Green and Co., NY, 1949 // UAH bookplate, Gift of the Patrons of UAH Library // Card pocket on back free endpaper is stamped, "Mount Providence Junior College Library, Baltimore, Md." // "Wayne General and Technical College, Orrville, Ohio."

Columbia University in the City of New York

THE LIBRARIES

BURGESS LIBRARY

Figure BX955.C66

BX1566.P4, *The Persecution of the Catholic Church in German-Occupied Poland,* H.E. Cardinal Hlond, Primate of Poland, Burns Oates, London // Embossed circle [Come to think about it, aren't all embossing devices circular? Probably has to do the physics of even-pressure stamping.] on title page. "War Department, Washington, D.C.," (outer circle) "Pentagon Library." (inner circle) // Pg. v, "Library of Congress, Surplus & Duplicate." // hand-printed in pencil on pg. iii (Preface page) "Gift-Source Unknown 4/30/45" The Pentagon was built in 16 months, between September 11, 1941 and January 15, 1943. The idea was only conceived on July 17, 1941, less than two months before construction began.

BX1754.G521917, *The Faith of Our Fathers,* James Cardinal Gibbons, John Murphy Company, Baltimore, MD, 1917 (88th Edition) // Embossed stamp on title page, "St. Francis Health Resort, Denville, N.J." and in the center, "The Sisters of the Sorrowful Mother."

BX1802.M23, *Authority in the Church,* John L. McKenzie, S.J., Sheed and Ward, NY, 1996 // Embossed on title page, "St. Mary-of-the-Woods Library." This is a women's college about five miles north of Terre Haute, Indiana.

BX1912.M23, *The Secular Priesthood,* Rev. E. J. Mahoney, D.D., Professor of Moral Theory, S. Edmunds College (Ware, England), Burns Oates & Washburne LTD., London, Publishers to the Holy See, 1930 // Library of Congress Surplus and Duplicate stamp on first free endpaper // Front cover verso has a small stick-on, "Personal Property of Rev. Joseph A. Shavlin."

BX2182.P581939, *Meditations for Religious,* Rev. Raoul Plus, S.J., Frederick Pustel Company, NY, 1939 // Stamped on first free endpaper, "Barat College, President's Office." Barat College is in Lake Forest, Illinois, a Lake Michigan suburb of Chicago.

BX2230.F61917, *The Mass,* Adrian Fortesque, Longmans, Green and Company, 39 Paternoster Row, London, 1917 // Written in the middle of the first free endpaper, "Ex Libris, Wm. W. Ridgeway" and on the bottom of the same leaf is a small sticker, "The Old Corner Book Store, Inc., Boston, Mass." This bookstore is still in existence, but now goes by the name, Globe Corner Bookstore.

BX3746.C5R651966, *Missionary and Mandarin,* Arnold H. Rowbotham, Russell & Russell, NY, 1966 // "Fort Knox Education Center, Fort Knox, Kentucky" on title page.

BX4205.E9, *Personality Development in the Religious Life*, John J. Evoy, S.J., Sheed and Ward, NY, 1963 // Pencil cursive on first free endpaper, "Sister Mary ____?, Cathedral Convent" and stamped "Bishop Gilmore Convent, 720 Madison Avenue, Helena, Montana 59601."

BX4629.P3N62, *The Biography of a Cathedral*, Robert Gordon Anderson, Longmans, Green and Company, NY, 1945 // Bookplate on the front cover verso, "United States Coast Guard Academy Library, Figure BX4629.P3N62. On the title page is embossed, "U.S. Coast Guard Academy Library, New London, Conn." // In pencil, "NA5550.N7A6" // Date stamped on left side of first Contents page, "Dec 13, 1945."

Figure BX4629.P3N62

BX4668.3.D852C31960, *Father Dujarie*, Tony Catta, Catholic Life Publications, Bruce Press, Milwaukee, 1960 // First free endpaper, "Holy Trinity High School Library, Discarded 9/85" (in cursive). The location of this high school was blacked out. An Internet search produced several similarly named schools, so the location will remain a mystery.

BX4705.G55114A31986, *Faith, Sex, Mystery*, Richard Gilman, Simon and Schuster, NY, 1986 // Stamped on title page, "NAS Branch Library, Bldg U-16, Norfolk, VA 23511-5117, 444-3583." The UAH censor missed the notation on the title page, but blacked it out in several other locations.

BX4705.M259A3, *Rig for Church*, William A. Maguire, Fleet Chaplain, Pacific Fleet, The Macmillan Company, NY, 1942 // Stamped on the title page, "Library, St Augustine H.S., 64 Park Place, Brooklyn 17, NY" // Partial remnant of a decorative bookplate on first free endpaper.

BX5995.L35W5, *Alfred Lee, First Bishop of Delaware*, Congregation of St. Andrew's Church, Wilmington, Delaware, Jas. B. Rodgers Printing Company, 54 N. Sixth Street, Philadelphia, 1988 // Front cover verso has two bookplates of John Stuart Groves. The smallest is gold and burgundy with five flying doves diagonally in front of two library shelves. The second is bigger with a crest in the center with a banner across the bottom which states "Liberty & Independence". Across the top blacked out is "Delawareana, From the Collection of John Stuart Groves." Groves was a well-known book collector whose collection was disbursed in the 1930s. An Internet search by his name produced a large number of books on sale by book sellers which feature his bookplate. Figures BX5995.L35W5-1 &2.

Fig. BX5995.L35W5-1

BX6495.F68A3, *The Living of These Days*, Harry Emerson Fosdick, Harper and Brothers, NY, 1956 // Small label at bottom of first free endpaper, "Fra G. Deitrick, 181 Boulder Trail, Bronxville, NY."

BX6793.S4B8, *Memoir of Elder Elijah Shaw*, by his daughter, L.J. Shaw, Philadelphia, 1852 // Cursive on first free endpaper, "Adna Browns, North Hampton, N.H." // UAH bookplate, "Lloyd S. Johnson in memory of Wayne L. Johnson, Former Professor Mathematics."

BX6943.P4, *Christian Science*, Robert Peel, Henry Holt and Company, NY, 1958 // Stamped on first free endpaper, "Naval Air Station, Guam."

BX7635.B3, *The Quiet Rebels*, Margaret H. Bacon, Basic Books, Inc., NY, 1969 // Bookplate on front cover verso, "Mitchell Memorial Library, Mississippi State University."

BX7780.H6A4, *Hopewell Friends History, 1734-1934*, Joint Committee, Shenandoah Publishing House, Strasburg, Virginia, 1936 // Small mailing address sticker in middle of front cover verso, "Mrs. H.A. Knorr, 1401 Union Street, Pine Bluff, Arkansas."

Figure BX5995.L35W5-2

BX8495.P543S6, *Life and Times of George F. Pierce*, George G. Smith, Hancock Publishing Company, Sparta, Georgia, 1888 // Large cursive on first free endpaper, "A.M.R. Branson, Augusta, Arkansas, Oct. 28th 1888, 1.25."

BX9715.N4, *The Hallelujah Army*, Harry Edward Neal, Chilton Company, NY, 1961 // On title page is a two-inch diameter embossed stamp, "Department of the Army, Washington D.C., Army Library."

BX9869.C8A31904, *Autobiography of Moncure Daniel Conway*, Houghton Mifflin and Company, The University Press, Cambridge, 1905 // Front cover verso is a superb bookplate undisturbed by the UAH accession personnel, likely because the first free endpaper was stuck to the cover, as there is a significant imprint of the bookplate on it. "Ex Libris" at the top and "Fanny and Casper Rowe" at the bottom. In between is a wonderful crest, a lamp of learning, 2 piles of 3 books each, a quill and inkpot on 1 pile, and an ink stamp on the other pile. Figure BX9869.C8A31904.

CB19.T575, *Acquaintances*, Arnold J. Toynbee, Oxford University Press, London, 1967 // Stamped on front cover verso and back cover recto, "Library – NAF Sigonella, U.S. Navy Property;" stamped on first free endpaper, "NAF SIG Library, Box 470, Naval Air Facility, FPO New York 09523,"

Figure BX9869.C8A31904

which is also stamped on top, bottom and open edges of the leaves. Sigonella is on the southeast coast of Sicily, Italy. It is a few miles south of the town of Catania, and has provided support to the events following eruptions of the Mount Etna volcano, which is about 25 miles north of Catania.

CB19.T6, *Civilization of Trial*, Arnold J. Toynbee, Oxford University Press, NY, 1948 // Front cover verso bookplate depicts a two-masted, Oriental-style boat in a circle (sun?). "Ex Libris, E. Craighill Brown," and under the right bottom corner is "1/49" as in year of purchase of reading. Figure CB19.T6.

CB77.S5, *History of Medieval and Modern Civilization*, Charles Seignobos, Charles Scribner's Sons NY, 1907 // Cursive on first free endpaper, "Frederich P. Jecusco, Bates, 1912."

CB103.0683, *Man and Crisis*, Jose Ortega y Gasset, W.W. Norton and Company, NY, 1958 // "Property U.S. Army Armor School" at eight places, inside both covers, first and last free endpapers, etc.

CB151.P53, *Science in the Cause of Man*, Gerhard Piel, Alfred A. Knopf, NY, 1961 // Stamped in four places, "Huntsville Public Library, Huntsville, Alabama"

CB156.D34131974, *In Search of Ancient Gods*, Erich von Daeniken, G.P. Putnam's Sons, NY, 1974 // "Maxwell Community Library, Maxwell Air Force Base, Ala., Property U.S. Air Force" on copyright page and inside back cover.

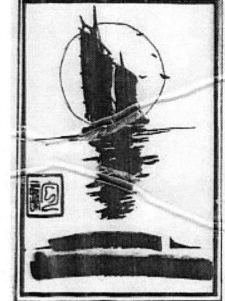

Figure CB19.T6

CB161.I51967, *Mankind 2000*, Robert Jungk, Allen & Unwin, London, 1969 // Stamp on front cover verso, "Institute for Space Studies, Library Room 710, 22? Broadway, R____, NY 18625?" This is apparently the current Goddard Institute of Space Studies, located at 2880 Broadway Ave. at the corner of West 112th Street.

CB161.T6, *Toward the Year 2018*, Foreign Policy Association, Cowles Education Corporation, NY, 1968 // "Base Library, Marine Corps Base, Camp Pendleton, Calif, 92959" on the title page.

CB195.H3, *The Racial Basis of Civilization*, Frank H. Hankins, Alfred A. Knopf, NY, 1926 // "Morris Gilmore Caldwell" red stamp on front cover verso and "Morris G. Caldwell" stamped in black on first free endpaper.

CB251.J3, *The Interplay of East and West*, Barbara Ward, W.W. Norton and Company, NY, 1957 // "Property of U.S. Defense W_____ School" on both inside covers and end leaves.

CB301.L513, *God and Magic*, Ivar Lissner, G.P. Putnam's Sons, NY, 1961 // "Library, United States Naval Home" stamped in 12 places. This is apparently is located in Gulfport, Mississippi.

CB401.W45, *The Age of Reason*, Leo Weinstein, George Braziller, NY, 1965 // Stamped on title page, "Wheeler Basin Regional Library, Headquarters, Decatur, AL, This Book Provided by Alabama Public Library Service."

CB440.L47, *Space: Its Impact on Man and Society*, Lillian Levy, W.W. Norton and Company, NY, 1965 // On title page (readable) and three other stamped places, "Base Library Andrews Air Force Base, Washington 26, D.C., Property of USAF."

CB478.M81963, *Technics and Civilization*, Lewis Mumford, Harcourt Brace and Company, NY, 1934 // Bookplate on front cover verso, a torch, crossed signal flags, four books, eagle bookends, "THE SIGNAL CORPS REFERENCE LIBRARY" and on the bottom of the bookplate is, "GPO 16-30142-1." GPO stands for Government Printing Office. Title page is embossed, "War Department, Washington, D.C., Pentagon Library and on bottom right is stamped in red, "Office of the Chief Signal Officer, The Signal Corps Reference Library, Washington, D.C." The UAH accession censor missed several locations, which helped to discern the blacked-out words. On page v is stamped, "Jul 14 1943" and in pencil cursive, "Phil Bk Co 2.95; Transfer/Signal Corps Lib (43/4035) 4/30/45."

Figure CT107.H261930

CC75.B47, *Archaeology and the Universe*, Leo Biek, Frederick A. Praeger, NY, 1963 // Bookplate on front cover verso, "Class B 571.018, Book B475a, Accession 199655, Mississippi State crest, Mitchell Memorial Library, Mississippi State University."

CC363.C651961, *The Last Pharaohs*, Leonard Cottrell, Holt, Rinehart and Winston, NY, 1961 // Previous owners were effectively blacked out by the UAH censors on front cover verso, first free endpaper and title page, but on page 101 is stamped "Base Library, Camp Pendleton, Calif."

CJ89.C5531974, *The Beauty and Lore of Coins*, Elvira and Vladimir Clain-Stefanelli, Redwood Publishers LTD, Croton-on-Hudson, NY, 1974 // Elliptical stamp, "Property of Library, U.S. Postal Service" on front cover verso, first free endpaper and pre-title page. Also on the first free endpaper is a 6 x 8-inch bookplate of the publisher, "With the compliments of the Publisher" and the signature, "Gerald Stearn" in red ink. Apparently it was sent direct from the publisher to the USPS.

J. Keene Fleck

Figure CT34.G7S7

CT34.G7S7, *English Biography Before 1700*, Donald A. Stauffer, Harvard University Press, Cambridge, Massachusetts, 1930 // Bookplate on the front cover verso: man rummaging through a container of disorderly books, as in a sale, and the name on the bottom, "J. Keene Fleck." Figure CT34.G7S7. Fleck was a librarian at the Princeton University Library during, at least, the 1950s and 1960s. He was on the editorial board for *The Princeton University Library Chronicle* in the mid-1960s and was appointed as supervisor of the Book Acquisition Division in 1961. (Google.com)CT107.H261930, *The Book of Courage*, Hermann Hagedorn, The Smithsonian Company, Oakland, Calif., 1930 // Bookplate of first free endpaper is a silhouette of three children outside, Figure CT107.H261930, and two swallows in the sky, "This Book Belongs to Martha Jackson."

CT120.M361981, *Makers of Modern Culture*, Justin Wintle, Facts On File, Inc., NY, 1981 // On verso of dedication page, "Station Library, NSF, Diego Garcia." Diego Garcia is a long way from Huntsville. It is an island in the British Indian Ocean Territory (BIOT) located about 1,000 miles south of the Indian Sub-Continent at 7 Degrees South Latitude and 72 Degrees, 25 Minutes East Longitude. The U.S. Naval Support Facility (NSF) provides communications, airfield and ship support to American forces. There are about 1,700 military and 1,500 civilian contractors on the island, along with about 50 British military. The island is in

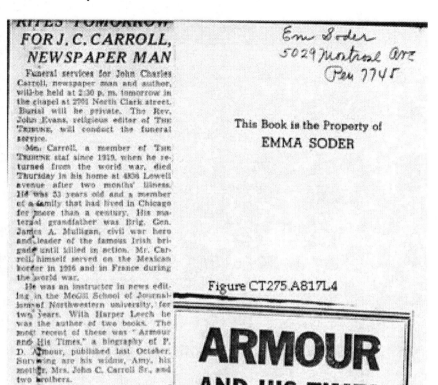

Figure CT275.A817L4

the shape of a horseshoe with a perimeter of about 40 miles and the average elevation is four feet above sea level, with the highest at 22 feet. It is identified on a map as the Chagos Archipelago. Wonder how this book got off the island and into the Salmon Library?

CT275.A817L4, *Armour and His Times*, Harper Leech and John Charles Carroll, D. Appleton-Century Company, NY, 1938 // Sticker on front cover verso, "This Book is the Property of EMMA SODER." Above the sticker in cursive, "Em Soder, 5029 Montreal Ave, Pen 7745." Pasted on the front cover verso is an undated newspaper obituary of co-author J.C. Carroll, who died the year after this book was published. Figure CT275.A817L4.

CT275.C578A31950, *Life of an American Workman*, Walter P. Chrysler, The Curtis Publishing Company, NY, 1937 // Stamp inside both front and back covers, "Library, Chrysler Corporation Space Division, Huntsville, Alabama."

CT275.F2A3, *The Autobiography of an Individualist*, James O. Fagan, Houghton Mifflin Company, NY, 1912 // Circular sticker on bottom left of cover (highly unusual), Century Club, California," which is also stamped on first free endpaper and a mostly-removed sticker at top of same endpaper // Stamped in red on front cover verso, "From the San Francisco Chapter, American Red Cross." // Bottom left of back cover recto is a small sticker, "Paul Elder & Co., San Francisco." Paul Elder was a well known bookstore in the city and carried the cachet, "the bookstore for San Francisco's elite."

CT275.F565F8, *Jubilee*, Robert H. Fuller, The Macmillan Company, NY, 1928 // Bookplate on front cover verso, Sailing ship and "McCruden." Figure CT275.F565F8. Later in the research, G540.H75 had

McCruden's bookplate, but this book had cursive on the first free endpaper, "Dr. McCruden, London, 12/5/32."

CT275.G6H631969, *The Goulds*, Edwin P. Hoyt, Weybright and Talley, NY, 1969 // "Naval Air Station Library, Norfolk, VA" stamped on front cover verso, title page and back cover recto.

CT275.K4574D38, *Ethel*, Lester David, The World Publishing Company, NY, 1971 // Stamped on copyright page and back cover recto, United States Air Force, Main Library, FL 3647, Lackland AFB, Tex."

CT275.M43A39, *Onions in the Stew*, Betty MacDonald, J.B. Lippincott Company, NY, 1954 // Cursive on first free endpaper, "To "That Brewster (Farm) Boy" Danbury's Champion Chicken Checker, J Roy Allen, from his boy, J. Rutledge Allen, Christmas 1955." Do you know what a "chicken checker" is? How about "chicken sexer?" Somebody has to check out the sex of those young chicks and put them in the right category.

CT275.T73W5, *A Builder of the New South*, George Tayloe Winston, Doubleday, Page and Company, NY, 1920 // Sticker on front cover verso, "Talladega College Library, Talladega, Alabama, Presented by A.S. Thompson."

EXTRACTS FROM THE PANAMA CANAL LIBRARY RULES

LIBRARY CARDS: Borrowers must present their library cards whenever a book is taken, returned or renewed. If card is lost borrower is responsible for books drawn on it.

DAMAGES TO BOOKS: Borrowers are financially responsible for any damages, as determined by the Library, caused through mutilation of books by tearing, pencil marking, turning of pages, etc.

TIME: Books may be kept 14 days, except recent fiction and books in great demand, which are limited to 7 days, as shown on date slip. Magazines may be borrowed for a period of 4 days except current numbers and bound volumes.

RENEWALS: A 14-day book may be renewed upon application unless it is reserved for another borrower. A 7-day book cannot be renewed. When renewing by mail or telephone state date borrowed, author, title, and borrower's name. An overdue book may not be renewed by telephone.

FINES: Each 14-day book kept overtime is subject to a fine of 2 cents a day, and each 7-day book, 4 cents a day. Magazines, 2 cents a day.

Figure CT788.B48B4

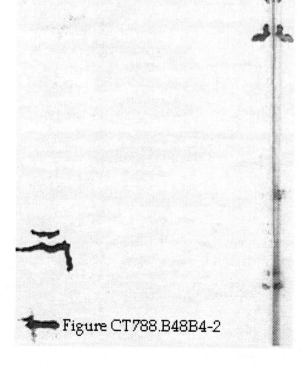

Figure CT788.B48B4-2

CT275.V23 4V3, *Queen of the Golden Age*, Cornelius Vanderbilt, Jr., McGraw-Hill Book Company, NY // Bottom of first free endpaper, "Library U.S. Naval Station, Argentia, Newfoundland." This is a little town in Placentia Bay in southeast Newfoundland. Wonder how the Navy found it, and what they do there? The subject of Vanderbilt's book is his mother, and what a nice title. This is an excellent way to make sure her money goes his way.

CT782.S81925, *Eminent Victorians*, Lytton Strachey, 17th printing, The Knickerbocker Press, 1925 // Small sticker on bottom left of first free endpaper, "The Studio Shop, Birmingham, Alabama, 406 N. 2d Street, Dial 3-7703."

CT788.B48B4, *India Called Them*, Lord Beveridge, George Allen & Unwin, Ltd., London, 1947 // Bookplate, 2.5 x 6 inches on front cover verso, "The Panama Canal Library, Balboa Heights, Administration Building." Figure CT788.B48B4-1. On first free endpaper is a stamp, "DDT 5 '54." // There are genuine "bookworm" tunnels in the front cover and the leaves through page eight, as well as in the back cover and last free endpaper. Figure CT788.B48B4-2. Based on the wormholes, it is assumed that the book received a DDT spraying in May 1954. DDT was developed in 1939 by the Swiss chemist, Paul Muller, working for J.R. Geigy. Panama has a moist climate, which was probably perfect for the bookworm. The silverfish is one candidate for a bookworm, although there are other possibilities.

CT788.L83A3, *Unkilled For So Long*, Sir Arnold Lunn, George Allen & Unwin, Ltd., London, 1968 // Sticker on bottom of title page, "Christian Classics, 205 Willis Street, Westminster, MD 21157."

CT3990.W36C641974, *Between Tradition and Modernity*, Paul A. Cohen, Harvard University Press, Cambridge, Massachusetts, 1974 // Stamp on front cover verso and title page, "Foreign Service Institute, Library, Department of State."

Figure CT275.F565F8

D13.B5613, *The Historian's Craft*, Marc Bloch, Alfred A. Knopf, NY, 1963 // Cursive on second free endpaper, "Lawrence Geddie, 302 W. 34th, Austin, June 1971."

D16.9.M274, *Shapes of Philosophical History*, Frank Manuel, Stanford University Press, Stanford, California, 1965 // Front cover verso stamped, "Worcester State College." This is apparently in Worcester, Massachusetts.

D20.I66v2, *History of Mankind*, Volume II, Luigi Paretti, Harper & Row, NY, 1965 // Title page is stamped, "Public Library, Birmingham, Alabama, Parke Memorial." "Discarded by B'ham Public Library" is stamped on front cover verso, first free endpaper, title page recto and verso, and back cover recto.

D21.L261950, *The World's History*, Frederic C. Lane, et al, Harcourt, Brace and Company, NY, 1950 // Front cover verso has a stamp, "Property of the Board of Education, Newtown High School, Elmhurst, NY" and below it is a glued-on sign-out paper for the students, "Board of Education, City of New York" as the first of six signatures is "Joseph Campagna, Class 205H, Date Issued 9/15/50, Condition old." The last signature was in 1958. The title page has a 1&1/4 x 2 inch stamp with a double-lined border, "Property of Board of Education, City of New York, Oct. 1950." // There is also a UAH / Willy Ley bookplate.

D24.B321889, v1 & v2, *Historic Events and Strange Oddities*, S. Baring Gould, Methuen & Company, 18 Bury Street, W.C., London, 1891 // Both volumes have a UAH / Willy Ley bookplate on the front cover verso. The second free endpaper of Volume 1 is a simple title page with cursive at the top, "Walter Phelps Dodge, Torquay '92." This last item seems to place the book in the possession of Dodge, a British lawyer and noted biographical historian, at the English Channel "British Riviera" in the vicinity of Torbay and Torquay on the southwestern coast of England in 1892.

D24.65, *Fifty Letters of History*, Curtis Gentry, Thomas Y. Crowell Co., NY, 1930 // Front cover verso has a circular stamp, "Dr. L. L. Hill, ___ So. Perry Street, Montgomery, Alabama." This stamp places the book in the possession of Dr. Luther Leonidas Hill, who performed the first open heart surgery in the Western Hemisphere when he sutured a stab wound in a young boy's heart in 1902. Hill studied medicine in London under Dr. Joseph Lister, a pioneer in antiseptic surgery and for whom Listerine mouth wash is named. Dr. Hill practiced from 1884 until 1932. He was the father of U.S. Senator Lister Hill of Alabama.

D27.F731957, *Peter Freuchen's Book of the Seven Seas*, Peter Freuchen, Julian Messner, Inc., NY, 1957 // Stamp on title page, "Base Library, Camp Pendleton, Calif."

D57.V3v.1&v.2, *A Political and Cultural History of the Ancient World*, C.E. Van Sickle, The Riverside Press, Houghton Mifflin Company, NY, 1895 // Stamped on the title page and the back cover recto, "Howard College Library, Birmingham, Alabama" and overstamped "Released from Collections of Howard College Library." Stamped below in larger letters, "NUCLEAR." Volume 1 has tape on all corners of both covers, while Volume 2 has a sticker, "Heckman Bindery, Inc., Aug 85, N. Manchester, Indiana 46962." Howard College is the arts and sciences college of Samford University, Birmingham, Alabama.

D106.M31922, *Post Mortem*, C. MacLaurin, George H. Doran Company, NY, 1922 // Fancy bookplate on front cover verso with the name, "Samuel Robert." The bookplate is at Figure D106.M31922 and contains the following verse:

Figure D106.M31922

> "When thou art wanted by a friend
> Right welcome shall he be
> To read, study, not to lend,
> But to leave with me.
> Not that borrowed knowledge"
> Does diminish learning's store;
> But books, I find, when often lent
> Return to me no more.

D113. Verdiere, Libraire, Quai Des Augustius, Nº 25, Paris, F71824, 16 Volumes, *Collection, Des Chroniques, Nationales Françaises*, J.A. Buchon, 1826 // On each title page are two cursive stamps. The first is "f. de St. Cyr" with an extravagant double loop below it continued from Cyr and the second is in an ellipse "Le Cte de. Palis." St. Cyr is the famous French military school.

D118.E52, *Introduction to the Middle Ages*, Ephriam Emerton, Ginn & Company, Boston, 1896 // Front cover verso has sticker, "M.J. Kling, Harvard, 02."

D217.M66, *A History of European Diplomacy, 1815-1914*, R.B. Mowatt, Edward Arnold & Co., London, 1922 // First free endpaper stamped, "Carlton Chu Pei Chen, Georgetown University, Washington, D.D." This is the first of seven books attributed to this individual, so be on the lookout for further intriguing information about him, especially his name and locations.

D220.F82K421926, *The Fugger News-Letter*, edited by Victor von Klarwill, G.P. Putnam's Sons, NY, 1926 // Front cover verso has a bookplate with the name, "Caroli Moran." It also contains the words, "Lucent in Tenebris," which means roughly, Light into Darkness. Figure D220.F82K421926.

D299.N4, *Modern Europe: A Popular History*, Thomas P. Neill, Doubleday & Company, NY, 1970 // A stamped overlooked by the UAH censors on fourth leaf verso, "Property of U.S. Air Force, Base Library, FL 5540, APO, NY 09194." The "09" APO indicates someplace outside the country to the east of New York City, the primary APO for the East Coast.

D413.C6A31941d, *Looking for Trouble*, Virginia Cowles, Harper & Brothers, NY, 1941 // Sticker address label on second leaf, a simple title page, "Y. de Treville, 853 Seventh Avenue, New York, NY, Apt. 7C."

D413.L9A3, *Assignment in Utopia*, Eugene Lyons, Harcourt, Brace and Company, NY, 1937 // Two circular embossed stamps on title page, #1, "War Department, Washington, DC" around outer circumference and "War Department Library" in center, and #2, same outside circumference, but inside is "Pentagon Library." On closed vertical leaves is "The Army Library, Washington, DC." Explanation was provided at BX1566.P4.

Figure D220.F82K42dSer1926

D425.G81936, *Inside Europe*, John Gunther, Harper & Brothers, NY, 1936 // Address label on front cover verso, Harve Mossawir, Jr., 1202 Owens Drive, S.E. Huntsville, Alabama // Cursive writing on front cover verso, "March 23, 1936, Eva Mae Sellers, Montgomery, Ala."

D427.K31934/35, *Kalender der Weltgeschichte 1934-1935*, 2 volumes, Essener Verlagsanstalt, Essen, 1937 // Cursive on front cover verso, "John Rison Jones, Jr., Paris, 1955" // UAH gift bookplate from John Rison Jones.

D442.S8, 1920-23, *Survey of International Affairs*, 1920-1925, Vol. 1, Arnold J. Toynbee, Oxford University Press, London, 1925 // UAH gift bookplate from John Rison Jones on front cover verso // Small sticker on bottom of front cover verso, "Blackwells, Oxford, England // First free endpaper has pencil cursive, "FB Bourdillon." // 1925 Supplement has cursive writing on front cover verso, "John Rison Jones, 3 Rue Segures, Paris 1954 // 1931 Volume, first free endpaper has in cursive, "John Rison Jones, Jr., Alexandria, VA 1959 and a UAH gift bookplate // 1932 Volume has stamped on the

Figure D443.S48

first free endpaper, "Historical Office, Department of State, Reference Copy." The markings in this book have led to the following probability of its accession. F.B. Bourdillon was an Englishman and a member of the Royal Institute of International Affairs (RIIA) in the 1920s. In 1922 he was secretary to the Boundary Commission that was involved in the conflicts in Northern Ireland. In 1926 Bourdillon was secretary of the Economic Group of the RIIA as he sent the invitations to the prospective participants. It is logical that Bourdillon would obtain copies of international affairs documents that were published in England. It seems logical that Bourdillon's heirs may have disposed of his library to Blackwell's bookshop in Oxford. Blackwell's opened its doors at 50 Broad Street, Oxford, on 1 January 1879 in a tiny room of only 12 feet square. In 2005 it was Oxford's largest bookshop, with more than 200,000 titles in stock covering every subject, discipline and interest. The shop includes the Norrington Room, which is under Trinity College, Oxford, which opened in 1966. It is in the *Guinness Book Of Records* for having the largest display of book for sale in one room anywhere in the world. The room has over 10,000 square feet and houses 160,000 on three miles of shelving. John Rison Jones confirmed, per phonecon, 1 December 2005, that he bought the volumes cited above at Blackwell's Bookshop when he was studying European history. He did live at the Paris address cited above while on a Fulbright scholarship. He also worked at the Department of State as a historian.

D443.B4, *World Chancelleries*, Edward Bell Price, The Chicago Daily News, Chicago, 1926 // The third free endpaper has a presentation copy plate to Hon. Lister Hill, #302.

D443.D78, *The End of Economic Man*, Peter F. Drucker, The John Day Company, NY, 1939 // Title page has a circular embossed stamp from the War Department, previously discussed at BX1566.P4, and an ink stamp, "Property of War Department, Bureau of Public Relations, Intelligence and Analysis Branch Library," Peter Drucker was the foremost management guru of the last 70 years and he died on 11 November 2005 at age 94, just 20 days before I handled this book.

D443.S48, *Can Europe Keep the Peace?*, Frank H. Simonds, Harper & Brothers, NY, 1931 // Second free endpaper has a bookplate, "L.E. Frechtling." Figure D443.S48.

D469.G7S4, *Britain and the Arab States*, M.V. Seton-Williams, Luzac & Company LTD, 46 Great Russell Street, W.C. 1, London, 1948 // Front cover verso has a Department of State stamp and an address label in the lower left corner, "Arthur Probsthain, Oriental Bookseller, 41 Gt. Russell Street, London, W.C. 1. // First free endpaper has a stamp, "Foreign Service Library, Department of State" and the frequently present Library of Congress surplus duplicate stamp. Arthur Probsthain is one of the oldest book stores in central London, with a history of almost 100 years. It specializes in Oriental and African books and is located opposite the British Museum. Great Russell Street, other than having a great name, is also the location of three other antiquarian book stores in London so it is a wonderful area for book lovers. The British Museum is the home of the circular Reading Room, which was the British Library until a new building was completed in the 1990s about one mile north of the British Museum. The Reading Room is absolutely magnificent and worth a visit.

D505.G532, *Outbreak of the World War*, German documents collected by Karl Kautsky, Oxford University Press, NY, 1924 // UAH gift bookplate from John Rison Jones // Title page has a stamp, "Royal Economic Society."

D511.D34, *The European Anarchy*, G. Lowes Dickinson, The Macmillan Company, NY, 1916 // Title page has a two-inch diameter punched-through-leaf, "Advance Copy, For Review, Not For Sale."

D511.093, *The Russian Imperial Conspiracy*, 1892-1914, Robert Owen, no publisher cited 1926 // Sticker of complimentary copy by the author. Figure D511.093.

D521.B8.v2, *Nelson's History of the War*, John Buchan, Thomas and Sons, London, undated // 24 volumes in series // UAH gift bookplate, Richard C. Pope // Bottom of back cover recto is a small blue sticker, "Brentano's Booksellers and Stationers, New York // In Volume 2 was a folded paper and a copy is at Figure D521.B8.v2

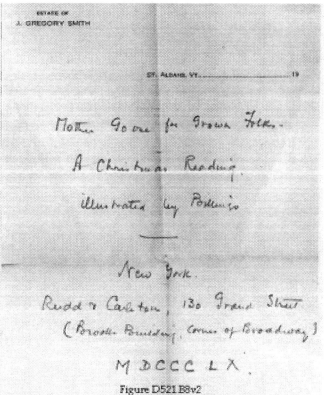

Figure D521.B8v2

D523.G48, *More That Must Be Told*, Phillip Gibbs, Harper & Brothers, NY, 1921 // Front cover verso bookplate, "Irma S. Byrne." Figure D523.G48.

D523.I87, *The Next War*, Will Irwin, E.P. Dutton & Company, NY, 1921 // Front cover verso bookplate, "Ex Libris" across top, "Irene" down left side, "Samuel" down right side, and "Gordon" across bottom. Figure D523.I87.

D526.2.M161939, *History and Rhymes of the Lost Battalion*, Buck Private McCollum, fortieth printing, Bucklee Publishing Co., no town cited, 1939 // First free

Figure D619.A41917ab

Figure D523.G48

endpaper recto has embossed stamp. Outside circle "Disabled American Veterans, The World War" and inner circle "Montfaucon Chapter, No. 27, Toledo Ohio." Toledo, Ohio is my hometown, having lived there until I entered the United States Army at age 23. Mountfaucon, France has a massive Doric column over two hundred feet high commemorating the Meuse-Argonne Offensive during the final two months of World War I. It is located about 19 miles northwest of Verdun and 6 miles south of the Meuse-Argonne American Cemetery.

D568.4.l42M91966, *T.E. Lawrence*, Sulieman Mousa, Oxford University Press, London, 1966 // Stamp on title page, "Camp Libraries, Camp Lejeune, N.C."

D570.P32v1, *Newton D. Baker*, Frederick Palmer, 2 volumes, Dodd, Mead & Company, NY, 1931 // Ink cursive on first free endpaper, "To Ed Booth from Bill Bennis (?), October 30, 1931."

D619.A41917ab, *Diplomatic Correspondence between the United States and Belligerent Governments Relating to Neutral Rights and Commerce*, Volume II, Oxford University Press, NY no date // Unidentified names under naval motif bookplate. Figure D619.A41917ab.

D619.3.J641918a, *The German Secret Service in America*, John Price Jones and Paul Merrick Hollister, Small, Maynard & Company, Boston, 1918 // Front cover verso, "W.J. Hall from Maurice, x-mas 1918" // Sticker on bottom of first free endpaper, "Chas. E. Lauriat Co. Importers & Booksellers, 385 Wash'n St. Boston." Charles E. Lauriat Company was founded in 1852.

Figure D523.I87

D627.G3P81916, *To Ruhleben and Back*, Geoffrey Pyke, Houghton Mifflin Company, Boston, 1916 // Stamp on front cover verso, "UNITED STATES SOLDIERS HOME LIBRARY ." Ruhleben was a camp for British subjects interned as prisoners-of-war during World War I. All British subjects living in Germany in 1914 were put in this camp, which was located six miles west of the center of Berlin on the east side of the town of Spandau, which became well known after World War II as the prison for Nazi leaders. About 5,500 males between the ages of 17 and 55 were in the camp by spring 1915. The internees were released at the end of the war in 1918, but the author of this book must have been released in 1916, because of the publication date. The U.S. Soldiers Home was established in 1851 in Washington, D.C. It occupies 320 acres of park in the northwest quadrant of the city. The home is now known as the U.S. Soldiers' and Airmen's Home, since the establishment of a separate Air Force after World War II.

D639.D45A5, *The British Revolution and the American Democracy*, Norman Angell, B.W. Huebsch, NY, 1919 // Front cover verso had stamp, "Library of Michael H. Kennedy, 1524 Laird Ave., Dayton, OH 45420."

D640.L27, *A Minstrel in France*, Harry Lauder, Hearst's International Library Co., NY, 1918 // First free endpaper contains a cursive note written at Christmas 1918. It appears to say, "This book is written by a father who with his wife mourn for a dear son and who overcame their sorrow, as you both have done, by thinking of and ministering to others." Figure D640.L27. Was the son lost during World War I?

D644.T3, *The Truth About the Treaty*, André Tardieu, The Bobbs-Merrill Company, Indianapolis, 1924 // Front cover verso has a defaced bookplate, "Of the Library of Henry H. Baish," courtesy of the UAH accession censors, at Figure D644.T3. I discovered a Henry H Baish who was from Altoona, Pennsylvania and apparently was the first secretary of the Pennsylvania Public School Employees' Retirement Act I 1918, but have no solid evidence the book belonged to him. Perhaps there was another clue on the defaced part of the bookplate.

D720.L271936, *The World Since 1914*, Walter Consuelo Langsam, The Macmillan Company NY, 1937 // Stamped in nine places, "James D. Kennedy, Jr., 144 Woodridge Place, Leonia, New Jersey." Good thing there were nine stamps, so I was able to discern the entire information, no thanks to the censors who tried to shut me out.

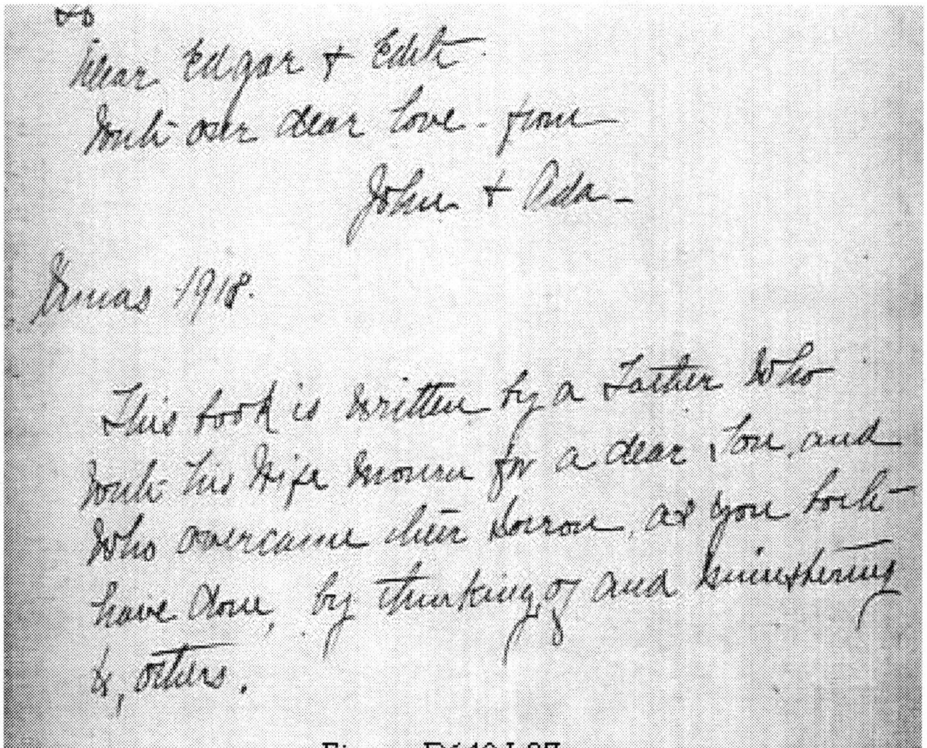

D741.C581965, *None So Blind*, Ian Colvin, Harcourt., Brace & World In., NY, 1965 // Very nice untouched stamp on bottom of title page overlooked by the UAH accession personnel, "U.S. Naval Station Library, Auxiliary Service Collection, U. S. Naval Station, Norfolk, Virginia 23511."

Figure D640.L27

D741.J68, *Munich, A Tale of Two Myths*, Thomas Brooks Jones, Dorrance and Company, Philadelphia, 1977 // First free endpaper, "USAOTEA Technical Library, Property of U.S. Army." USAOTEA is the U.S. Army Operational Test and Evaluation Agency.

D742.A8J6, *Pacific Partner*, George H. Johnston, Duell, Sloan and Pearce, NY, 1944 // Title page stamped in red, "U.S. Naval Proving Ground."

D742.N4N3, *New Zealand*, Walter Nash, Duell, Sloan and Pearce, NY, 1943 // Front cover verso has a stamped bookplate, "Conrad Library." Figure

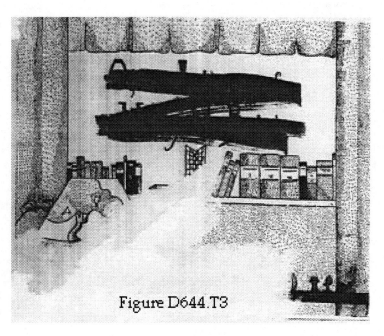

Figure D644.T3

Figure D742.N4N3

D742.N4N3. // Embossed stamp on title page, "Seamen's Church Institute of NY, 25 South Street."

D743.D261960, *Der Zweite Weltkrieg* (The Second World War), Hellmuth Gunther Dahms, Rainer Wunderlich Verlag, Tubingen, Germany, 1966 // First free endpaper has embossed stamp, "Library of Gerhard H.R. Reiseg" and in the center are the larger initials, "GHR."

D743.G666, *American Strategy in World War II: A Reconsideration*, Kent Roberts Greenfield, The Johns Hopkins Press, Baltimore, 1963 // Front cover verso, title page and back cover recto have a red stamp, "Property of United States Air Force, Travis A.F. Base Library." // Also Library of Congress surplus and duplicate. Travis AFB is midway between San Francisco and Sacramento, California and is the gateway for almost all military flights to the Pacific region.

D743.S8, *Preview of History*, Raymond Gram Swing, Doubleday, Doran and Company, Inc., NY, 1943 // First free endpaper has hand printed, "Jennie Giehl Language Prize to Leatrice Resnick, South Side High School, January, 1944."

D743.U531945c, *George Marshall's Report, The Winning of the War in Europe and the Pacific*, Simon and Schuster, NY, 1945 // Front cover verso and title page, "Collier Library, University of North Alabama, Florence, Alabama.

D744.R32, *The Redemption of Democracy*, Hermann Rausching, Alliance Book Corporation, NY, 1941 // Front cover verso and title page stamped, "TIME INC, EDITORIAL LIBRARY."

D745.2.M34, *Up Front*, Bill Mauldin, Henry Holt and Company, NY, 1945 // First free endpaper has bookplate, "Ex Libris, Mollie & Martin Soffer." Figure D745.2.M34.

D478.R66v2, *The Secret History of the War*, Waverly Root, Charles Scribner's Sons, NY, 1945 // First free endpaper and title page stamps, "U.S. Naval Hospital, Norman, Oklahoma."

D753.M48, *Beyond German Victory, 1940*, Helen Hill and Herbert Agar, Reynal & Hitchcock, NY, 1940 // Cursive on first free endpaper, "For Lister Hill from Helen Hill with regards." See D24.65 for reference to Lister Hill, who had two sisters, but if Helen was his sister it seems as if her words would portray more warmth.

Figure D742.2.M34

THE EMPORIA GAZETTE

My Dear Friend:

June 27th

Here is a book you should read, not because I wrote the introduction to the book, but because it states fairly, I think, the case of the United States in this crisis. I fear we are all in for a bad quarter of a century, in any event, and a worse time, if England is defeated. Well — at any rate look over this little book, with your lens turned. With kind personal regards. I am

Sincerely yours
W. A. White

Figure D753.W45

D753.W45, *Defense for America*, Quincy Wright and 14 others, The Macmillan Company, NY, 1940 // Front cover verso and first free endpaper have a cursive stamp, "Pete Darman" (?) Pasted on the free endpaper preceding the title page is a folded letter, Figure D753.W45. The author of the inserted letter was William Allen White, the owner of *The Emporia Gazette*, Kansas. He was one of America's greatest journalists for 50 years and had opinions on almost everything, which he wrote since he owned the paper. This is a classic example of Freedom of the Press, if you own it.

D754.B8M3, *The Brazilian-American Alliance*, Princeton University Press, Princeton, NJ, 1973 // Front cover verso, first free endpaper and other locations, "Library, U.S. Armor School, Fort Knox, Kentucky." // Title page is stamped, but not blacked out as usual, "Salvaged from Library, Acct. L 24.2"

D755.5.A3, *Years of Expectation*, Henry H. Adams, David McKay Company, Inc., NY, 1973 // Last free endpaper book pocket, "Crew's Library, U.S.S. Orion, (AS-19), Naval General Library, Chief of Naval Personnel, C-46." The first USS Orion was a coaling ship of World War I vintage. The second USS Orion was a submarine tender built in 1941 and decommissioned in 1993. Her last home port was La Maddalena, on the northern tip of Sardinia, Italy, where she supported US submarines in the Mediterranean Sea.

D755.6.A3, *Years to Victory*, Henry H. Adams, David McKay Company, Inc., NY, 1973 // Title page and back cover recto, "Warrior Preparation Center, Library, APO 09012" and "Library FL 2566, _____ Field, Syracuse, NY, 13225." A Warrior Preparation Center is a US Air Force facility to train staffs for war fighting through simulations. This one was located in Germany.

D756.G6131959, *The Battle of France*, 1940, Colonel A. Goutard, Ives Washburn, Inc., NY, 1959 // Cursive on first free endpaper, "B.T. Seehan, Lt Col, Artillery, Heidelberg, Germany, 1960."

D756.5.A7M261984, *A Time for Trumpets*, Charles B. MacDonald, William Morrow and Company, NY, 1985 // Stamped on book pocket on first free endpaper, "Det 1, 10 TRW / Library APO 09120" and a sticker, "7119 ABF / Library, APO 09120." The above unit is Detachment 1, 10th Tactical Reconnaissance Wing, somewhere in Europe.

Figure D763.I82R66

D761.G46v1, *Les Fossoyeurs, 1943*, Éditions De La Maison Française, Inc., NY, no date // Simple title page has red stamp, "U.S. Government, Office of War Information, New York, Library."

D762.P3L34, *Is Paris Burning?*, Larry Collins, Pocket Books, NY // Second free endpaper is blurb page and is stamped, "Salem College Library, Discard." This is from Salem College in Winston-Salem, North Carolina.

D763.I82A55, *Anzio*, Martin Blumenson, J.B. Lippincott Company, NY, 1963 // Sticker on first free endpaper, "James H. Higgins, 8232 Crestline Circle, N.W., Huntsville, AL 35805." "5.00"

D763.I82R66, *Inside Rome With the Germans*, Jane Scrivner, The Macmillan Company, NY, 1945 // First free endpaper has a bookplate of a library shelf, lamp and a house in background. Figure D763.I82R66. Also there is stamped, "Boysville High, BOYSVILLE, Clinton, Michigan." Boysville is a treatment center for juveniles.

D764.Z4871969, *Marshal Zhukov's Greatest Battles*, Georgi Zhukov, Harper & Row, NY, 1969 // UAH gift bookplate, LTC James C. Schaaf Jr.

Figure D764.3.L4S313

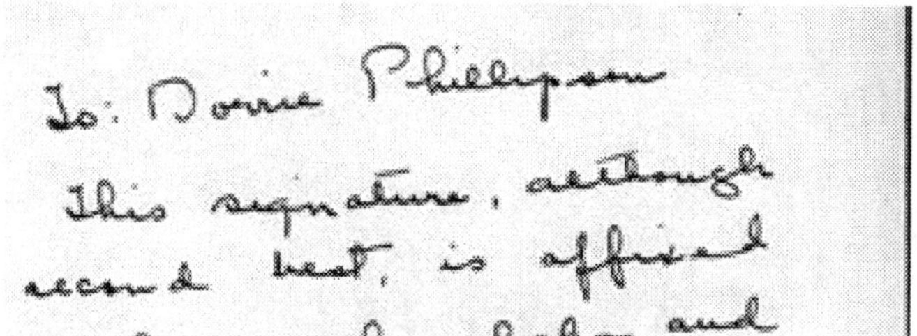

D764.3L4S313, *Siege and Survival*, Elena Skrjabina, Southern Illinois University Press, Carbondale, Illinois, 1971 // Stamped on first free endpaper and title page, "Parke Library, Birmingham Public Library." There is also a Birmingham Public Library bookplate. Figure D764.3L4S313.

D766.3.B8, *Greece and Crete 1941*, Christopher Buckley, Her Majesty's Stationery Office, London, 1952 // Title page stamped, "Naval Air Station, Library, Norfolk, VA."

D767.L4, *They Call It Pacific*, Clark Lee, The Viking Press, NY, 1943 // Writing on dedication page is at Figure D767.L4.

Figure D767.L4

D767.P7, *The Marines War*, Fletcher Pratt, William Sloane Associates, Inc., NY, 1948 // Front cover verso sticker, "Bruce Ward, 3735 Cowley Way, San Diego, Calif. 92109"

D767.6.S56, *Defeat Into Victory*, Field Marshal The Viscount Slim, David McKay Company, Inc., NY, 1961 // Stamped on front cover verso and title page, "Air University Library, Maxwell Air Force

Base, Ala, Property of U.S. Air Force, Discarded." Also Library of Congress surplus and duplicate. These marking were appreciatively unmarked by the UAH censors.

D769.A533vol.6pt.12, *U.S. Army in World War II, The Technical Services*, Leo Brophy, Department of the Army, Washington, D.C., 1959 // Front cover verso bookplate, "Technical Library, Department of the Navy, Bureau of Ships." "Bureau of Ships" also stamped of first free endpaper and title page.

D773.I55, *First Fleet*, Reg Ingraham, The Cornwell Press, Cornwell, NY, 1944 // Stamped on front cover verso and back cover recto, "Naval Library, Naval Bureau Weapons Center, Dahlgren Laboratory, Dahlgren, Virginia, 22448."

D787.L831977b, *Luftwaffe: A History*, Harold Faber, Times Books, NY, 1977 // Cursive on front cover verso, "To Jim, With Highest Regards For Your Air Force Career, 5/16/1980. Your Son-In-Law, Roger."

D804.G42A42v12, *Trials of War Criminals*, Nuernberg Military Tribunals // Stamp on first free endpaper, "Surgeon General's Library, U.S. Navy."

Figure D807.U6A52v5

D804.R9Z3, *Death in the Forest*, J.K. Zawodny, University of Notre Dame Press, Notre Dame, Indiana, 1962 // Stamp on back cover recto, "Wayne General & Technical College, Orrville, Ohio 44667."

D805.F8F42, *The Devil in France*, Lion Feuchtwanger, The Viking Press, NY, 1941 // Front cover verso bookplate, "Winthrop College," Figure D805.F8F42. The college library carried the name, "Carnegie Library." Andrew Carnegie apparently provided the funds with which to construct the building, as he did for over 1,900 libraries in the United States.

D807.U6A52v5, *Preventive Medicine in World War II*, Medical Department, U.S. Army // Bookplate on front cover verso, "Consultation-Research-Publication-Instruction" on top, a world map and an owl in the center, and" The Dyer Institute of Interdisciplinary Studies, New Hope, Bucks County, Pennsylvania."

D810.C4P2, *Evacuation Survey*, Richard Padley, George Routledge & Sons, LTD, London, 1940 // Front cover verso bookplate, "Property of Public Roads Administration Library," not further identified.

D811.B4751945, *Keep Your Head Down*, Walter Bernstein, Book Find Club, NY, 1941 // Cursive on first free endpaper, "This book belongs to: Shirley Heller, 779 New Lots Ave., Brooklyn 8, N.Y."

D811.M36, *The Road Past Mandalay*, John Masters, Harper & Brothers, NY, 1961 // Embossed stamp on first free endpaper, "Library of Paul X. Kelley," with a large "PXK" in the center.

Figure D811.5.S24

Figure D811.5.M3

D811.Y573, *The Two Worlds of Jim Yoshida*, Jim Yoshida, William Morrow & Company, Inc., NY, 1972 // Title page has a stamp, "Station Library, U.S. Naval Radio Station, Sugar Grove, W. VA 26815."

D811.5.B76, *Suez to Singapore*, Cecil Brown, Random House, NY, 1942 // Pencil cursive on simple title page, "Robert T. Pollock, New York, 1192 Park Ave."

D811.5.D3751943, *The Germans came to Paris*, Peter de Polnay, Duell, Sloan and Pearce, NY, 1943 // Stamped on front cover verso and first free endpaper, "Station Library, U.S. Naval Station, Melbourne, Florida" and "Property of Station Library, NWL, Dahlgren, VA." NWL is Naval Weapons Laboratory.

D811.5.M3, *Women of Britain*, Beatrice Curtis Brown, Harcourt, Brace and Company, NY, 1941 // First free endpaper bookplate, "Ex Libris, Maynard's Book Shops" with a sailing ship. Figure D811.5.M3.

D811.5.M4, *Tell the Folks Back Home*, U.S. Senator James M. Mead, D. Appleton-Century Company, NY, 1944 // Cursive on first free endpaper, "To Lister Hill with good wishes from his friend, Jim Mead, Washington, D.C., June 28 44." The "with good wishes" was written smaller, as if it was an afterthought. Mead was a senator from New York, 1938-47.

D811.5.P9, *Ernie Pyle in England*, Ernie Pyle, Robert M. McBride & Company, NY, 1941 // Cursive on first free endpaper, "to W.D. Alsbaugh by Arthene & Wentz, Father's Day, 1946. 5.00"

D811.5.S24, *From the Land of Silent People*, Robert St. John, Doubleday, Doran & Co., Inc., NY, 1942 // Bookplate on first free endpaper of Betty Smith. Figure D811.5.S24.

D825.W367, *Where Are We Heading?*, Sumner Welles, Harper & Brothers, NY, 1946 // Front cover verso bookplate, "John O. Watz." Figure D825.W367.

D842.S451964, *Nationalism and Communism*, Hugh Seton-Watson, Frederick A. Praeger, NY, 1964 // First free endpaper bookplate, "Post Library, Redstone Arsenal, Huntsville, Alabama, Property of U.S. Army." Figure D842.S451964.

D843.H54, *The Crouching Future*, Roger Hilsman, Doubleday & Company, NY, 1975 // Stamp on title page verso and back cover recto, "Station Library, MCAS, Kaneohe." MCAS is Marine Corps Air Station and Kaneohe is on the beautiful eastern shore of Oahu, Hawaii Islands, surrounded on three sides by water.

D845.C61964, *The Politics of the Atlantic Alliance*, Alvin J. Cottrell, Frederick A. Praeger, NY, 1964 // "Library of U.S. Defense Intelligence School" stamped in red on front cover verso, first free endpaper, last free endpaper and back cover recto.

D847.S9, *Soviet and Chinese Communists Power in the World Today*, Rodger Swearingen, Basis Books, Inc., NY, 1966 // Stamped on titled page, "Naval Station Library, Argentia, Newfoundland." This is cross-referenced to CT275.V234v3.

Figure D825.W367

D907.B53, *Europe, A Geographical Survey*, J.F. Bogardus, Harper & Brothers, NY, 1934 // Front cover verso bookplate, "U.S. Board of Geographical Names." Figure D907.B53. Stamp on title page, "U.S. Department of the Interior, Office of Geography Library, Washington 25, DC.

D919.F161912, *My Unknown Chum*, Agueecheek (a pseudonym), The Devin-Adair Co., NY, 1912 // Stamped in seven places, "Holy Trinity High School, Chicago 22, Illinois."

D919.W55, *European Notes on What I Saw in the Old World*, M.B. Wharton, James P. Harrison & Company, Atlanta, Georgia, 1884 // Circular stamp on front cover verso, "Dr L.L. Hill, 122 So. Perry Street, Montgomery, Alabama" and cursive on second free endpaper, "L.L. Hill M.D. Montgomery, Alabama, Feb. 17th 1885." Cross reference to D24.65.

D921.G451934b, *European Journey*, Philip Gibbs, Doubleday, Doran & Company, In., NY, 1934 // Bookplate on front cover verso, "Ruby & Max Bloomstein." Figure D921.G451934b.

Figure D921.G451934b

D967.S7, *Traveller's Tales*, "The Princess," G.P. Putnam' Sons, NY, 1912 // Front cover verso bookplate, "James W. Ligon RA." Figure D967.S7.

DA16.G7381969, *Empire Into Commonwealth*, Sir Percival Griffiths, Ernest Benn Limited, London, 1969 // Front cover verso bookplate, "Miami University Library, Oxford, Ohio." Figure DA16.G7381969. Embossed stamp on title page, "Miami University Library, Oxford, Ohio."

DA28.1.B451954, *The Royal Family*, Pierre Berton, Alfred A. Knopf, NY, 1955 // Stamped on title page verso, "Property of AFL 5518 Base Library, 7513th Air Base Group, RAF Mildenhall, Suffolk" (England). Royal Air Force Base Mildenhall is about 70 miles north of London. It was and still remains the principal base utilized by the U.S. Air Force for flights from and to the United States and Europe.

Figure D967.S7

Figure D842.S451964

DA32.A891899v1, *Rise and Growth of the English Nation*, 3 volumes, W.H.S. Aubrey, D. Appleton and Company, NY, 1896 // Cursive on first free endpaper, "Laura Farber Fitch McQuiston, Fort Sheridan, Illinois." On second free endpaper is cursive, "Laura from Charlie, Fort Sheridan, Illinois." This appears to be the same Laura Fitch McQuiston who was the author of an article in the *St. Nicholas Magazine,* March 1915 and received a letter from Mark Twain in 1901.

DA32.H9, *History of the British People*, Edward Maslin Hulme, The Century Co., NY, 1924 // Front cover verso bookplate, "Harold Hulme" underneath, across the top, "Overhulme" and along sides and bottom, "Francimur Sed Numgian Flegtimur." Figure DA32.H9. It is presumed that Harold was the son of Edward, the author.

DA32.M936, *First Steps in the History of England*, Arthur May Mowery, Silver, Burdett and Company, NY, 1902 // Stamped on title page, "Public School 40, ?13 1904, Albert Sh???, Principal."

DA 86.R51953, *The Navy as an Instrument of Policy*, Admiral Sir Herbert Richmond, Cambridge University Press, Cambridge, United Kingdom, 1953 // Stamped on back cover recto, "Property Puget Sound Naval Shipyard, Bremerton, Washington, Please Return."

Figure DA16.G7381969

DA86.22.R2W3, *Sir Walter Raleigh*, Walter Waldman, St. James Library, Collins, London, 1928 // Front cover verso sticker, "Robert G. Albion, Widener Library, Harvard."

DA110.T35, *Notes on England*, H. Taine, Henry Holt and Company, NY, 1874 // Sticker on first free endpaper, "From the Library of Robert F. Campbell, Ashville, N.C." and cursive on sticker, "John Boone Trotti, July, 1954."

DA130.H41879, *Chronicles and Memories of Great Britain and Ireland During the Middle Ages*, Thomas Arnold, Longman & Co., Paternoster Row, London, 1879 // Bookplates on front cover verso and first free endpaper. Figures DA130.H41879-1 &-2, There are two Watford's in England. Stamped on first free endpaper and title page, "Bellarmine College, Joques Library, Plattsburgh N.Y." Embossed on the preface page, "LeMoyne College Library." LeMoyne College is in Syracuse, New York.

Figure DA32.H9

DA256.L31975, *Henry V*, Margaret Wade, Secker & Warburg, London, 1975 // Sticker on bottom left of front cover verso, "Foyles, The World's Greatest Bookshop, 119-125 Charing Cross Road, London, W.C.Z." This is a similar Foyles' sticker to BT75.07190?, but the words are different.

DA315.L46, *Tudor Dynastic Problems, 1460-1571*, Mortimer Levine, George Allen & Unwin LTD, London, 1973 // UAH giftplate of Dr. John C. Wright on front cover verso. On first free endpaper in cursive, "For Dean John Wright, with my compliments and good wishes, Mortimer Levine."

DA320.H2811966v1, *Nuge Antique*, Sir John Harrington, J. Wright, Denmark-Court, Strand, London, 1804 // Cursive on first free endpaper, "Tredell (?) Jenkins (?) 1978"

DA355.H1761892, *Society in the Elizabethan Age*, Hubert Hall, Swan Sonnenschein & Co., Paternoster Square, London, 1892 // Small sticker on bottom right of front cover verso, "H. Cleave, Bookseller, 9, New Bond Street Place, Bath." (England)

DA355.W261946, *Elizabeth and Leicester*, Milton Waldman, Collins, 14 St. James Place, London, 1944 // Stamp on first free endpaper, a climbing bear and R D. Figure DA355.W261946.

DA391.M23, *The Wisest Fool in Christendom* (King James I and VI), William McElwee, Harcourt, Brace and Company, NY, 1958 // Stamp on first free endpaper, "F. Nelson Breed, Wilton, Conn."

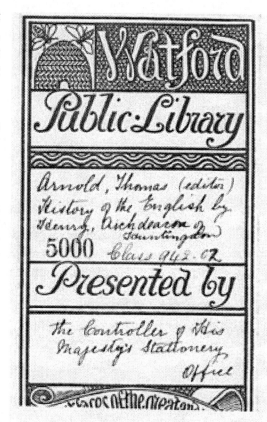

DA391.S75, *James I of England*, Clara & Hardy Steeholm, 1938 // Bookplate "The Public Library of Dark Harbor, Maine, November 1938 by Book Club, Figure DA391.S75. Isleboro, Maine // "The Old Corner Book Store, Inc., Boston, Maine."

Figure DA130.H41879-1

Figure DA391.S75

Figure DA355.W261946

DA407.N5L6, *The First Duke and Duchess of Newcastle Upon-Tyne*, T. Longueville, Longmans, Green, & Co., 39 Paternoster Row, London, 1910 // Bookplate on front cover verso, "Sir Hugh Nicholas Jackson." Figure DA407.N5L6.

A470.C61945, *The Common People, 1746-1938*, G.D.H. Cole, Methuen & Co., London, 1938 // First free endpaper and title page stamp, "No. 2 School of Cookery, R.A.F., Innsworth." Royal Air Force Innsworth, is in Gloucester, England, and is the location of the RAF Personnel and Training Command. It is about 90 miles northwest of London.

DA533.F3, *Victorians Day in England*, Anna Maria Fay, Houghton Mifflin, NY, 1923 // Front cover verso bookplate, "Ex Libris, D.H. Frank." Figure DA533.F3. A voracious reader is sitting on a haphazard pile of books. The figure resembles the man in "The Bookworm" drawing by Karl Spitzweg, which I have hanging on the wall outside my work room. It is a shame that the UAH censor made those ghastly black marks across a wonderful bookplate that symbolizes the bibliophile.

A556.I61926, *England*, William Inge, Ernest Benn Limited, London, 1926 // Sticker on lower right of front cover verso, "R.G. Glaisher, Bookbuyer & Bookseller, 25 Hillgate Hill, London, N.19. Books Bought."

DA566.4.B8, *Here is England*, Elizabeth Burton, Ariel Books, NY, 1965 // Stamp on front cover verso, "Property of United States Air Force, Chicksands Base Library." Chicksands is near Shefford, England, about 35 miles north of London and 22 miles southwest of Cambridge. In 1950 the US Air Force Security Service established a radio squadron there. The antennas were tall towers in a circle designed to detect Soviet high frequency radio signals and provide the direction of the signal source.

Figure DA407.N5L6

The antenna array nomenclature was AN/FLR-9, but everybody called it the "Elephant Cage" There were about 80 towers in the array of 260 meters in diameter, each several hundred feet high, hence the name elephant cage. It obviously worked because there were no elephants around, as the joke went. The site was deactivated in 1995 and dismantled in 1996.

Figure DA533.F3

DA588.C681949, *No Cause for Alarm*, Virginia Cowles, Hamish Hamilton, London, 1949 // Front cover verso bookplate, "Ex Libris, Millicent Turle Roelker." Figure DA588.C681949. The censor did not get at this nice bookplate of a lady wearing a bustle

Figure DA588.C681949

superimposed over a French poodle. The scene in the bookplate apparently is connected to graphics associated with the English author, Charles Dickens. Millicent Turle was married on January 12, 1905 to Alfred Roelker, a graduate of Amherst College in 1895. Roelker received his law degree from Columbia University in 1898 and practiced in New York City from 1898 onwards. He served as a captain in a machine gun battalion in World War I.

DA676.8.A1O771867, *Citizens of London and Their Rulers, 1060-1867*, B.B. Orridge, William Tegg, Pancras Lane, Cheapside, London, 1867 // Bookplate on front cover verso of Earl of Arran featuring his crest and two horses, topped by the English lion. Figure DA676.8.A1O771867. The Earl of Arran is a peerage in both Ireland and Scotland. Based on lineage information available, this bookplate appears to be

Figure DA676.8.A1O771867

associated with the Ireland branch, which is still being passed on in the family Gore. This book, published in 1867, possibly belonged to the 6th Earl of Arran, who lived 1868-1958, and was succeeded by the 7th Earl, 1903-1958. The 9th Earl, born 1938, was elected into the House of Lords as Baron Sudley in 1999.

DA677.1.H61926a, *Roman London*, Gorden Home, George H. Doran Co, NY, 1926 // Cursive on first free endpaper, "Hannal More Academy, June 7th-1927, This prize is given to Eunice Lehman for excellence in the reading of Virgil, and in Latin composition, and for her scholarly attitude toward the subject. Mary Lee Labl(?)." Hannal More is a private special education school in Reisterstown, Maryland, just northwest of Baltimore. In 2005 the school had 135 students.

DA685.S143D2, *History of St. James Square*, Arthur Dasent, Macmillan Company, London, 1895 // Circular stamp on front cover verso, "Cullum Library, Bury St. Edmunds." First free endpaper cursive, "G. Milner-Gibson-Cullum." There was a pressed leaf between pages 72-73. Bury St. Edmunds is in England about 65 miles northeast of London.

DA687.69L8, *The Guildhall of the City of London*,

Figure DA687.69L8-1

Sir John James Baddeley, Eden Fisher & Company, LTD, London, 1912 // Front cover verso presentation copy bookplate. Figure DA687.69L8-1. On the bottom of the plate is the cursive, "Clarence Hayden, Esquire, who entered the corporation, October 1909." Above the bookplate is written in cursive, "To M.E. Robinson, from her Father. September 1921." On the second and third free endpapers are pasted newspaper clippings of a picture (Figure DA687.69L8-2) and obituary (Figure DA687.69L8-3) of the above cited Clarence Hayden, who passed away at his home in Sutton-on-Sea, a coastal town 120 miles north of London.

DA690.G45A81957, *King Arthur's Avalon*, Geoffrey Ashe, Collins, St. James Place, London, 1957 // Bottom left corner of front cover verso is a small sticker, "Books and Careers, 485 Oxford Street, London, W.1 GROsvenor 5664." The capital "GRO" is exactly the way they were printed on the sticker. It looks as if the printer realized there was not enough space to capitalize the rest of the letters in the word and changed to lower case or perhaps it is a telephone number.

THE STANDARD. SATURDAY, APRIL 28, 1928.

SUTTON-ON-SEA J.P.'s DEATH.

MR. CLARENCE HAYDEN, J.P.,
of Link's View, Sutton-on-Sea, who died on Wednesday at the age of 76 years. A detailed report of the deceased gentleman's career appears in our Horncastle and Louth editions.

Figure DA687.69L8-2

DA783.4.M3, *Robert the Bruce*, Herbert Maxwell, G.P. Putnam's Sons, London, 1897 // Bookplate on front cover verso from Virginia Traveling Library, Figure DA783.4.M3. Punched through title page, "Virginia State Library." Stamp on back cover recto, "Received, T.L. Div, Jan 30 1908, Virginia State Library."

DA787.A2L3, *A Letter from Mary Queen of Scots to the Duke of Guise, January 1562*, John Hungerford Pollen, Edinburgh University Press, Edinburgh, Scotland, 1904 // Front cover verso bookplate from George Lorimer. Figure DA787.A2L3.

DA890.G55M81925, *The Streets of Glasgow and: Their: Story*, David Murray, Aird & Coghill, Limited, Glasgow, Scotland, 1925 // Front cover verso has a blacked out bookplate, "Gift of William Stanley Hoole, Dean of the University Libraries, 1969-1971, University Librarian, 1944-1969, Professor, Graduate School of Library Science, 1971-1974, The University of Alabama." Stamped on cover, first free endpaper and title page, "S.S.C. Library, Edinburgh."

DA965.D4B71956a, *De Valera*, Mary C. Bromage, The Noonday Press, NY, 1956 // Embossed stamp on dedication page, "Columbus Public Library, Columbus, Ohio."

DB19.S35131967, *Imago Austria*, Otto Schulmeister, et.al., Verlag Herder & Co., Vienna, 1967 // Large sticker on title page, "Donated by the Republic of Austria." Cursive on first free endpaper, "1979 Donated by Professor Dr" above a stamp, "Dr. jur. Siegmund Seiger, 2685 University Avenue, Apartment 64B, Bronx NY 10468." Front cover verso has UAH bookplate, "Gift of the Austrian Institute for the Hertha Heller Retirement Fund."

DB215.K4, *Czechoslovakia*, Robert J. Kerner, University Press, Berkeley, California, 1949 // Title page stamp, "Bureau of the Census Library."

DB217.M3N49, *Masaryk*, Edward Polson Newman, Campion Press Limited, London, 1960 // Front cover verso stamp, "Library, Branch 2, U.S. Information Agency."

DC33.4.E46v1, *Old Court Life in France*, Frances Elliot, 2 volumes, G.P. Putnam's Sons, NY, 1893 // Bookplate on front cover verso, "Lawrence and Alicia Harnecker," which features books, a river and a castle. Figure DC33.4.E46v1.

DC33.7.S4, *French Perspectives*, Elizabeth Shepley Sergeant, Houghton Mifflin Company, NY, 1916 // Sticker on front cover verso, "Sylvia C. Bowditch, 77 Woodland Road, Jamaica, Plain, Mass."

DC34.N6813, *The French*, Francois Nourissier, Alfred A. Knopf, NY, 1968 // Front cover verso bookplate, "Charles White," candles and books. Figure DC34.N6813. First free endpaper has a UAH gift bookplate by Dr. John C. White.

DC126.L3v1, *Historie de le Régence et de La Minorite de Louis XV (History of the Regency of the Minority of Louis 15th)*, 2 volumes, Par P.-E. leMontey, Paulin, Paris, MDCCCXXXII // Front cover verso small sticker, "Librarie, Raymond Clavreuil, 37. Rue St. Andre des Arts, Paris VII."

Figure DA687.69L8-3

DC135.B5A31902v2, *Memoirs and Letters of Cardinal de Bernis*, Hardy, Pratt & Company, Boston, 1902 // Front cover verso stamp, "Library of Virginia Military Institute, Lexington, Virginia."

DC137.5.B8204, *L'Amour Le Plus Tendre*, Jeanine Delpech, Librarie Academique Perrin, Paris, 1964 // Large sticker on first free endpaper, "Offert par l'Alliance Française, 101, Boulevard Rasparl-Paris 6ᵉ."

DC203.Y612v2, *Napoleon as a General*, Count Yorck von Wartenburg, no publisher, no date // Bookplate on front cover verso, "COLONEL N. BUTLER BRISCOE." Figure DC203.Y612v2. Title page stamp, "Copy No. 1, Education Center, Fort Knox, Kentucky."

DC242.H871968, *Waterloo: Day of Battle*, David Howarth, Antheneum, NY, 1968 // First free endpaper stamp, "Property of US Army, Post Library, Fort Campbell, Kentucky."

DC251.T1361906c1, *Les Origines de La France Contemporaine*, H. Taine, Librarie Hachette, Paris, 1906 // Title page stamp, "Biblioteca de: Melchor de La Garza; Saenz: Donado A: Biblioteca Benjamin Franklin."

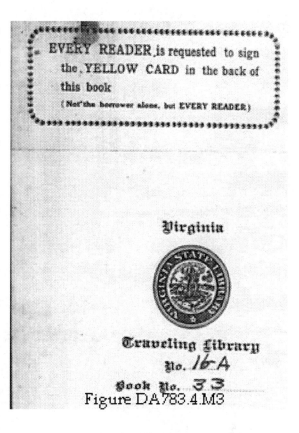

Figure DA783.4.M3

VIRTUTIS GLORIA MERCES
EX LIBRIS GEORGE LORIMER.

Figure DA787.A2L3

DC285.H31905a, *Count Halzfeldt's Letters 1870-1871*, J. L. Bashford, E.P. Dutton and Company, NY, 1905 // Front cover verso bookplate, "From the Library of Munroe Smith, Bryce Professor of European Legal History" and first free endpaper and title page stamp, "Property of Athens College Library." Although not stated in the book, the Bryce Professor of International Legal History is an endowed chair at Columbia University in New York City.

DC285.W33v1&2, *Recollections of a Minister to France*, E. B. Washburne, Charles Scribner's Sons, NY, 1887 // Embossed stamp

Figure DC33.4.E46v1

on title page, "Harry S. Truman Library, Independence, Missouri."

DC290.B85, *Franco-German War of 1870-'71*, L.P. Brockett, J.W. Goodspeed & Co., NY, 1871 // Cursive on first free endpaper, "G.L. Foleys Book, Norwich, Ohio, July 5th 1871" and stamp, "The Lora Allen Memorial Library, Norwich, Ohio." and another stamp, "The Allen Museum, Norwich, Ohio." Norwich seems to be an unincorporated community about 10 miles east of Zanesville, Ohio, and is also 5 miles west of New Concord, the home of astronaut John Glenn.

DD90.S821945a, *A Short History of Germany*, S.H. Steinberg, The Macmillan Company, NY, 1945 // Stamp on front cover verso, first free endpaper, last free endpaper verso and back cover recto, "Chester V. Easum, University of Wisconsin, Madison, Wisconsin."

Figure DC34.N6813

DD222.F8, *Germany of Today*, George Stuart Fullerton, The Bobbs-Merrill Company, Indianapolis, 1915 // Cursive on first free endpaper, "Uncle John from Mary & Margaret, August 1916."

DD231.B43A42, *Memoirs of Count Bernstorff*, Random

Figure DC203.Y612v2

House, NY, 1936 // First free endpaper stamp, "Bertrand Smith's Book Store, Acres of Books, 633 Main St., Cincinnati, Ohio."

DD231.B8A17v1, *Prince von Bülow Memoirs 1897-1903*, Putnam, London, 1930 // This is the first time I encountered a sticker on the front of the cover. It was in the form of a shield or crest, green, and had, "Boots, Booklovers Library." It is amazing that it was still there after many years.

DD231.H5W5, *Wooden Titan*, John W. Wheeler-Bennett, William Morrow & Co., NY, 1940 // Front cover verso had a Yale University bookplate. Figure DD231.H5W5.

DD247.H5T57, *They Wanted War*, Otto D. Tolischus, Reynal & Hitchcock, NY, 1940 // Sticker on front cover verso, "M. Lincoln Schuster, 11 East 73rd Street, New York City, BUTTERFIELD 8-2878." Note the two sizes of letters in Butterfield. This was the

YALE UNIVERSITY
LIBRARY

WITHDRAWN FROM
YALE UNIV. LIBRARY

Figure DD231.H5W5

New York City telephone prefix system of 50 years ago. There was 1960 movie, BUTTERFIELD 8, starring Elizabeth Taylor, Laurence Harvey and Eddie Fisher.

DD801.A347A21874, *Alsace 1871-1872*, E. About, Librarie Hachette ET, Paris, 1874 // Stamped on first free endpaper, second free endpaper and third free endpaper, "Eigentum Des Deutschen, Ausland-Instituts, Stuttgart." (Property of the German Foreign Institute,Stuttgart)

DD801.S13F55, *The Saar Struggle*, Michael T. Florinsky, The Macmillan Company, NY, 1935 // Front cover verso bookplate, Paul Kramer. Figure DD801.S13F55.

DF220.B3131967, *Lion Gate and Labyrinth*, Hans Bauman, Random House, NY, 1967 // Title page stamp, "Field Library, 7551 Support Sq., APO New York 09607." Stamp on title page verso, "Property of U.S. Air Force, Base Library, FL 5540, APO New York 09194." Stamp on title page verso, "Property of U.S. Air Force, USAFE Field Library Center, AFL 5510, APO US Forces 09633." Notice that there are three different numbered units and three different APO numbers.

Figure DD801.S13F55

DF220.H381968c, *Dawn of the Gods*, Jacquetta Hawkes, Random House, NY, 1968 // Bookplate on front cover verso, "James D. Ramer." Figure DF220.H381968c. James D. Ramer founded the University of Alabama Graduate School of Library and Information Science and was the first Dean in 1971.

Figure DF220.H381968c

DF725.M2121913, *Rambles and Studies in Greece*, J.P. Mahaffy, The Mcmillan Company, NY, 1913 // Cursive of first free endpaper, "Tom Davis, 1925, NY."

DF727.B4, *Marvelous Greece*, Ethyl S. Beer, Walker and Company, NY, 1967 // Stamped on first free endpaper and title page, "Base Library AFL 5620, 50th Combat Support Group, APO New York 09109."

DF859.A9213, *By Fire and Axe*, Evangelos Averoff-Tossizza, Caratzas Brothers, New Rochelle, NY, 1978 // Back cover recto bookplate, "Pentagon Library." Figure DF859.A9213.

DG207.T21T3351951, *On Britain and Germany*, Tacitus, Penguin Books, Harmondsworth, Middlesex, England, 1948 // Bookplate on original first free endpaper, "Charles Coker."

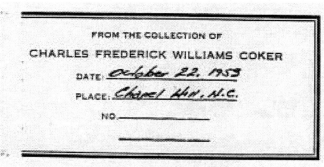

FROM THE COLLECTION OF
CHARLES FREDERICK WILLIAMS COKER
DATE: *October 22, 1953*
PLACE: *Chapel Hill, N.C.*
NO.

Figure DG207.T21T3351951

Figure DG207.T21T3351951.

DG271.S31906, *Imperial Purple*, Edgar Saltus, Brentano's, NY, 1892 // Cursive on first free endpaper, "Albert Brush, 133 West 56th, New York, NY."

DG427.H8571838, *Italian Journeys*, W.D. Howells, The Riverside Press, Cambridge, England, 1883 // Cursive on first free endpaper, "M.B. Saffold, Denver, Colo, July 5, 1907."

DG551.S85, *The Union of Italy*, 1815-1895, W. J. Stillman, Cambridge University Press, 1899 // First free endpaper cursive, "Susan A. Harper, 730 W. Adams St., Chicago, Ill."

Figure DG677.O48

DG677.O48, *Makers of Venice*, Mrs. Oliphant, H.M. Caldwell Company, NY, no date // Stamp on front cover verso of scroll and two high flames. Figure DG677.O48.

Figure DH188.O4119v2

DH188.O4119v2, *The Complete Works of John L. Motley*, v11, Society of English and French Literature, NY, 1874 // Front cover verso has a bookplate of a man beside a stream. "Ex Libris, Lee W. Parke, Books-My-Silent-Faithful-Friends-Are-They." Figure DH188.O4119v2.

Figure DK32.W46

DH404.G66, *Belgium*, Jan-Albert Goris, University of California Press, Berkeley, California, 1945 // First free endpaper stamp, "Library, American University, Moscow."

DK28.H5, *Red Plush and Black Bread*, Marguerite Higgins, Doubleday & Company, Garden City, NY, 1955 // Bookplate on front cover verso from Illinois Bell Telephone

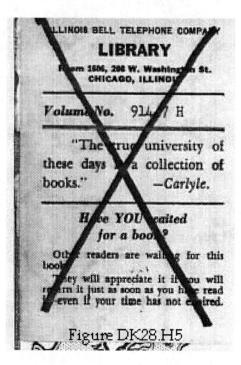

Figure DK28.H5

46

Company. Figure DK28.H5. The bookplate has one of my favorite sayings by Thomas Carlyle, the 19th century Scottish essayist and historian. The quote is not what one would expect from a telephone company.

DK32.W46, *Land of Milk and Honey*, W.L. White, Harcourt, Brace and Company, NY, 1949 // Bookplate on first free endpaper has a horse and rider, "Jane Esty, Her Book." Figure DK32.W46.

DK71.L3, *The March of Muscovy*, Harold Lamb, Doubleday & Company, Garden City, NY, 1948 // Title page stamp, "Naval Training Station Library, Great Lakes, Illinois." Great Lakes Naval Training Station has a longstanding and continuing history as the premier U.S. Navy training facility.

DK170.K351935b, *Catherine*, Gina Kaus, Halcyon House, NY, 1935 // Front cover verso bookplate with a torch, book and "Hassmer." Figure DK170.K351935b.

DK189.U43, *Russia's Failed Revolution*, Adam B. Ulam, Basic Books, Inc., NY, 1981 // Stamp of lion head and "The New York Public Library," on front cover verso, first free endpaper, and title page verso. For those unfamiliar with the front of the NY Public Library, there are two huge lions, one on either side of the steps from the street.

Figure DK170.K351935b

DK219.6.A4A31932a, *Once a Grand Duke*, Alexander, Grand Duke of Russia, Garden City Publishing Company, Garden City, NY, 1932 // Stamped on title page, "U.S. – T.V.A. LIBRARY." Work on the Tennessee Valley Authority's dam between Huntsville and Guntersville started in 1936. The TVA sent a professional librarian to establish libraries throughout Madison, Jackson and Marshall Counties to support the activities of the TVA and make a better life for the residents of the counties. The TVA library was separate from the Huntsville Public Library, but had its office in the basement of the Huntsville Library. TVA established over 50 library stops in stores and homes throughout the area. There was a 10 x 25-feet room just for a library in the community center building in the TVA village established about one half mile from the Guntersville Dam. When the dam was completed in 1939 and the village dismantled, the TVA professional became the director of the Huntsville Library. For more details, see my book, *From Carnegie to Fort Book*, ISBN 0-7414-2488-6, which is available in all locations of the Huntsville Madison County Public Library system.

DK268.L5P61943a, *Maxim Litvinoff*, Arthur Upham Pope, Fischer, NY, 1943 // Pasted over the "Fischer" is a sticker, "Martin Secker & Warburg LTD, 7 John Seal, Bloomsbury, W.C. I" This is the first instance I've encountered where a publisher put his sticker over another publisher. I'm sure there is a logical reason. Written in cursive on the first free endpaper, "Chen Chu Pei, Calcutta, India, Jan 14, 1946, on the way to the States." Please refer back to D217.M66. This individual had several books in the Salmon Library. The story seems to be that the man cited was Chinese, and came to the United

States by way of India. It was absolutely fascinating to find such an entry. He possibly bought the book in India to read on his long passage to the America. In addition, the time is less than a year after the terrible turmoil of World War II.

DK270.C6, *Communist Propaganda Techniques*, John C. Clews, Frederick A. Praeger, NY, 1964 // Title page verso and other locations stamped, "U.S. Air Force Base Library, Whiteman AFB, MO" // "USAF FL 4609, Kincheloe AFB, MI 49788." Both of these bases were part the nuclear Strategic Air Command (SAC) during the Cold War. Kincheloe was located in Michigan's upper peninsula, south of Sault Ste. Marie, and was inactivated in the 1970s. Whiteman was east southeast of Kansas City, and was inactivated in the 1990s.

DK274.S6525, *The Soviet Union*, Foy D. Kohler, University of Miami Center for Advanced International Studies, Miami, FL, 1975 // Stamp on title page verso and back cover recto, "Property of U.S. Air Force, Base Library, Hancock Field, NY, 13225." Hancock Field was activated as part of World War II and inactivated in 1983. It now serves as the airport for Syracuse, New York.

DK274.S71985, *USSR Foreign Policies After Détente*, Richard F. Starr, Hoover Institution Press, Stanford University, Stanford, CA, 1985 // Title page verso stamp, "July 1985, Received, Library, Naval War College, Newport, RI."

DK275.A4B531967b, *Svetlana*, Enzo Biagi, Funk & Wagnalls, NY, 1967 // Stamps on title page, "Carroll College Library, Helena, Montana, 59601" and "Discarded from Carroll College Library."

DK275.A45A3613, *Involuntary Journey to Siberia*, Andrei Amalrik, Harcourt Brace Jovanovich, Inc., NY, 1970 // Stamp on simple title page, "Santa Barbara Public Library, County Fund Purchase." The state is assumed to be California.

DK275.A53S641983, *Yuri Andropov*, Vladimir Solovyov, Macmillan Publishing Company, NY, 1983 // Title page stamp, "Library, U-16, Naval Air Station, Norfolk, Virginia 23511."

DK276.M51961, *Russians as People*, Wright Miller, E.P. Gutton & Co., NY, 1961 // Bookplate on front cover verso, "Burgess Library, Columbia University." Figure DK276.M51961.

DK407.P5, *The New Poland*, Charles Phillips, The Macmillan Company, NY, 1923 // Cursive on first free endpaper, "Inscribed for Frank Rice: friend & comrade of "the good old days" in the New Poland: Charles Phillips, Dec 23/23."

DK418.5.R9C31944, *Poland and Russia*, Ann Su Cardwell, Sheed & Ward, NY, 1944 /// Front cover verso bookplate, "Park College Library." This college is at Parkville, Missouri, a northern suburb of Kansas City, Kansas.

DK756.S241969, *Siberia*, George St. George, David McKay Company, Inc., NY, 1969 // First free endpaper stamp, "U.S. Army RVN, Spec Svc Libraries APO 90348." The translation is RVN for Republic of Vietnam and Special Services, which are all the morale and related activities. This is my first

THE LIBRARIES

COLUMBIA UNIVERSITY

URGESS LIBRARY

Figure DK276.M51961

accession from Vietnam, where I served for one year, March 1966-March 1967.

DL113.S581956a, *Denmark*, Sacheverell Sitwell, B.T. Batsford, LTD, London, 1956 // First free endpaper stamp, "USAF Library, RAF Station, Upper Heyford." Upper Heyford is about 15 miles north of Oxford, England, and was an active U.S. Air Force base from World War II until 1994, when it was returned to the English Ministry of Defence.

DL305.S26, *Daughter of Fire*, Katharine Scherman, Little, Brown and Company, Boston, 1976 // Title page stamp, "This Book Provided by Project: LEARN (Books For People) Interchurch Council, 781-7071, NOT FOR RESALE." UAH Gift bookplate from Del Williams.

DL631.W553, *Sweden in the Sixties*, Ingemar Wiksell, Almquist & Wiksell, Stockholm, 1967 // Stamp on simple title page, "Export-Import Bank of the United States, Oct 16, 1968, Library."

DP42.A86, *Beyond the Pyrenees*, Marcel Aurousseau, Alfred H. King, NY, 1931 // Bookplate on front cover verso, "William Bradley Randall, Pelham Manor, N.J." Figure DP42.A86.

Figure DP42.A86

DP42.021937a, *Farewell Spain*, Kate O'Brien, Doubleday, Doran & Company, Garden City, NY, 1937 // "Emporium Circulating Library, Nov 9, 1937." Found no clues on this location.

DP48.E462, *Old Court Life in Spain*, Frances Elliot, Brentano's, NY, no date // Front cover verso bookplate, "David F. Hieras" and a print of *The Bookworm*, by Karl Spitzweg. Figure DP48.E462. Spitzweg lived from 1808 to 1885 and the Internet is full of Spitzweg art so there are apparently no copyright issues about using it.

Figure DP48.E462

DP59.R651997, *Los Borbones destronados*, Carlos Rojas, Plaza & Janes, Barcelona, Spain, 1997 // Cursive on second free endpaper, "For Herbert Francis, with five hundred years of friendship and a very big "Abuzo.", Carlos Rojas."

DP264.F7A82, *Francisco Franco*, Joaquin Arrarás, The Bruce Publishing Company, Milwaukee, 1938 // Front cover verso stamp, "Library, St. Augustine's H.S., 64 Park Place, Brooklyn,"

DP650.C421969, *Carlota Joaquina*, Marcus Cheke, Books for Libraries Press, Freeport, NY, 1947 // Title page stamp, "The Library, Indiana State University Evansville Campus, WITHDRAWN."

DR10.B4, *Central and South East Europe 1945-1948*, R.R. Betts, Royal Institute of International Affairs, London, 1950 // Front cover verso bottom left small sticker, "Arthur Probsthain, Oriental Bookseller,

41 Gt. Russell Street, London, W.C.1." Arthur Probsthain was still in business in 2006. Great Russell Street is well known because the British Museum's main entrance is on that street and Probsthain is directly across the street.

DR60.2.R5 (oversize), *Bulgarien*, Erich Rinka, Sachenverlag, Dresden, Germany, 1956 // Front cover verso bookplate of Army Map Service. Figure DR60.2.R5.

DR98.P55C5, *Plovdiv*, Konstantin Chalatscher, Fremsprachenverlag (foreign language publisher), Sofia, Bulgaria, 1965 // Stamp on first free endpaper, "Army Map Service Library, Washington, D.C., Jan 22, 1966."

DS32.A81957, *Asia's Who's Who*, Pan-Asia Newspaper Alliance, Hong Kong, 1957 // Title page stamp, "The Ford Foundation, The Library."

DS33.3.L31968b, *Asian Frontiers*, Alastair Lamb, Frederick A. Praeger, 1968 // Title page verso stamp, "Property of US Air Force Base Library, Eglin AFB, Florida 32542. Eglin is a large base in Florida's panhandle surrounding the town of Fort Walton Beach.

DS35.P455, *Changing Politics of Modern Asia*, René Peritz, D. Van Nostrand Company, NY, 1973 // Stamp on title page verso, "Library, Armed Forces Staff College." This college is in Norfolk, Virginia and has students from all military services. The students better understand the different missions and capabilities, and therefore, perform better in a joint (multi-service) operation.

Figure DR60

DS44.M51973, *The Middle East*, Peter Mansfield, Oxford University Press, London, 1973 // Stamp on front cover verso and back cover recto, "Property of the DIA Library." DIA is the Defense Intelligence Agency, includes all services, and is the highest level military intelligence organization.

JOHN F. MANGELS

Figure DS49.G7181936

DS48.H27, *Under the Flag of the Orient*, Marion Harland, Historical Publishing Company, Philadelphia, 1897 // Book was rebound by Heckman Binding, Inc., N. Manchester, Indiana, 46962 in March 1986. Stamped on the original first free endpaper, "Library, Crichlow School, Volume No.___, Murfreesboro, Tennessee." And below is cursive, "Mrs. W.E. Reeves, Teacher, 8th Gr." Title page has a stamp, "Fisk University Library." Fisk was founded in 1866 in Nashville, Tennessee, about 30 miles northwest of Murfreesboro.

DS49.G7I81936, *Japan Must Fight Britain*, Lt.-Comdr. Tōta Ishimoru, I.J.P. (Imperial Japanese Navy), Hurst & Blackett, Ltd, London, 1936 // Front cover verso bookplate of a sailing ship and "Ex Libris, John F. Mangels." Figure DS49.G7I81936. Cursive on first free endpaper, "Chen Chu Pei, Two months after the liberation of Manila, the world famous metripalis (sic) in the East, 20 April 1945." So far, Chen Chu Pei is the only person who has provided such wonderful narrative about the books in his hands. Note the title and date, five years before Japan attacked the United States to start World War II.

DS49.5.P61923a, *By Camel and Car to the Peacock Throne*, R. Alexander Powell, Grosset & Dunlap, no city, 1923 // Title page stamp, "Property of the Regional Library, Huntsville, Alabama." "Regional Library" refers to the remaining library stations which continued after the Tennessee Valley Authority completed Guntersville Dam. See DK219.6.A4A31932a.

DS56.M3, *The Romance of Excavation*, David Masters, Dodd, Mead and Company, NY, 1923 // Front cover verso bookplate of strong words by Richard Pope. Figure DS56.M3. Pope's bookplate was covered by a UAH gift bookplate, with the donor of Richard Pope, but the glue dried on the UAH sticker so it came loose, happily to reveal the superb bookplate underneath.

DS63.&65, *Dynamite in the Middle East*, Khalil, Tolah, Philosophical Library, NY, 1955 // Title page stamp, "NEWSWEEK LIBRARY."

DS119.7.E5, *Between Enemies*, Amos Elon, Random House, NY, 1974 // Front cover verso and last free endpaper stamp, "Base Library, Pope Air Force Base, NC." Pope AFB is immediately adjacent to Fort Bragg, and there are no visible signs of a dividing line between the two bases. Pope provides the aircraft for the huge number of parachutists stationed at Bragg. I was stationed at Bragg for two years in the early 1970s.

Figure DS56.M3

Figure DS141.L67

DS121.55.V44v1, *Ages in Chaos*, Immanuel Velikovsky, Doubleday & Company, Garden City, NY, 1952 // Stamp on first free endpaper, second from back free endpaper, and last free endpaper recto, "Institute for Space Studies, Library-Room 710, 288 Broadway, New York, NY 10025."

DS141.L67, *Israel*, Ludwig Lewisohn, Boni & Liveright, NY, 1925 // Front cover verso bookplate of a man in a turban writing with a quill pen, "Ex Libris, Gordon." Figure DS141.L67.

DS486.D3S81967, *Archaeology and Monumental Remains of Delhi*, Carr Stephen, Kitab Mahal, Allahabad, 1967 // Front cover verso stamp, "Ex Libris, Myron Bement and Katherine Dennis Smith."

DS518.7.M66, *Soviet Far Eastern Policy 1931-45*, Harriet L. Moore, Princeton University Press, Princeton, NJ, 1945 // First free endpaper cursive, "Chen Chu Pei, Graduate School, Georgetown University, Washington, D.C." // Back cover recto cursive, "Carlton Chu Jue(?) Chen, 1946." This is now the fourth book by what seems to be the same person, except that the names are not consistent and sometimes in different order. See DS49.G7181936, D217.M66, and DK268.L5P61932a.

DS518.8.J6, *The United States and Japan's New Order*, William Johnstone, Oxford University Press, London, 1941 // Obliterated bookplate on front cover verso, "International Relations Club, Pro Patria Per Orbis Concordian, Given by the Carnegie Endowment For International Peace to encourage the study of international relations." // Obliterated bookplate on first free endpaper, "Park College Library, Parkville, Missouri."

DS518.8.K56, *Wider War*, Donald Kirk, Praeger Publishers, NY, 1971 // Stamp on first free endpaper, "Library MCAS, Beaufort, S.C." MCAS is Marine Corps Air Station.

DS518.8.L31954, *Solution in Asia*, Owen Lattimore, Little, Brown and Company, Boston, 1946 // Sticker on front cover verso, "In Memoriam, Roland McMillan Harper, 1878-1966, Botanist and Geographer."

DS518.8.U8, *The China Story*, Freda Utley, Henry Regnery Company, Chicago, 1951 // Stamp on front cover verso, first free endpaper and back cover recto, "Carlton C. Chen, 99-05, 63rd Drive, Rego Park 74, N.Y." I think this the fifth book by C.C. Chen.

DS557.A6M76, *No Place To Die*, Hugh A. Mulligan, William Morrow & Company, NY // First free endpaper sticker, "James H. Higgins, 823 Crestline Dr., Huntsville, AL 35805."

DS557.A6S281970, *The Road from War*, Robert Shaplen, Harper & Row, NY, 1966 // Title page verso stamp, "3 Nov 1970, Received, Mahan Library, Naval War College, Newport, R.I." The library was named after Alfred Thayer Mahan, 1840-1914, an American naval officer, who in 1890 wrote *The Influence of Sea Power Upon History, 1600-1783*. The book was studied by naval leaders from countries around the world, as it was the most important treatise on that subject.

DS685.F7, *Between Two Empires*, Theodore Friend, Yale University Press, New Haven, CT, 1965 '' Small sticker on bottom right of first free endpaper, "Savile Book Shop, 3236 P St., N.W., Washington 7, D.C."

DS735.B8, *Nations of the World*, Mayo W. Hazeltine, Peter Fenelon Collier, NY, 1848 // Title page stamp, "Boys Club of Knoxville, Inc., 312 W. Vine Ave., Knoxville, 16, TENN." // Stamp on front cover verso, "Huntsville Boys Club, Inc., 300 Fifth Avenue, Huntsville, Alabama."

DS738.C523C671974b, *The Chinese Red Army*, Gerard H. Corr, Schocken Books, NY, 1974 // First free endpaper stamp, "USAOTEA Technical Library." The initials stand for U.S. Army Operational Test

Agency, a group that tests Army developmental material from the soldiers' perspective before it is approved for distribution to the troops in the field.

DS740.N6, *Chinese Communism*, Robert C. North, McGraw-Hill Book Company, NY, 1966 // First free endpaper and last endpaper verso stamp, "Naval Station Library, Guam, Marianas."

DS740.4.H751925, *China and Her Political Entity*, Oxford University Press, NY, 1926 // Cursive on first free endpaper, "Carlton Chu Pei Chen, New York University, New York City." So we meet again. This seems to be the name finally settled on by our immigrant friend from the other side of the world, as confirmed by EC335.M45.

DS740.5.R8M48, *The Duel of the Giants*, Drew Middleton, Charles Scribner's Sons, NY, 1978 // Title page stamp, "Illinois Valley Library System." This was one of 21 library systems in Illinois, along with the Western Illinois System from which the Salmon Library has hundreds of books.

DS740.5.R8S33, *Tsars, Mandarins, and Commissars*, Harry Schwartz, J.B. Lippencott Company, NY, 1964 // Front cover verso bookplate of Conrad H. Eadon, with a global map. Figure DS740.5.R8S33.

DS809.H4451895a, *Out of the East*, Lafcadio Hearn, Houghten, Mifflin and Company, NY, 1895 // Bookplate on front cover verso, "Armstrong College Library." Figure DS809.H4451895a.

Figure DS740.5.R8S33

1952

Presented to

Armstrong College Library

In Memory of

Alexander R. Lawton

and

Ella B. Lawton

by their son

Alexander R. Lawton

Figure DS809.H4451895a

DS881.9.H31969, *Japan: Images and Realities*, Richard Halloran, Alfred A. Knopf, NY, 1969 // Front cover verso stamp, "Return to: The Agency Library – VOA Br., Room 2139 – HEW." VOA is guessed to be Voice of America, America's radio station to Eastern Europe and other places around the world.

DS895.F75C3, *Still the Rice Grows Green*, John C. Caldwell, Henry Regnery Company, Chicago, 1955 // Small sticker on bottom right of front cover verso, "HB, Honolulu Book Shops." Honolulu Books Shops is still active at 1450 Ala Moana Blvd. in the huge Ala Moana Shopping Center.

DS895.F75R5, *Formosa Under Chinese Nationalist Rule*, Fred W. Riggs, The Macmillan Company, NY, 1952 // Title page verso stamp, "Post Library, Camp Drum, N.Y., Property of U.S. Army." Camp Drum is located in northwest part of the state near Watertown. Its lineage goes back to 1809, although it was not officially designated until 1908. It was used by three divisions during World War II. It was in an inactive status for many years until it again became the home of the reactivated 10th Mountain Division in 1984 and designated Fort Drum.

DT1.H3vol9, *Tribes of the RIF*, Carleton Stevens Coon, Peabody Museum of Harvard University, Cambridge, Mass., 1931 // Front cover verso bookplate of Conrad H. Eadon. Figure DT1.H3vol9. Look at the figure as it was defaced by the UAH accession censor. Fortunately the key motivation words were left intact, "Great The Gift That Bringeth Knowledge." Fortunately the UAH censor blacked over a punch-through stamp on the title page, which makes it even more readable.

DT12.C559, *The African Giant*, Stuart Cloete, Houghton, Mifflin Company, Boston, 1955 // First free endpaper stamp, "Main Post Library, Fort Bragg, N.C., Property of U.S. Army."

DT12.F31941, *Behind God's Back*, Negley Farson, Harcourt, Brace and Company, NY, 1941 // Bookplate on simple title page, "Helen O'Brian, Her Book." Figure DT12.F31941.

Figure DT1.H3vol.9

DT12.L51944, *Focus on Africa*, Richard Upjohn Light, American Geographical Society, NY, 1044 // Title page stamp, "United States Air Force, Headquarters, Aeronautical Chart Service, Technical Library," and stamp on back cover recto, "2nd & Arsenal, St. Louis, 18, MO."

DT18.I813, *The New Leaders in Africa*, Rolf Italiaander, Prentice-Hall, Inc., Englewood Cliffs, NJ, 1961 // Title page stamp, "Southern Illinois Regional Library, S.I.U. Library, Carbondale, Illinois." S.I.U. is Southern Illinois University.

DT31.Z3, *International Relations in the New Africa*, I. William Zartman, Prentice-Hall, Inc., Englewood Cliffs, NJ, 1966 // First free endpaper stamp, "Leicester Junior College Library, Withdrawn 4/86." This college is in Leicester, just west of Worcester, Massachusetts.

DT215.W3, *Rivers to the Sea*, Walt Wandell, You & Europe Publications GmbH, Wiesbaden, Germany, 1966 // Stamp on second free endpaper, "U.S. Air Force Base Library 4887, Luke AFB, AZ 85301."

DT351.S79v1, *In Darkest Africa*, Henry M. Stanley, Charles Scribner's Sons, NY 1890 // Small sticker on back cover recto, "Protective Ass'n, Publishers & Booksellers."

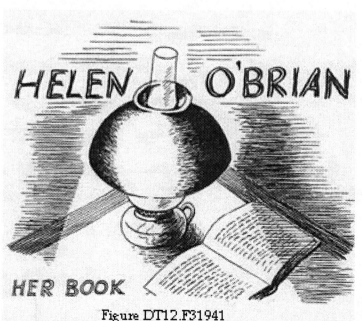

Figure DT12.F31941

DT434.E22H51964, *Journey to the Jade Sea*, John Hillaby, Simon and Schuster, NY, 1964 // Last free endpaper stamp, "Naval Security Station Library, 3801 Nebraska Avenue, Washington, D.C. 20390"

DT471.C7, *Pagans and Politicians*, Michael Crowder, Hutchinson of London, 1959 // Small sticker on bottom left of front cover verso, "Claude GILL Books, 485, Oxford Street, London, W.I., GRO 5664."

DT471.W38, *Dream of Unity*, Claude E. Welch, Cornell University Press, Ithaca, NY, 1966 // Stamp on front cover verso, back cover recto, card envelope and 3 sides of the leaves (top, bottom and fore-edge), "Station Library, Marine Air Station, North Island, San Diego, Calif, 92135."

SCHOOL LIBRARY

COLLEGE OF EDUCATION

DT498.R6, *Letters from Africa*, Homer T. Rosenberger, The American Peace Society, Gettysburg, PA 1965 // Stamp on page 183, "Bureau of Public Roads Library, Received May 26, 1965."

DU411.M32, *New Zealand*, Ngaio, Marsh, The Macmillan Company, 1964 // Front cover verso bookplate, "University of Alabama, College of Education." Figure DU411.M32.

CLASS

BOOK

ACCESSION NO.

Figure DU411.M32

DU700.04, *White Shadows in the South Seas*, Frederick O'Brien, The Century Co., NY, 1919 // Cursive on first free endpaper, "J__t(?) V. Cunliffe, 1920."

DU740.5.P61063, *Kapauku Papuan Economy*, Leopold Pospisil, Department of Anthropology, Yale University, New Haven, Conn, 1963 // Multiple stamps, "U.S. International University, Walter Library." The exact location could not be determined with confidence.

E36.C18v2, *Pioneer Laymen of North America*, Rev. T. J. Campbell, S.J. (Society of Jesuits), The America Press, NY, 1915 // Stamp on first free endpaper and third free endpaper, "Donated to the Library of Mount St. Charles Library." Mount St. Charles Academy is in Woonsocket, Rhode Island.

E40.M6, *The Romance of North America*, Hardwick Moseley, Houghton, Mifflin Company, Boston, 1958 // Cursive on first free endpaper, "Marie Cecile Page, 4870 MacArthur Blvd. N.W. Washington, D.C."

E78.N75A451986, *The Knife River Flint Quarries*, Stanley A. Ahler, State Historical Society of North Dakota, Bismarck, N.D., 1986 // Stamp on front cover, "North Dakota State Depository Document." It is most unusual for a stamp to be on the front cover and remain despite the handling.

Merrill Memorial Library
Yarmouth, Maine.

Figure E162.B972

E99.E7P6, *Kabloona*, Gontron de Poncins, Reynal & Hitchcock, Inc., NY, 1941 // Small sticker bottom left on first free endpaper, "Smith & Hardwick, South's Largest Book Store, Birmingham, Alabama." Title page stamp, "Library, University College, University of Alabama, 35294.

E99.T6S97, *Tlingit Myths and Texts*, John R. Swanton, Government Printing Office, Washington, D.C., 1909 // Stamp on first free endpaper, "This book is the property of the Indian Office Library."

E162.B972, *Travels Through North America*, Rufus Rockwell Wilson, A. Wessels Company, NY, 1904 // Front cover verso bookplate, "Merrill Memorial Library, Yarmouth, Maine." Figure E162.B972. Small sticker on back cover recto, "Joseph McDonough Co., Scarce and Fine Books, Albany, NY."

E162.F53vI, *Men, Women and Manners in Colonial Times*, Sydney Geo. Fisher, J.B. Lippencott Company, NY, 1898 // Front cover verso circular bookplate, "Ex Libris, Isaac Hobart Brooks" with a small sailing ship. Figure E162.F53vI -1. Cursive on first free endpaper, "To Mrs Grant from Mrs Witten." Volume II of the same title has the same cursive writing, but the bookplate is different. It has a larger bookplate with a larger sailing ship and crest. Figure E162.F53vI -2.

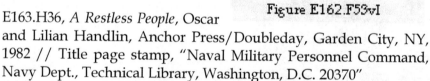

Figure E162.F53vI

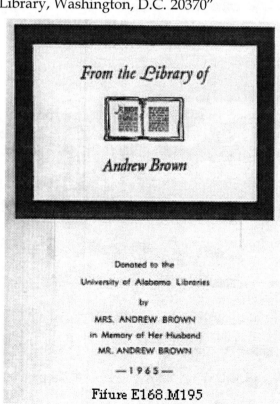

E163.H36, *A Restless People*, Oscar and Lilian Handlin, Anchor Press/Doubleday, Garden City, NY, 1982 // Title page stamp, "Naval Military Personnel Command, Navy Dept., Technical Library, Washington, D.C. 20370"

Figure E162.F53vII

E168.M195, *The Americans at Home*, David Macrae, E.P. Dutton & Co., NY, 1952 // Front cover verso bookplate, "Andrew Brown." Figure E168.M195.

From the Library of

Andrew Brown

Donated to the
University of Alabama Libraries
by
MRS. ANDREW BROWN
in Memory of Her Husband
MR. ANDREW BROWN
—1965—

Fifure E168.M195

E168.O332, *Orpheus in America*, Jacques Offenbach, Indiana University Press, Bloomington, Indiana, 1957 // Multiple stamps, "Library, U.S. Naval Hospital, Oakland, California." Back cover recto sticker, "John Cole's book & craft shop, 7871 Ivanhoe Avenue, La Jolla, California."

E169.G44, *People of Destiny*, Phillip Gibbs, Harper & Brothers Publishers, NY, 1920 // Bookplate on second free endpaper, table and lamp, "Dec 25, 1920," and the last name blacked out by the UAH censor. Figure E169.G44.

E169.P46, *Cities of America*, George Sessions Perry, McGraw-Hill Book Company, Inc., NY, 1947 // First free endpaper stamp, "Library, Mt. St. Mary's Seminary, Norwood, Ohio."

E169.02.M485, *The Fifties*, Douglas Miller, Doubleday and Company, Garden City, NY, 1975 // First free endpaper stamp, "USS CANOPUS." The USS Canopus (AS34) was a submarine tender commissioned in 1963 and decommissioned in 1994. It had a crew of approximately 1,200 personnel, was 196 meters in length and had a speed of 18 knots. On 29 November 1970 a fire broke out onboard while the ship was docked at Holy Loch, Scotland. It was carrying nuclear-armed missiles and two U.S. submarines were moored alongside. The fire was brought under control after four hours and three men were killed. In 2003 the Canopus was towed to England for scrap.

Figure E169.G44

E169.1.F75, *U.S.A.*, Russell W. Davenport, Prentice-Hall, NY, 1951, // First free endpaper stamp, "Library of Foreign Policy Association." The FPA is well known to me because it annually publishes a booklet, *Great Decisions*, which contains 10-12 pages of discussion on each of eight foreign policy issues. This booklet was the text for a discussion group I initiated at the Academy for Lifetime Learning at The University of Alabama in Huntsville in 1994. That course is still a popular course at the Academy in 2006.

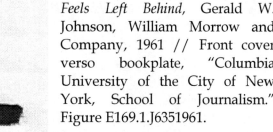
Figure E169.1.J6351961

E169/1G615, *Ess, Ess, Mein Kindt (Eat, Eat, My Child)*, Harry Golden, G.P. Putnam's Sons, NY, 1963 // Multiple stamps, "This Provided by the Alabama Public Library Service."

E169.1.J6351961, *The Man Who Feels Left Behind*, Gerald W. Johnson, William Morrow and Company, 1961 // Front cover verso bookplate, "Columbia University of the City of New York, School of Journalism." Figure E169.1.J6351961.

Figure E169.1.N52

E169.1.N52, *American Social History as Recorded by British Travellers*, Allan Nevins, Henry Holt and Company, NY, 1923 // Bookplate on front cover verso of a house, "Marlboro College Library" (Figure E169.1.N52) and a sticker, "Gift of Robert H. Cory, Jr." Title page has an embossed stamp, "Marlboro College Library, Marlboro, Vermont."

E169.1.V29, *The Age of Conformity*, Alan Valentine, Henry Regnery Company, Chicago, 1954 // First free endpaper cursive, "To Robert Lusser, In part payment for knowledge of Burckhardt, Norman

Preioda and Eleanor, 6-21-55." There is a strong possibility that Robert Lusser was the German engineer and aircraft designer who was a member of Wernher von Braun's rocket team at Peenemünde, Germany and later worked in Huntsville, Alabama with von Braun's team during the period 1953-59. Lusser lived 1900-69. The Burckhardt referred to is Jacob Burckhardt, the noted Swiss historian, 1818-97, who wrote *The History of the Renaissance in Italy*. He was the first historian who widely publicized the term Renaissance, although he was not the first to coin the term. Contrary to the perceptions of some folks about the Nazis who were brought to the United States after World War II to work on rockets and missiles, they were very educated by American standards and had a rich knowledge of the arts and literature.

E171.A05C33, *History of the United States of America*, Ernest Cassara, Gale Research Company, Detroit, MI, 1977 // Title page stamp, "Morale Support Activities, Post Library, EA205, Edgewood Arsenal, Aberdeen Proving Ground, MD." Edgewood Arsenal is the Army's center for chemical weapons and is located on a peninsula next to Aberdeen Proving Ground.

E172.A611916, *Annual Report of the American Historical Association, 1916, v1*, Washington, D.C., 1917 // Front cover verso bookplate and title page embossed stamp, "Library, Department of Commerce."

E175.9.S34, *New Viewpoints in American History*, Arthur M. Schlesinger, The Macmillan Company, NY, 1925 // Front cover verso stamp, "Property of the Georgia State Womans College at Valdosta." My word processing spell check rebelled at "Womans," since the word is neither properly plural nor possessive. The college's website confirmed that spelling.

E176.S843, *American Men of Mind*, Burton E. Stevenson, Doubleday, Page and Company, Garden City, NY, 1913 // Front cover verso bookplate of a child with books. Figure E176.S843.

This Book belongs to

Figure E176.S843

E178.C3, *The Seafarers*, Robert Carse, Harper & Row, NY, 1964 // First free endpaper stamp, "Library, USS Bennington, CVS 20, FPO San Francisco, Calif. 96681." The Bennington was an aircraft carrier commissioned in 1944. It was named after the town in Vermont which was the site of an American victory over the British on 16 August 1777. The British suffered 207 dead and 700 captured, while the American losses were 30 killed and 40 wounded. Much needed small arms, cannon and wagons were captured.

E178.P35, *The United States*, Theodore Calvin Pease, Harcourt, Brace and Company, NY, 1927 // Cursive on first free endpaper, "Walter Mathews, Phi Chi House, 2320 West End Ave., 119 Louise Street, Lambda Chi Alpha House, Larkinsville, Alabama." The evidence seems to say that Walter Mathews was from the small town of Larkinsville, about 5 miles directly west of Scottsboro, and lived in two fraternity houses in Tuscaloosa. A single individual, however, seldom changes fraternities.

E181.A52, *Fighting Generals*, Curt Anders, G.P. Putman's Sons, NY, 1965 // Title page verso stamp, "Base Library, WP AFB, Property of USAF. WP is Wright-Patterson Air Force Base in Dayton, Ohio, which is the home of the Air Force Museum.

E181.B68, *Bliss, Peacemaker*, Frederick Palmer, Dodd, Mead and Company, NY, 1934 // Front cover verso cursive, "Harry Bennett, Smithborough, Mass, Christmas, 1934, H.T.B."

E181.C43, *The Life of Lieutenant General Chaffee*, William Harding Carter, The University of Chicago Press, Chicago, IL, 1917 // Front cover verso bookplate and title page embossed stamp, " Messiah College Library, Grantham, Penna." Grantham is about 12 miles southwest of Harrisburg.

E181.W859, *Leonard Wood*, Eric Fisher Wood (not related as stated in the preface), George H. Doran Company, NY, 1920 // Front cover verso cursive, "Earl E. Chase, East Main St. Bennington, VT."

E182.R68J6, *Rear Admiral John Rogers*, Robert Erwin Johnson, United States Naval Institute, Annapolis, MD, 1967 // Cursive on first free endpaper, "For John Fraser with the high regard and best wishes of Robert Edwin Johnson [Author], Tuscaloosa, 29 December 1967." The inscribed words indicate that this should be considered a "presentation" copy by the author, since he obviously knew the recipient previously.

E183.7.W271934, *Study of International Relations in the United States*, Edith Ware, Columbia University Press, NY, 1934 // Front cover verso sticker, "University Book Shop, 69 University Place, New York 3, NY." First free endpaper stamp, "Institute of Pacific Relations, International Research Secretary." Title page embossed stamp, "Harry S Truman Library, Independence, Missouri." The Institute of Pacific Relations was founded in 1925 at the University of British Columbia, Canada. This book may be one of very few that have three different locations cited by evidential stamps.

E183.7.W37, *Foreign Policy Begins at Home*, James P. Warburg, Harcourt, Brace and Company, NY, 1944 // First free endpaper cursive, "For the Honorable Lister Hill with highest esteem and warm personal regards, James P. Warburg." Warburg was a member of the internationally banking extended family of the same name. Whether he was really friends with Alabama senator Lister Hill is not known. Perhaps Warburg was just using his book as a way to influence foreign policy and made a big thing about flattering a senator. At any rate, this book will qualify as an "association" copy, inasmuch as Hill was a well known personality.

E183.8.G3T73, *The Dollar Drain and American Forces in Germany*, Gregory F. Treverton, Ohio University Press, Athens, OH, 1978 // Title page stamp, "DARCOM Technical Library, 5001 Eisenhower Avenue, Alexandria, Virginia 22333." DARCOM stands for [Army] Development and Readiness Command, the four-star general command in charge of all Army material development and sustainment. It is now named the Army Material Command (AMC) and will be moving to Redstone Arsenal in 2008-9 as part of the Department of Defense Base Realignment and Closure (BRAC) decisions in 2006.

Figure E184.G3F3vI

E183.8.I4T3, *India and America*, Phillips Talbot, Harper

and Brothers, NY, 1958 // Title page embossed stamp, "U.S. Bureau of the Budget Library, Washington, D.C."

E184.A1G52, *Understanding Minority Rights*, Joseph B. Gittler, John Wiley & Sons, Inc., London, 1956 // Front cover verso bookplate, "Library, United States Department of Justice." Title page stamp, "Civil Rights Division, April, 02, 19__(?)"

E184.G3F3v1, *The German Element in the United States*, Albert Bernhardt Faust, Houghton Mifflin and Company, NY, 1909 // Front cover verso bookplate of Edward F. O'Connor with a sailing ship in an archway. Figure E184.G3F3v1. It appears that the bookplate owner might be a California lawyer who has written at least two books on intellectual property law.

E185.61.L57, *My Face is Black*, C. Eric Lincoln, Beacon Press, Boston, 1964 // Front cover verso stamp, "Center for Family and Community in Home Economics, P.O. Box 2967, University, Alabama."

E185.61.L691971, *The Healing of a Nation*, David Love, W.W. Norton & Company, Inc., NY, 1971 // Title page stamp, "Department of Housing and Urban Development, Feb 16, 1972, Washington, D.C,, 20410."

A million candles have burned themselves out. Still I read on. —Montresor.

Figure E185.8.R6

E185.61.O471976, *Black-White Racial Attitudes*, Constance E. Obudho, Greenwood Press, Westport, Connecticut, 1976 // Stamp on contents page, "Technical Library, Building 45, Dec 3, 1976, Johnson Space Center, Houston, Texas 77058."

E185.8.M24, The Negro and Apprenticeship, F. Ray Marshall, The Johns Hopkins Press, Baltimore, MD, 1967 // Title page stamp, "Property of EEOC Library." EEOC = Equal Employment Opportunity Commission.

E185.8.R6, *Employment, Race, and Poverty*, Arthur M. Ross, Harcourt, Brace & World, Inc., NY, 1967 // First free endpaper bookplate, "Naval Electronic Systems Command, Washington, D.C. 20360." Figure E185.8.R6, which has an open book, two candles, and the sentences, "A million candles have burned themselves out. Still I read on. –Montresor." What a wonderful thought.

BERTRAND WALKER

Figure E188.F541v1

E185.93, *Race Relations in Minnesota*, The Governor's Interracial Commission, Saint Paul, MN, 1948 // Title page stamp, "Housing and Home Finance Agency, Office of the Administrator, Library Reference Service."

E185.97.J76W4, *Lost Boundaries*, W.L. White, Harcourt, Brace and Company, NY, 1947 // First free endpaper stamp, "Property of Muscle Shoals Regional Library, State of Alabama, Public Library Service."

E188.F541v1-3, *John Fiske's Historical Writings VIII*, John Fiske, Houghton, Mifflin and Company, Boston, 1899 // Front cover verso bookplate of a sailing ship and the name "Bertrand Walker." Figure E188.F541v1-3.

E207.G9G741871v1-3, *The Life of Nathanael Greene*, George Washington Greene, Hurd and Houghton, NY, 1871 // Title page stamp, "Social Library, Hollis N.H." Hollis is a small town of 6,760 people six miles west of Nashua in southern New Hampshire. The Hollis Social Library was incorporated in 1799.

E211.B971899, *Conciliation With America by Edmund Burke*, Joseph Rushton, Ainsworth & Company, Chicago, 1899 // Cursive on first free endpaper, "Nellie Ethel Smith, October 8, 1920."

E312.71931v1, *Writings of Washington, Vol. 1, 1745-1756*, John C. Fitzpatrick, Editor, U.S. Government Printing Office, 1931 // Front cover verso bookplate of George Washington. Figure E312.71931v1. This bookplate was pasted on the cover verso, but I'm not sure that he ever had such a plate or whether the GPO made it up to enhance the book appearance.

Figure E340.B4R6

Figure E312.7.1931v1

E340.B4R6, *Thomas Hart Benton*, Theodore Roosevelt [26th President], Houghton, Mifflin and Company, Boston, 1887 // Front cover verso bookplate, "The Winthrop Club, Springfield Club, Mass." Figure E340.B4R6.

E382.P271861vII, *Life of Andrew Jackson*, James Parton, Mason Brothers, NY, 1861 // Front cover verso bookplate of borrowing instructions from a blacked out place in Maine. Figure E382.P271861vII.

E404.B55, *Rehearsal for Conflict*, Alfred Hoyt Bill, Alfred A. Knopf, NY, 1947 // First free endpaper cursive, "E. Sherman Webb, Jr., 4/25/51."

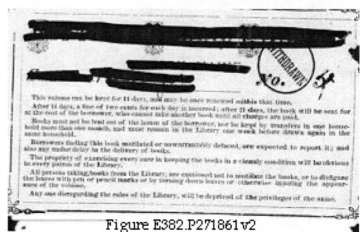

Figure E382.P271861v2

E415.9.D73C3, *Stephen A, Douglas*, Clark E. Carr, A.C. McClung & Co., Chicago, 1909 // Second free endpaper cursive, "Mr. E.P. Chambers. Presented by his friend, Clark C. Carr, the author, Galesburg, IL, June 2nd 1910."

E467.1.L4B77, *Lee the American*, Gamaliel Bradford, Jr., Houghton Mifflin and Company, Boston, 1912 // Title page punch-through stamp, "Brooklyn Public Library."

E467.1.S85C6, *Alexander H. Stephens*, Henry Cleveland, National Publishing Company, Philadelphia, 1866 // Front cover verso bookplate, "W.C. Bradley Memorial Library, Columbus, GA." Title page stamp, "Public Library, Columbus, GA."

E467.1.W67E41901, *The Life of John Ancrum Winslow*, John M. Ellicott, G.P. Putman's Sons, NY, 1902 // Bookplate on front cover verso, "Newburgport Public Library from the Peabody Fund." Figure E467.1.W67E41901. Newburgport is in the extreme northeast corner of Massachusetts.

E655.R661893, *Fighting for Honor*, Theodore F. Rodenbough, G.W. Dillingham, NY, 1893 // Second free endpaper bookplate, "William Stanley Hoole." Figure E655.R661893.

Figure E467.1.W77E41901

Figure E655.R661893

E661.B3v I&II, *Twenty Years of Congress*, James G. Blaine, The Henry Bill Publishing Company, Norwich, CT, 1884 // Front cover verso bookplate, "Deborah Cook Sayles Public Library, Pawtucket, Rhode Island." Figure E661.B3vI&II.

E664.B78vI&II, *The Life and Times of Samuel Bowles*, George S. Merriam, The Century Company, NY, 1885 // Second free endpaper stamp, "Henry B. Gardner."

Figure E661.B63v1

E664.G73H3, *Henry W. Grady*, Joel Chandler Harris, Cassell Publishing Company, NY, 1890 // First free endpaper cursive, "W/T. Swift to Fred M. Swift, Aug. 30th / [18]90, Price $3.00."

E664.P15H4v1, *The Life and Letters of Walter H. Page*, Burton J. Hendrick, Doubleday, Page and Company, Garden City, NY, 1922 // Cursive on first free endpaper, "To Al Harris, from the three grandchildren of the author, John H. Page, Shelby H. Page, Allison F. Page." Note that Hendrick was really only the compiler and editor.

E664.P72P7, *The Autobiography of Thomas Collier Platt*, B.W. Dodge & Company, NY, 1910 // Front cover verso stamp, "Willard C. Fisher, Jan 22 1912." E741.J481982, The Dark Ages, Marty Jezer, South End Press, Boston, 1982 // Title page stamp, "Taylor Memorial Public Library, Cuyahoga Falls, Ohio," and a UAH gift bookplate from Del Williams.

Figure E744.B858

E743.5.H55D471962, *Seeds of Treason*, Ralph de Toledano, Henry Regnery Company, Chicago, 1962 // First free endpaper cursive, "For Huntington Cairns, who knew the answers all along – with very best wishes, Ralph de Toledano." [author] Huntington Cairns was a lawyer, author of a book about Plato and the secretary – treasurer of the National Gallery of Art in 1945.

E744.B858, *Containment or Liberation*, James Burnham, The John Day Company, 1952 // Front cover verso bookplate, "Library, National War College," Figure E744.B858, and a punched through stamp on the title page, "Library, The National War College." The National War College is located at Fort Lesley J. McNair, at the junction of the Potomac and Anacostia Rivers, in Washington, D.C. Fort McNair is the oldest Army post still active today.

E744.H69, *Blood is Cheaper than Water*, Quincy Howe, Simon & Schuster, NY, 1939 // First free endpaper and page 15 stamp, "Reference Library, The March of Time."

E748.B318A3, *That Reminds Me*, Alben W. Barkley, Doubleday & Company, Garden City, NY, 1954 // First free endpaper stamp, "Property, U.S. Army, Sandia Base Library." Sandia is in Albuquerque, New Mexico and is the location for the development of nuclear warheads for Army weapons systems.

Figure E748.G5356

E748.B846A3, *Farewell to Foggy Bottom*, Ellis Briggs, David McKay Company, NY, 1964 // Front cover verso stamp, "Federal Aviation Agency," and stamp on title page, "FAA Library."

E748.B94B942, *The Letters of Archie Butt*, Lawrence F. Abbott, Doubleday, Page & Company, Garden City, NY, 1924 // First free endpaper cursive, "To Father from Juah(?) and Frank, Christmas, 1924."

E748.G53S6, *Carter Glass*, Rixley Smith, Longman, Green and Co., NY, 1939 // Second free endpaper bookplate, "Lister Hill." Figure E748.G53S6.

E748.S883A3, *On Active Service in Peace and War*, Henry L. Stimson, Harper & Brothers, NY, 1947 // Title page embossed stamp, "International Center for Scholars, Woodrow Wilson."

E757.R75, *The Long Trail*, Kermit Roosevelt, The Metropolitan Magazine, NY, 1921 // Cursive on first free endpaper, "To Col. William B. Thompson, with best wishes for a Merry Christmas 1921, From his devoted servant, J. Rocchia."

E786.D28, *The Inside Story of the Harding Tragedy*, Harry M. Daugherty, The Churchill Company, NY, 1932 // Front cover verso cursive, "Property of Harold T. Hamer(?), 7162 Washington St., Springfield, Illinois."

E786.G22, *The Desert is Yours*, Erle Stanley Gardner, William Morrow & Company, NY, 1963 // Stamps in five places, "Post Library, Army Electronic Proving Ground, Fort Huachuca, Arizona."

E796.C95, *The Presidency vs. Hoover*, Samuel Crowther, Doubleday, Doran and Company, Inc., Garden City, NY, 1928 // Cursive on first free endpaper, "Congratulations & Best wishes, ???, Jan 3, 1930, From her cousins, Rosalie & L???, Dec 31, 1929."

E801.J65, *Hoover off the Record*, Theodore G. Joslin, Doubleday, Doran & Company, Inc., Garden City, NY, 1934 // First free endpaper stamp, "Ethel G. Romspert, 1947 Far Hills Ave., Dayton, Ohio 45419."

E806.C67, *The Prospect of American Democracy*, George S. Counts, The John Day Company, NY, 1938 // Punch-through stamp on title page, "Mississippi A&M College," and front cover verso stamp, "Mississippi State College, General Library." Mississippi A&M College became Mississippi State University in 1932.

E807.R649v2, *F.D.R., His Personal Letters*, Edited by Elliott Roosevelt, Duell, Sloan and Pearce, NY, 1948 // Front cover verso stamp, "Property of U.S. Army, Onkel Tom Library, HQ Berlin Mil Post, APO 342, U.S. Army." The library's name mystifies me. Onkel is German for uncle. Uncle Tom appears to refer to the famous book, *Uncle Tom's Cabin*. The Army normally does not use clever or whimsical names for facilities. The APO number has only 3 digits, indicating an early date of the American occupation of Germany. "Onkel Tom Library" is not logical, but it existed at one time.

Presented by
E 813

Class

Book   H6

Access No.   41635

Figure E813.H6

E807.S8, *"Hi – Ya" Neighbor*, Ruth Stevens, Tupper and Love, Inc., NY, 1947 // Second free endpaper cursive, "With best wishes, Ruth Stevens." [author]

E813.B4, *The Iron Curtain Over America*, John Beaty, Wilkinson Publishing Company, Dallas, TX, 1951 // Front cover verso stamp, "St. Vincent Remore(?) Priory, New York City."

E813.G61956, *The Crucial Decade*, Eric F. Goldman, Alfred A. Knopf, NY, 1959 // First free endpaper stamp, "Property of Library, U.S.

Naval Ammunition Depot, Charleston, S.C."

E813.H6, *Addresses Upon the American Road*, 1948-1950, Herbert Hoover, Stanford University Press, Stanford, CA, 1951 // Front cover verso bookplate, "Industrial College of the Armed Forces." Figure E813.H6. There was also a stamp, "NDU Withdrawn." Refer back to E744.B858, which describes the location of National War College. The Industrial College of the Armed Forces was located at Fort McNair with the National War College. Each college served different purposes, but at the same level of military education, which is the highest formal education in the Armed Forces. NDU is the National Defense University, a new name for the consolidation of the two colleges previously discussed.

E814.1.T7, *Souvenir*, Margaret Truman, McGraw-Hill Book Company, NY, 1956 // Stamp on top of closed leaves, "Base Library, Pepperrell AFB." When I first saw the name, Pepperrell, I wondered why, after over 40 years associated with the military, I had never heard of Pepperrell Air Force Base. This base was located five miles from St. John's, Newfoundland, Canada. It was the location of the 642nd Air Control & Warning Squadron, a radar site looking east over the Atlantic Ocean. The base was established during World War II and became even more important during the Cold War with the Soviet Union. It was on the great circle route for aircraft going to and from Europe, both friendly and Soviet. The radars picked up the location of all aircraft and passed the information to other locations for identification or interception. Pepperrell AFB was located about 75 miles from Argentia, the Navy base mentioned in CT275.V234V3 and D847.S9.

TELEVISION INFORMATION OFFICE
LIBRARY
666 5TH AVENUE
NEW YORK 19, NEW YORK
SEP 24 1962

LINCOLN OUT-OF-PRINT
BOOK SEARCH LTD.
Mount Hygeia Road   Box 100
Foster, Rhode Island 02825 U.S.A.
(401) 647-2825

Figure E840.K7

E835.B55, *Herblock's Here and Now*, Herbert Block, Simon and Schuster, NY, 1955 // Cursive of first free endpaper, "For Judy Morse, as a reminder to come back to Washington, With best regards from Herb Block." There was also a UAH gift bookplate from Willy Ley.

E838.5.C3751977, *A Government as Good as Its People*, Jimmy Carter, Simon and Schuster, NY, 1977 // Stamp on front cover verso and contents page, "Library, ERC, Cincinnati, U.S. Environmental Protection Agency, 26 W. St. Clair Street, Cincinnati, OH 45268."

E840.H37, *The New Age of American Foreign Policy*, Frederick H. Hartman, The Macmillan Company, London, 1970 // Stamp on top and bottom of closed leaves, "Dr. Krish Bhansall, Box 842, State College, MS 39762."

E840.K7, *The Great Debates*, Sidney Kraus, Indiana University Press, Bloomington, IN, 1962 // First free endpaper stamp and book sellers sticker. Figure E840.K7.

"The true University of these days is a Collection of Books."
—CARLYLE.

1813
COMMODORE OLIVER HAZARD PERRY
THE HERO OF LAKE ERIE

Perry Public Library
Perry, New York
1913

Figure F7.A223

E840.O93, *The Next Phase in Foreign Policy*, Henry Owen, The Brookings Institute, Washington, D.C., 1973 // Title page stamp, "Department of Transportation, Aug. 7 1975, Library, FOB 10A Branch."

F7.A223, *Revolutionary New England, 1691-1776*, James Truslow Adams, The Atlantic Monthly Press, Boston, 1923 // Bookplate on front cover verso, "Perry Public Library." Figure F7.A223. Perry, New York was obviously named after the naval hero as stated on the bookplate. Perry is nowhere near the water, however. I was most pleased to note the quotation from Thomas Carlyle about a collection of books, as it fits my current avocation of reading books, writing about books and giving courses about books.

There are 50,000 numbered copies of this first edition of

A Southern Album

of which this is copy number

17221

It is signed by the author

F27.K32C6, *Kennebec*, Robert P. Tristram, Coffin, Farrar and Rinehart, NY, 1937 // Second free endpaper cursive, "To Arline, In memory of a happy visit to the counties of Maine, July 1937, With best wishes, Charlie."

F124.N436, *Progressive Democracy*, Alfred E. Smith, Harcourt, Brace and Company, NY, 1928 // Front cover verso stamp, "Jonathan C. Day, General Agent, State of Virginia, Manhattan Life, 1122 Mutual Building, Richmond, VA, Phone: Randolph 277."

Figure F210.S68

Figure F215.F22

F128.47.T961927, *"Boss" Tweed*, Denis T. Lynch, Blue Ribbon Books, NY, 1927 // First free endpaper cursive, "Howard Bernard Shaw, 65-35 Yellowstone Blvd., Forest Hills 75, NY."

F128.5.G294, *William Jay Gaynor*, Mortimer Smith, Henry Regnery Company, Chicago, 1951 // Front cover verso and back cover recto oval stamp, "Library, Willard M.L. Robinson, New York."

F128.5.S35, *Girl from Fitchburg*, Bernandine Kielty Scherman, Random House, NY, 1964 // First free endpaper cursive, "To Basil Davenport, Affectionately, Bernandine, Jan 8, 1964." Author inscription.

F128.68.A1T63, *New York Walk Book*, Raymond H. Torrey, American Geographical Society, NY, 1923 // Front cover verso sticker, "The Library of Richard A. Peterson." That sticker was pasted over a stamp, "Thomas ????lls, Vasser College."

F129.B8A38, *From Ararat to Suburbia*, Selig Adler, The Jewish Publication Society of America, Philadelphia, 1960 // Back cover recto stamp, "Mount Providence Junior College, Library, Baltimore, Md."

F158.52.B7, *Our Philadelphia*, Frank Brookhouser, Doubleday & Company, Inc., Garden City, NY, 1957 // First free endpaper cursive, "Best Wishes – Frank Brookhouser." Author inscribed.

F196.L31951, *Washington Confidential*, Jack Lait, Crown Publishers Inc., NY, 1951 // First free endpaper stamp, "The Book Nook Used Books, 208 & 1/2 W. Side Sq., Huntsville, Ala, Price $1.29."

F199/B265, *The Bonus March and the New Deal*, John Henry Bartlett, M.A. Donohue & Company, Chicago, 1937 // First free endpaper cursive, "To Hon. W$^{\underline{m}}$ O. Douglas from John H. Bartlett, , Jan 3 – 1938." This book qualifies as a "presentation copy" because it was presented by the author to a well-known person, in this case, Associate Justice of the Supreme Court (1939-1975), William O. Douglas, 1896-1980.

F209.D16, *Liberalism in the South*, Virginius Dabney, The University of North Carolina Press, Chapel Hill, NC, 1932 // Bookplate on front cover verso, "Walter Mahon Jackson." Figure F209.D16. Stamp on first free endpaper, "Hunter Dickinson Farish, Williamsburg, Virginia."

F210.S68, A Southern Album, Irwin Glusker, Oxmoor House, Inc., Birmingham, AL, 1976 // Front cover verso bookplate, #17221 and a picture of a church. Figure F210.S68.

F215.F22, *Seeing the Sunny South*, John T. Faris, J.B. Lippincott, Philadelphia, 1921 // Front cover verso bookplate, "Muhlenberg College." Figure F215.F22.

F215.S9, *American Adventures*, Julian Street, The Century Co., NY, 1917 // Bookplate on front cover verso, "Ernest F. Tyler." Figure F215.S9.

Figure F215.S9

F229.L43, *The Virginia Committee System and the American Revolution*, James Miller Leake, The New Era Printing Company, Lancester, PA, 1917 // Front cover verso bookplate, "Library of the University of Missouri," lower half covered by UAH sticker. Figure F229.L43. Title page punch-through stamp, "University of Missouri Library."

F232.J2v57, *The James River Basin*, Virginia Academy of Science, Richmond, VA, 1950 // Title page cursive, "Mrs. J.L. Camp, Jr., with the compliments of the Virginia Academy of Science, Marcellus H. Stow."

F262.K5J6, *The Story of Kinston and Lenoir County*, Talmage C. Johnson, Edwards & Broughton Company, Raleigh, NC, 1954 // Front cover verso cursive, "W. Oliver ???, 917 Holt Drive, Raleigh, NC."

Library

University of Alabama

In Huntsville

Figure F229.L43

Figure F289.C3

F289.C3, *The Early Settlement of Georgia*, James Etheridge Callaway, The University of Georgia Press, Athens, GA 1948 // Front cover verso bookplate, "WC Henson," Figure F289.C3, and first free endpaper cursive, "W.C. Henson, 1/8/49."

F292.W17S2, *Wayfarers in Walton*, Anita B. Sams, Foote & Davies, Doraville, GA, 1967 // Inscribed by author on first free endpaper, "Wish best wishes, Anita B. Sams."

F326.3A71962, *Alabama Mounds to Missiles*, Helen Morgan Akens, The Strode Publishers, Huntsville, AL, 1967 // First free endpaper, cursive, "Roland H. Harper, Bought at Grove Hill, Ala, 2-2-63, $4.95."

F326.5.M2, *Alabama Historical Sketches*, Thomas Chalmers McCorvey, University of Virginia Press, Charlottesville, VA, 1960 // Inscription by author on first free endpaper, "To my friend Dean Marten ten Hoor, a truly great scholar, from Thomas C. McCorvey, Mobile, Ala, December 1960." Second free endpaper cursive, "April 15 – 1971, With our very best wishes to a T. Henry Walker and family, our long and good friends for many years – with our love – Marie and Marten." Marten ten Hoor, 1890-1967, was born in the Netherlands and received his undergraduate degree from Tulane University. He was the co-author of the Tulane fight song in an alumni contest in 1925. He was the dean of the Tulane College of Arts and Sciences 1937-44. He was later dean of the College of Arts and Sciences at The University of Alabama where a hall is named after him in 1963, which houses classrooms and offices for American studies, anthropology, history, philosophy and political science.

Figure F327.B18351853

F327.B18351853, *The Flush Times of Alabama and Mississippi*, Joseph G. Baldwin, Americus Book Co., Americus, GA, 1853 // Front cover verso bookplate of a man and frog, "Ward L. Miner, 2-12-48." Figure F327.B18351853.

F330.3.P751973, *Alabama Politics*, "Shorty" Price, Vantage Press, NY, 1973 // Cursive on first free endpaper, "Dec. 10, 1973, Best wishes and Merry Christmas to a fine young lady of Ozark, [presumed Alabama] Miss Virginia Sallie. I hope you enjoy reading my book, Shorty Price." Front cover verso has a UAH gift bookplate from Virginia Gellerstedt, assumed to be the same Virginia.

F336.M75v1-2, *Publications of the Mississippi Historical Society*, Franklin L. Riley, Oxford, MS, 1898 // First free endpaper cursive, "N.R. Drummond, Columbia, Miss."

F335.K4, *Mighty Mississippi*, Bern Keating, National Geographic Society, 1971 // Second free endpaper with a photo stamp, "U.S. Navy Library, 7N___adly, Street, London, W1."

F394.G2M3, *Death from the Sea*, Herbert Molloy Mason, Jr., The Dial Press, 1972 // Stamp on fore edge of leaves, "U.S. Naval Hospital General Library, Box 7636, APO San Francisco 96630."

F435.T28, *Notable Men of Tennessee*, Oliver P. Temple, The Cosmopolitan Press, NY, 1912 // First free endpaper cursive, "To Dr. W.P. Stevenson, With best regards of Samuel T. Wilson, June 6, 1919."

F454.F482, *Filson's Kentucke*, Willard Rouse Jillson, John P. Morton & Company, Louisville, KY, 1929 // Author's inscription on first free endpaper, "To P.H. Dunn, A new salvation and an old subject – Kentucky! From W.R. Jillson, Frankfort, Ky, Jun. 18/30."

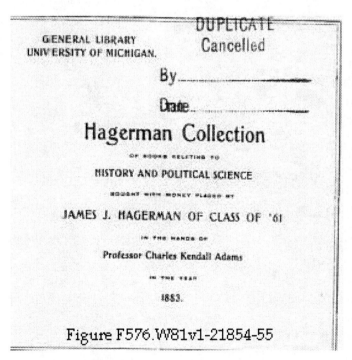

Figure F576.W81v1-21854-55

F484.3.M6, *A Trip from New York to the Falls of St. Anthony in 1845*, Stanley Pargellis, University of Chicago Press, Chicago, 1946 // First free endpaper cursive, "Lt Col B.T. Dechan(?), USA, HHB(?), 69th Artillery, Karlsruhe(?), Germany, June 1958."

F576.W81v1-2 1854-55, *Collection of Wisconsin State Historical Society*, Beriah Brown, Printer, 1855 // Front cover verso bookplate, "Hagerman Collection." First free endpaper stamp, "Garrett Biblical Institute, Evanston, Illinois." The Hagerman collection is from the University of Michigan Library.

F595.r17, *Our Great West*, Julian Ralph, Harper & Brothers Publishers, NY, 1983 // Oval stamp on front cover verso and back cover recto, "Bureau of Rolls & Library, Department of State, Oct 21, 1893."

F694.M13, *Iron Men*, C.H. McKennon, Doubleday & Company, Garden City, NY, 1967 // First free endpaper has a United States Post Office Service 4¢ stamp with a Lincoln head.

F782.N6P31965, *Where the Rockies Ride Herd*, Stephen Payne, Sage Books, Denver, CO, 1965 // Back cover recto stamp, "United States Air Force, Base Library, Francis E. Warren AFB." Warren AFB is next to Cheyenne, Wyoming.

F864.F165, *A Historical, Political, and Natural Description of California by Pedro Fages*, University of California Press, Berkeley, CA, 1937 // Title page oval stamp, "Smithsonian Institute National Museum, Oct 13, 1937."

F866.S25, *Under the Sky in California*, Charles Francis Saunders, Robert M. McBride & Co., NY, 1926 // Title page stamp, "Glendale [CA?] Public Library."

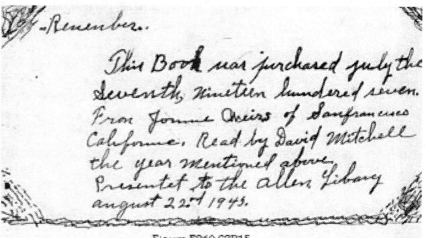

Figure F869.S3B15

F869.S3B15, *The Complete History of the San Francisco Disaster and Mount Vesuvius Horror*, Charles Eugene Banks, C.E. Thomas, 1906 // Cursive on third free endpaper, which is best seen at Figure F869.S3B15.

F869.S3C56, *Christopher of San Francisco*, George Dorsey, The Macmillan Company, NY, 1962 // Front cover verso stamp, "U.S. Air Force, Sheppard Air Force Base, AFL 3020." Sheppard is next to Wichita Falls, Texas in northeastern Texas just south of the Oklahoma border.

F910.S6, *The Frontier States*, Richard Austin Smith, Time-Life Books, NY, 1968 // Title page stamp, "Area Library, AFL 5638, 7500 Air Base Group, APO New York 89125." This air base group was located at Denham Air Station (an Air Force location without airplanes), which was located in western London about six miles north of Heathrow Airport.

F1210.D5, *The Days of Ofelia*, Gertrude Diamant, Houghton Mifflin Company, Boston, 1942 // Second free endpaper cursive, "To Mother, with all my love, Lister, 11/24/42." This is suspected to be from U.S. Senator Lister Hill of Alabama, as he and his father have several citations in this book.

F1432.P98, *The Southland of North America*, George Palmer Putnam, G.P. Putnam's Sons, NY, 1913 // Front cover verso small sticker on bottom right, "McClelland & Co., Booksellers, Columbus, O."

F1488.3.M661982, *Revolution in El Salvador*, Tommie Sue Montgomery, Westview Press, Boulder, CO, 1982 // Title page stamp, CINCUSAREUR, ATTN: AEAAG-AL, APO NY 09403." This was my address in Heidelberg, Germany for four years, 1975-79. The acronym will be spelled out with the key letters in bold italics. **C**ommander-*in*-**C**hief, **U**nited **S**tates **A**rmy, **E**urope, Attention: **A**rmy **E**urope **A**(Headquarters) **A**djutant **G**eneral- *AL* is a subordinate section.

F1776, *The Pageant of Cuba*, Hudson Strode, Harrison Smith and Robert Haas, NY, 1934 // Simple title page inscription by author, "For Mrs. W.T. Fitts, with cordial regard and esteem from Hudson Strode, May-1936."

F1911.M77v3, *Historia de Santo Domingo*, Don Antonio del Monte Y Tejada, Imprenta de Garcia Hermanos, Santo Domingo, 1890 // First free endpaper oval stamp, "Encuaderncion de Cadrira e Hllo, Calle Palau, ICCCTA."

F1915.R61973, *Haiti: The Black Republic*, Selden Rodman, The Devin-Adair Company, Old Greenwich, CT, 1954 // Title page stamp, "Peace Corps Information Service Division."

F1938.5.T7C7, *Trujillo*, Robert D. Crassweller, The Macmillan Company, NY, 1966 // Title page stamp, "Property of FBI Academy, Learning Resource Center."

F2161.E84, *The Buccaneers of America*, John Esquemeling, George Allen & Company, LTD, NY, 1911 // Cursive on simple title page, "Adolphus Koenig, Glenshaven, PA, from Lescy's Book Store of Philadelphia on June 3-1949."

F2223.B911914, *South America Observations and Impressions*, James Bryce, The Macmillan Company, NY, 1916 // Front cover verso and title page stamp, "Martin F. McGuire, Anthropology."

F2230.W57, *North West Amazons*, Thomas Whiffen, Duffield and Company, NY 1915 // First free endpaper cursive, "Owen S. Paxson, Devon, Pa., 11-6-1916."

F2235.3.A11950v2, *Obras Completas, Simon Bolivar*, Editorial Lex, La Habana, Cuba, 1950 // Stamp on Part I page, "Obsequio de la Direccion de Cultura y Bellas Artes del Ministerio de Educaccion Nacional."

F2235.F75, *Birth of a World*, Waldo Frank, Houghton Mifflin Company, Boston, 1951 // First free endpaper cursive, "Andrew J. Pereida, 356, Fairview Dr. Charleston, W. Va., Dec 9, 1951." The owner's full page of comments on the simple title page are at Figure F2235.F75.

F2508.Z8, *Brazil*, Stefan Zweig, The Viking Press, NY, 1941 // Front cover verso cursive, "Henrietta Fontaine Dent, 501 Randolph St., Eufaula, Ala."

F2521.F861894, *Historia de Revolta de 6 de Setembro de*

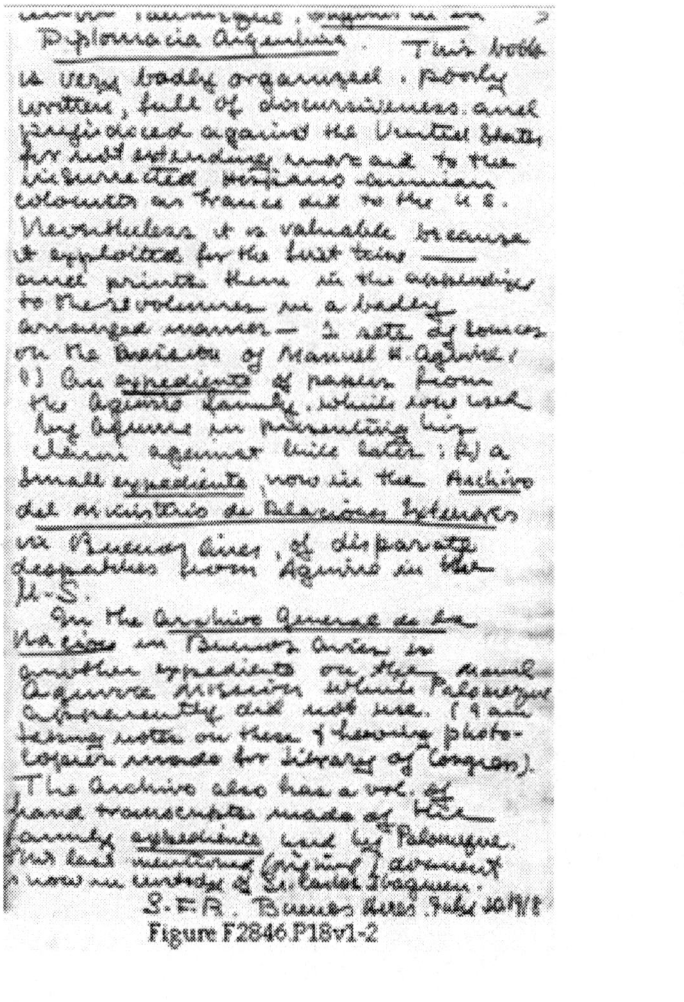

Figure F2846.P18v1-2

1893, Commercia de S. Paulo, Rio de Janeiro, 1894 // Bookplate on front cover verso, "Brasilian Booksellers."

F2846.P18v1/2, *Orijenes de la Diplomacia Arjentina*, Alberto Polomeque Establecimento Grafico, Robles & Cin, 1905 // Title page embossed stamp, "Harry S Truman Library, Independence, Missouri." First free endpaper verso cursive, "Samuel Benns(?) (Yale University) Buenos Aires, June 1938." On the first free endpaper recto was the owner's cursive, which is at Figure F2846.P18v1/2. He apparently did not think much of the book as he started out, "This book is very badly organized, poorly written, full of discursiveness, and prejudiced against the United States for not extending more aid to the insurrected Hispanio-American..."

F3423.F751932, *The Adventures of a Tropical Tramp*, Harry L. Foster, Robert M. McBride & Company, NY, 1932 // Second free endpaper cursive, "Wille(?), Hinckley Seager, San Francisco – '34."

G539.C61954a, *The Life and Times of General Two-Gun Cohen*, Charles Drage, Funk & Wagnalls Company, NY, 1954 // Title page stamp, "Pittsburg Public Library, Pittsburg, Kansas."

G600.A05A7v1, *Artic Bibliography*, Department of Defense, 1953 // Title page stamp, "Return to Nortronics Technical Information Center."

G606.K5, *Geography of the Northlands*, George H.T. Kimble, John Wiley & Sons, Inc., NY, 1955 // Stamp on top of closed leaves, "George W. Bledsole."

G7001928.N6M341979b, *Ice Crash*, Alexander McKee, St. Martin's Press, NY, 1979 // First free endpaper stamp, "USS Forrestal (CV-59)."

GC296.G9L4, *Der Grosse Fluss im Meer* (The Big River in the Sea), Hans Leip, Paul List Verlag, Munchen, Deutschland, 1954 // UAH gift bookplate and inscription which opens in part, "Mine young Hanns, Christmas 1955," and ends "Your Mother." Figure GC296.G9L4.

Figure GC296.G9L4

GF3.N381969, *No Deposit – No Return*, Huey D. Johnson, Addison-Wesley Publishing Company, Reading MA, 1970 // Stamp on simple title page, "EPA Regional VIP Library, Denver, Colorado."

GF31.H751933, *The Geographical Basis of Society*, C.C. Huntington, Prentice- Hall, NY, 1933 // Front cover verso cursive, "Murray J. Chilt??, 178 E. 13th Ave., Columbus, O," and "Edward A. Gage II, University, Virginia, 10 Preston Court." First free endpaper cursive, "Anthony H. Carter, 413 W. Illinois St., Urbana, Ill." This is the first item with three individual names on it.

GN6.B4, *An Anthropologist at Work*, Margaret Mead, Houghton Mifflin Company, Boston, 1959 // First free endpaper sticker, "Joseph Rich, 228 Raymond Rd., Hartford, Conn. 06107."

GN27.P4, *Studies in Human Biology*, Raymond Pearl, Williams and Wilkins Company, Baltimore, MD, 1924 // Department of Labor sticker on front cover verso and embossed stamp on title page.

GN575.G751916, *The Passing of a Great Race*, Madison Grant, Charles Scribner's Sons, NT, 1922 // First free endpaper cursive, "J.P. Bibb."

GN635.D9D8, *The People of Alor*, Cora du Bois, The University of Minnesota Press, Minneapolis, MN, 1944 // "M????, VA Hospital, Topeka, Kansas."

GN805.W76, *The Antiquary's Books*, Methuen Books, London, 1904 // First free endpaper cursive, "Eliot C. Curwen, Christmas 1908."

GN875.N4D9, *The Moa-Hunters of New Zealand*, T. Lindsey Buick, Thomas Avery and Sons Limited, New Plymouth, N.Z., 1937 // UAH gift bookplate Willy Ley and front cover verso sticker, "N.H. Seward PTY. LTD., 457 Bourke St. Melbourne, Aust. Scientific and Natural History Books."

GR520.M81954, *The Divine King in England*, Margaret Murray, Faber & Faber, LTD., London, 1954 // First free endpaper sticker on bottom left, "Lincoln Out-of-Print Book Search LTD., Mount Hygeia Road Box 100, Foster, Rhode Island 02825, U.S.A. (401) 647-2825."

GT450.W8, *Warm and Snug*, Lawrence Wright, Rutledge & Kegan, London, 1962 // Title page embossed stamp, "Adams County Public Library, 1945. Twelve states have an Adams County and there were no clues to further identify a specific state.

GT3530V37, *Twilight of the Kings*, Daniela Vare, John Murray, London, 1948 // Front cover verso stamp, "Property of American Merchant Marine Library Association, 45 Broadway, New York City."

Figure GVB61.W451969b

GV200.B498, *Ascent*, Jeremy Bernstein, Random House, NY, 19656 // Front cover verso stamp, "Base Library, George Air Force Base, California." George AFB was located just north of the San Gabriel Mountains near Victorville, and was the principal base for training pilots in the F-4 Phantom. It was closed by the military in 1992.

GV861.W451969b, *Acquiring Ball Skill*, H.T.A. Whiting, Lea & Febiger, Philadelphia, PA, 1969 // Front cover verso bookplate, "Joint Medical Library, Offices of the Surgeon General, Forrestal Building, Washington, D.C. 20314." Figure GV861.W451969b.

GV865.S67A34, *A False Spring*, Pat Jordan, Dodd, Mead & Company, NY, 1973 // First free endpaper stamp, "Property of Library, Naval Weapons Station, Charleston, S.C."

GV989.H36, *Lacrosse*, Mike Hanna, Hawthorn/Dutton, NY, 1980 // First free endpaper stamp, "Property of USS Carl Vinson Library." USS Carl Vinson (CV-70) is an aircraft carrier commissioned in 1982 and home-based at Bremerton, WA.

GV10-25.A5A8, *Trans-Africa Highways*, Peninsula Press Limited, Capetown, South Africa, 1949 // Sticker on front cover verso bottom left, "Van Schaik's Book Store, Pretoria." [South Africa]

GV1785.N6N61934, *Nijinsky*, Romola Nijinsky, Simon & Schuster, NY, 1934 // First free endpaper sticker, "Kamin Dance Bookshop and Gallery, 1365 Sixth Ave. at 56th St., New York 19 N.Y., Tel CIrcle 5-7955." Note the old telephone prefix of "CI." My word processing software automatically corrected my capital "I" and I had to go back to correct it.

H35.I6v19, *Intercollegiate Debates*, Egbert Ray Nichols, Noble & Noble Publishers, Inc., NY 1938 // First free endpaper cursive, "W.C. Blasingame, University, Ala."

HA29.C5651951, *Statistical Manual Methods of Making Experimental Inferences*, C.W. Churchman, Pitman-Dunn Laboratory, Frankford Arsenal, Philadelphia, PA, 1951 // Technical Library, Redstone Arsenal, Huntsville, Alabama."

Figure HB501.C85

HB103.K47H25, *A Guide to Keynes*, Alvin H. Hansen, McGraw-Hill Book Company, Inc., NY 1953 // First free endpaper cursive, "Edward M. Smith, 602A 12th St. Tuscaloosa, Ala."

HB161.S666, *The Synthetic Wealth of Nations*, Malcolm K. Graham, The Parthenon Press, Nashville, TN, 1937 // Title page stamp, "Social Security Board, Informational Service Library."

HB171.G614, *The Poverty of Nations*, Gilbert Goodman, The Ann Arbor Press, Ann Arbor, MI, 1960 // First free endpaper, simple title page, title page, and dedication page oval stamp, "Board of Governors of the Federal Reserve System Library."

HB171.5.F381958, *Economics for Modern Living*, Richard Feier, College Entrance Book Company, NY, 1958 // Title page stamp, "Yeshiva University High School, Amsterdam Ave. & 186th St., New York 33, N.Y."

HB501.C85, *In Defense of Capitalism*, James H.R. Cromwell, Charles Scribner's Sons, NY, 1937 // Front cover verso bookplate, "Lister Hill." Figure HB501.C85.

HB601.K71971, *Risk, Uncertainty and Profit*, Frank H. Knight, University of Chicago Press, Chicago, 1921 // Title page verso stamp, "United States Air Force, Bentwaters Base Library." Bentwaters AFB is about 13 miles northwest of Ipswich, England and about 6 miles from the English Channel. In 1980 Bentwaters and its nearby companion Woodbridge RAF base were involved in an alleged unidentified flying object (UFO) in Rendlesham Forest, which separates the two bases. The incident received considerable publicity.

HB871.F53, *Our Overcrowded World*, Todd Fisher, Parents' Magazine Press, NY, 1969 // Title page stamp, "Library Copy, NASA-Wallops Station, Wallops Island, VA." Wallops Island is a NASA test station location just south of the Maryland border on the Delaware/Maryland/Virginia peninsula. This part of Virginia is connected to the main body of Virginia by the Chesapeake Bay Bridge/Tunnel.

HC25.M61946, *Development of Economic Society*, George Matthews Modlin, D.C. Heath and Company, Boston, 1946 // Front cover verso bookplate, "University of Florida Libraries," and an embossed stamp on title page, "University of Florida Library."

HC55.C57, *Natural Resources and International Development*, Marion Clawson, The Johns Hopkins Press, Baltimore, MD, 1964 // Front cover verso bookplate, "Federal Trade Commission Library." Figure HC55.C57.

HC103.J451937, *A History of the Economic and Social Programs of the American People*, Walter W. Jennings, South-Western Publishing Company, NY, 1937 // First free endpaper stamp, "Edward K.

Figure HC555.C57

Austin, U of A Center, B'ham, Ala."

HC103.L5, *Economic Development of the United States*, Isaac Lippincott, D. Appleton and Company, NY, 1922 // First free endpaper cursive, "Martha C. Bennett, October 1926."

HC103.R58, *History of the American Economy*, Ross M. Robertson, Harcourt, Brace and Company, NY, 1955 // First free endpaper bookplate with no name. This is apparently for a school pupil, probably in high school based on the subject. It is too bad there is no name to trace backwards. Figure HC103.R58.

HC106.T851930, *American Economic Life*, Rexford Guy Tugwell, Harcourt, Brace and Company, NY, 1925 // Front

Figure HC103.R58

cover verso cursive, "Ray E. Tising, 2119E 21st Ave., Denver, Colorado." This is the first evidence that a college fraternity member actually touched an economics book, however, there is no evidence, such as underlining, folded corners or other possible markings, to make further statements that Tising might have read the book.

HC106.3.B448, *Productivity, Wages, and National Income*, Spurgeon Bell, The Brookings Institution, Washington, D.C., 1940 // First free endpaper oval stamp, "Treasury Department Library, Room 350."

HC106.3.C738, *The Crisis of the Middle Class*, Lewis Corey, Covici-Friede-Publishers, NY, 1935 // First free endpaper stamp, "Withdrawn from Rand Library." The Rand Corporation is a well-known problem-solving organization. It started in the defense business almost 60 years ago, and the name comes from the contraction, *R*esearch *and D*evelopment.

HC106.3.E65, *The Strategy of Raw Materials*, Brooks Emeny, The Macmillan Company, NY, 1938 // Title page embossed stamp, "Bluffton College, Bluffton, Allen County, Ohio.," with the Ohio seal of a sunrise, mountains and stacked grain in the foreground in the center of the stamp. Bluffton is about 80 miles south of my hometown of Toledo, and is one of many small liberal arts colleges which dot the Ohio landscape. It is unusual for a college to put the county name on its stamp.

HC106.3.F251938, *Capital Consumption and Adjustment*, Solomon Fabricant, National Bureau of Economic Research, NY, 1938 // Stamp on front cover verso, simple title page, objective page and title page, "Research Library, Works Progress Administration." For old-timers, the short name is WPA, a synonym for work opportunities during the 1930s' Depression. "Progress" was later officially changed to "Projects."

HC106.3.R575, *Capitalism in Crisis*, James Harvey Rogers, Yale University Press, New Haven, CT, 1938 // First free endpaper cursive, "Chen Chu-pei, 5 August 1945, Manila, P.I." This is absolutely astounding. We have tracked this previous owner, in alphabetical order, from Georgetown University, to New York University, to Calcutta, India in January 1946, and now to Manila, Philippine Islands, in August 1945. I had concluded that Calcutta was the earliest, but this is wonderful to reach back to Manila. Will we find earlier evidence?

HC106.6.M3881973, *Unfinished Business*, Paul M. Mazur, Nash Publishing, Los Angeles, CA, 1973 // Front cover verso and title page stamps, "Library, Federal Deposit Insurance Corporation, Apr. 1, 1975."

HC107.A131.T31, *The New South*, Holland Thompson, Yale University Press, New Haven, CT, 1921 // Front cover verso bookplate, History Reserve." Figure HC107.A131.T31.

HC110.P6W3, *Poverty: Power and Politics*, Chaim Isaac

Figure HC107.A131T31

Waxman, Grosset & Dunlap, NY, 1968 // Title page stamp, "Library, National Institutes of Health, Bethesda, Maryland 20014."

HC244.Z9C65, *Personal and Social Consumption in Eastern Europe*, Bogdan Mieczkowski, Preager Publishers, NY, 1975 // Title page recto stamp, "US Army Library, Wiesbaden, APO 09457," and title page verso stamp, "Lindsey Library, PL 5600, APO 09633, Tel: 6333,3093." Lindsey Air Station in Wiesbaden, Germany was the headquarters for all US Air Forces in Europe. In March 1973 the Headquarters moved to Ramstein Air Force Base, near Kaiserslautern, where it remains in 2006. It could be assumed that the Army inherited this book when the Air Force moved out of Wiesbaden. In 2008 or 2009, the top US Army headquarters in Europe, which has been in Heidelberg since the end of World War II, will move to Wiesbaden. Wiesbaden is on the Rhine River about 20 miles west of Frankfurt.

Figure HC253.R6

HC253.R6, *The Economic Interpretation of History*, James E. Thorold Rogers, G.P.Putnam's Sons, NY 1909 // Front cover verso bookplate, "Library, Bureau of Education, Department of the Interior," and title page embossed stamp, US Bureau of Education, Library." Figure HC253.R6.

HC255.A81964, *The Industrial Revolution*, 1760-1830, T.S. Ashton, Oxford University Press, NY, 1964 // Simple title page and title page stamps, "North Carolina, State Board of Education, Dept. of Community Colleges, Libraries."

Figure HC335.C515

HC335.C515, *A Critique of Russian Statistics*, Colin Clark, Macmillan and Co., Limited, London, 1939 // Front cover verso bookplate, "Library of the Embassy of the United States at Moscow." Figure HC335.C515.

Figue HC430.I5H6

HC427.9.E36, *Economic Trends in Communist China*, Alexander Eckstein, Aldine Publishing Company, Chicago, 1968 // Title page verso stamp, "Manpower Development Library – AID." AID stands for Agency for International Development.

HC430.I5H6, *China's Gross National Product and Social Accounts*, 1950-1957, William E. Hollister, The Free Press, Glencoe, IL, 1958 // Front cover verso bookplate of Joe Hunt, which features an old friend, *The Bookworm*, by Karl Spitzweg, previously seen at DP48.E462. Figure HC430.I5H6.

HC591.L6M3, *Foreign Investment and Development in Liberia*, Russell McLaughlin, Frederick A. Praeger, NY, 1966 // "Export-Import Bank, Washington, Library."

HD31.D7731974, *Management*, Peter Drucker, Harper & Row, Publishers, NY, 1973 // First free endpaper stamp, "HQS, Naval Material Command, Management Division Library."

HD31.M22, *The Professional Manager*, Douglas McGregor, McGraw-Hill Book Company, NY, 1967 // Stamp on front cover verso, first free endpaper and back cover recto, "Property of USAFE NCO Academy." USAFE is U.S. Air Forces Europe and NCO is Noncommissioned Officers.

HD31.M299, *Management by Participation*, Alfred J. Marrow, Harper & Row, Publishers, NY, 1967 // Title page stamp, "Portsmouth Naval Shipyard, Portsmouth, N.H., Library Bldg. No. 22."

HD31.M31934c, *Prohibiting Poverty*, Farrar & Rinehart, NY, 1934 // Front cover verso bookplate, "Ex Libris, Henry R. Luce (blacked out) and first free endpaper embossed stamp, "Ex Libris, Clare Boothe Luce," with a crest and two lions on their hind legs. This is by far the most notable bookplates from famous persons. Henry Luce founded *TIME* magazine and his wife was a famous playwright, author, congresswoman from Connecticut and ambassador to Italy.

Figure HD45.C51939

HD31.U76, *The Pattern of Management*, Lyndall F. Urwick, University of Minnesota Press, Minneapolis, MN, 1965 // Front cover verso and preface page stamp, "Library, Chrysler Corporation, Missile Division, Huntsville, Alabama."

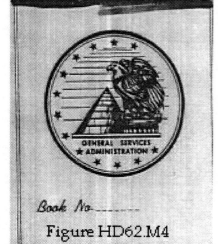

Figure HD62.M4

HD31.W1533, *Managing Yourself and Others for Executive Success*, Lynn W. Whiteside, Parker Publishing Company, Inc., West Nyack, NY, 1971 // Front cover verso stamp, "U.S. Postal Service, Library, 11th Floor North, 475 L'Enfant Plaza West, Washington, D.C. 20260."

HD38.B621978, *The New Managerial Grid*, Robert R. Blake, Gulf Publishing Company, Houston, TX, 1978 // Front cover verso, first free endpaper and fore edge stamps, "U.S. Naval School of Health Sciences, Bethesda, Maryland, 20614."

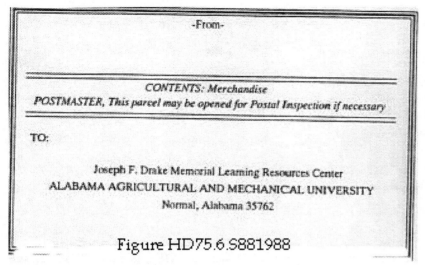

Figure HD75.6.S881988

"IBM Huntsville Library."

HD45.C51939, *Social Control of Business*, John M. Clark, McGraw-Hill Book Company, NY, 1939 // Front cover verso bookplate, "Library of the Ohio State University," and title page punch-through stamp, "Ohio State University." Figure HD45.C51939.

HD62.M4, *Profiting from Industrial Standardization*, Benjamin Melnitsky, Conover-Mast Publications, NY, 1953 // Front cover verso bookplate, "Property of General Service Administration." Figure HD62.M4.

HD75.6.S881988, *Sustainable Environmental Management*, R. Kerry Tirner, Westview Press, Boulder, CO, 1988 // Loose shipping label inside front cover to "Alabama Agricultural and Mechanical University." Figure HD75.6.S881988.

HD82.B58, *Laissez Faire and After*, O. Fred Boucke, Thomas Crowell Company, NY, 1932 // Front cover verso bookplate, "My Book, J.J. Mills (blacked out). Figure HD82.B58. This is the bookplate which is directly associated with the sciences, in this case, chemistry.

HD38.P315, *Current Perspectives in Organizational Development*, J. Jennings Partin, Addison-Wesley Publishing Company, Reading, MA, 1973 // Top and bottom edges stamp, "Property of MRDO, NORVA." NORVA is suspected to stand for Norfolk, Virginia, but I have no idea on the MRDO.

HD38.S53, *The Dynamics of Management*, Waino W. Swojanen, Holt, Rinehart and Winston, NY, 1966 // Front cover verso, first free endpaper and fore edge stamps,

Figure HD82.B58

HDB2.D38, *The Economics of Development in Small Countries*, William G. Demas, McGill University Press, Montreal, 1965 // Front cover verso bookplate, "Park College Library." Figure HDB2.D38. This is a very clean bookplate from Park College, as the previous citations, DK418.5 and DS 519, were blacked out by the UAH accession censors.

HD82.E33, *Economics and Public Policy*, Arthur Smithies, The Brookings Institute, Washington, D.C., 1955 " First free endpaper stamp, Sun Oil Company, Public Relations Department Library, 1600 Walnut Street, Philadelphia, Penna." "Discarded" over-stamped.

PARK COLLEGE
LIBRARY

DISCORD

Parkville, Missouri

Figure HD82.D38

HD1375.L4591932, *The Promotion of Commercial Buildings*, Charles H. Lench, Architectural Economics Press, NY, 1932 // First free endpaper stamp, "Thos J. Biggs, Major, Corps of Engineers, Area Engineer," and cursive "Thos J. Biggs, Jr., His Book, October-1933."

HD1694.A5H347, *The Economic Performance of Public Investments*, Robert H. Haveman, Johns Hopkins Press, Baltimore, MD, 1972 // Title page stamp, "Property of the United States Government, National Oceanic and Atmospheric Administration."

HD1694.A7M2, *The Politics of Water in Arizona*, Dean E. Mann, The University of Arizona Press, Tucson, AZ, 1963 // First free endpaper stamp, "Colorado River Basin, Project Field office, Public Health Service, DHEW, 1324 N. First St., Phoenix, Arizona, 85004."

HD2346.P6C3, *The Filipino Manufacturing Entrepreneur*, John J. Carroll, S.J., Cornell University Press, Ithaca, NY, 1965 // First free endpaper stamp, "Asia Training Center, UH/AID Library."

HD5504.A3S53, *Mediation*, William E. Simkin, The Bureau of National National Affairs, Inc., Washington, D.C. // Top edge stamp, "Office of the Staff Judge Advocate, SAMTEC," and back cover recto stamp, HQ SAMTEC, AFL 2527, Technical Library, Vandenberg AFB, CA 93437." SAMTEC is Space and Missile Test Center.

HD6483.F74, *Frontiers of Collective Bargaining*, John T. Dunlop, Harper & Row, NY, 1967 // Title page stamp, "Hospital Administration Library, U.S. Naval School of Hospital Administration."

HD7293.S73, *Housing*, 1970-1971, George Sternlieb, AMS Press, NY, 1972 // Title page stamp, "Library, West Georgia College, Carrollton, Georgia."

HD7413.E6I6, *George F. Johnson and his Industrial Democracy*, Huntington Press, NY, 1935 // Front cover verso stamp, "Library of Willard M.L. Robinson, ??"

HD9502.U52R42, *Refining the Waterfront*, David Morell, Oelgeschlager, Gunn and Hain, Publishers, Inc., Cambridge, MA, 1980 '' First free endpaper and title page stamps, "U.S. Department of Justice, Civil Division Library, Main Justice Building, Washington, D.C. 2053."

HD9545.E57, *Energy: Demand, Conservation and Industrial Problems*, Michael S. Macrakis, The MIT Press, Cambridge, MA, 1974 // Top edge stamp, "Property of NSWC, Crane, Indiana." NSWC is Naval Surface Warfare Center, which is located about 30 miles southwest of Bloomington.

HD9566.M37, *Horizontal Divestiture and the Petroleum Industry*, Jesse W. Markham, Ballinger Publishing Company, Cambridge, MA, 1977 // Title page stamp, "Property of U.S. Army, The Judge Advocate General's School Library." This school is in Charlottesville, Virginia.

HD9695.U52H4, *The Great Price Conspiracy*, John Herling, Robert B. Luce, Inc., Washington, D.C., 1962 // Front cover

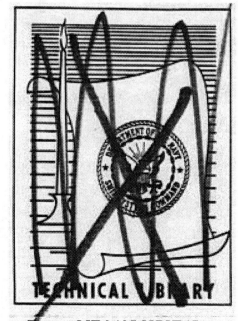

Figure HD9698.U52T43

verso and title page stamps, "Law Library, Office of the General Counsel, U.S. Atomic Energy Commission."

HD9698.A28M61952a, *The Traitors*, Alan Morehead, Charles Scribner's Sons, NY, 1952 // Front cover verso, "Nello Andrews, Huntsville, Alabama, August, 1956.

HD9698.U52N791977, *Nuclear Power Issues and Choices*, Nuclear Energy Policy Study Group, Ballinger Publishing Company, Cambridge, MA, 1956 // Top edge stamp, "U.S. Nuclear Regulatory Commission."

HD9698.U52T43, *Productive Uses of Nuclear Energy*, Perry D. Teitelbaum, National Planning Association, NY, 1958 // Front cover verso bookplate, "Department of the Navy, Ship Systems Command, Technical Library." Figure HD9698.U52T43.

HD9724.F3, *The Output of Manufacturing Industries*, 1899-1937, Solomon Fabricant, National Bureau of Economic Research, NY, 1940 // Title page oval stamp, "Federal Works Agency, Library." This agency was abolished in 1949.

HE356.A4R45, *Crooked Road*, David A. Remley, McGraw-Hill Book Company, NY, 1976 // First free endpaper stamp, "Sellenkirchen International Library" and title page stamp, "US Army Library, Baumholder Military Community, APO NY 09034." Baumholder is an American base in the western part of Germany. Sellenkirchen could not be found as a German town on a recent road atlas. The American military usually do not add the "international" into library

Figure HE745.C5

names, since most libraries are not international. I have no idea about this name.

HE396.C4G71989, *The National Waterway*, Ralph D. Gray, University of Illinois Press, Urbana, IL, 1989 // Title page stamp, "CEETL, Shinfo Center, Fort Belvoir, VA." CEETL is an office symbol designating Corps of Engineers, Engineering Topographical Laboratory.

HE745.C5, *The Clipper Ship Era*, Arthur H. Clark, G.P. Putnam's Sons, NY, 1910 // First free endpaper cursive, "John F. Stevens, Jr., Christmas 1926, John & Beatrice" and second free endpaper bookplate, Ex Libris, John F. Stevens, Jr." Figure HE745.C5. This is the first bookplate in color, as the sea is blue and the sail is orange.

Figure HE1843.M65

Figure HE1843.R6

HE1051.E61913a, *The Truth About the Railroads*, Howard Elliott, Houghton Mifflin Company, NY, 1913 // First free endpaper and title page stamps, "Flatbush Boy's Club, Community Center." Flatbush is a neighborhood in the Borough of Brooklyn, New York City. It is the Angelicization of the Dutch language *Vladbos* (approximately *wooded land*).

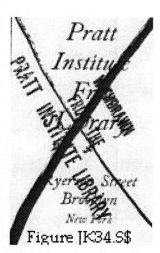

Figure JK34.S$

HE1843.M65, *Government Regulation of Railway Rates*, Hugo R. Meyer, The Macmillan Company, NY, 1905 // Front cover verso bookplate, "Daniel Willard." Figure HE1843.M65. Daniel Willard was president of the Baltimore & Ohio Railroad for over 25 years.

HE1843.R6, *Railroads*, William Z. Ripley, Longmans, Green and Co., NY, 1922 // Front cover verso sticker, "Dixie Business Book Shop." Figure HE1843.R6.

HE2708.I51895, *Ninth Annual Report of the Interstate Commerce Commission*, Government Printing Office, Washington, D.C., 1896 // Front cover verso bookplate, "University of Alabama Gift of Truman H. Aldrich." Figure HE2708.I51895.

HE2708.I51900, *Fourteenth Annual Report of the Interstate Commerce Commission*, Government Printing Office, Washington, D.C., 1901 // First free endpaper oval stamp, "Alabama Industrial and Scientific Society, Library."

HE2741.v3, *Railroads*, Homer Bews Vanderblue, The Macmillan Company, NY, 1923 // First free endpaper stamp, "Baltimore & Ohio R.R., Research Library, 117 B.&O. Bldg. Baltimore| 2, Md" and first free endpaper cursive, "To Mr. Willard from James J. Cornwell(?), 1/2/23"

Figure HE2708.I51895

HE2751.R21910, *The Railroad Library*, Slason Thompson, The Gunthorp-Warren Printing Co., Chicago, IL, 1910 // Front cover verso and first free endpaper bookplates, "Association of American Railroads." Figure HE2751.R21910.

HE2754.F3F8, *Joseph B. Eastman, Servant of the People*, Claude Moore Fuess, Columbia University Press, NY, 1952 // Front cover verso cursive, two inscriptions, Figure HE2754.F3F8, and back cover recto sticker, "Emily Mundy's Book Shop, Syracuse, New York."

HE6185.U5S31936, *United States Stamp Catalogue, 1936*, Hugo M. Clark, Scott Stamp & Coin Company, LTD., NY, 1935 // Front cover verso bookplate, "Library, Jacksonville University, Florida." Figure HE6185.U5S31936. Note that the print year was a year ahead of the stamp year.

HE6185.U5S31937, *United States Stamp Catalogue*, 1937, Hugo M. Clark, Scott Stamp & Coin Company, LTD., NY, 1936 // First free endpaper cursive, "Alexander Friches, 60 Anson Road, Cricklewood, London, N.W.2."

HE6226.S481946v1, *Standard Postage Stamp Catalogue*, Scott Publications, NY, 1945 // ▌ Front cover verso bookplate, "Alexander A. Klieforth," and a sailing ship. Figure HE6226.S481946v1.

HF1455.C5, *Tomorrow's Trade*, Stuart Chase, The Twentieth Century Fund, NY, 1945, Front cover verso bookplate (blacked out), "Pratt Institute Library, Brooklyn, New York." A later book, JK34.S4, had the additional address on Ryerson Street, but had a reasonable copy of the bookplate, Figure JK34.S4 (out of sequence).

Figure HE2751.R21910

HF3424.S65, *El Comercio en la Historia de Columbia*, Jose Raimundo Sojo, Editado por la Camara de Comercio de Bogota, no date, // First free endpaper cursive, "Luz Marina Celedón Slines(?), Tercer Semestre Economa, April 26, 1972, Universidad Taveriana."

Figure HE2754.E3F8

HF5386.H47, *Private Keepers of the Public Interest*, Paul T. Heyne, McGraw-Hill Book Company, NY, 1968, Front cover verso bookplate (blacked out), Nash Library, Science – Arts, Oklahoma University, Chickasha, Oklahoma, 73018." This was a nice bookplate at one time. Too bad!

HF5386.C58, *Philosophy of a Businessman*, E.M. Clark, University of Missouri, Columbia, MO, 1965 // Front cover verso bookplate, "Oklahoma College of Liberal Arts." Figure HF5386.C58.

HF5415.L33, *Case Histories of Successful Marketing*, Hector Lazo, Funk & Wagnalls Company, NY, 1950 // First free endpaper and title page stamps, "ARAMCO Technical Library." ARAMCO is the world famous Arabian American Oil Company, formed in 1933. In 1988 the name was changed

Figure HF5415..13.K425

to Saudi ARAMCO.

HF5415.O97, *Pricing for Marketing Executives*, Alfred R. Oxenfeldt, Wadsworth Publishing Company, San Francisco, CA, 1961 // Title page stamp, "Edward M. Smith, P.O. Box 34132, University, ALA, 35496."

HF5415.I3.K425, *Managerial Marketing: Perspectives and Viewpoints*, Eugene J. Kelly, Richard D. Irwin, Inc., Homewood, IL, 1958 // First free endpaper bookplate, "Ben R. Graves," and UAH gift bookplate. Dr. Benjamin R. Graves was the first president of The University of Alabama in Huntsville. See Z992.Y17 for a story about another book once belonging to Dr. Graves.

HF5549.B38, *Manual of Job Evaluation*, Eugene J. Benge, Harper & Brothers Publishers, NY, 1941 // First free endpaper stamp, "Received in Library, Aug. 10, 1954, Rohm & Haas Company, Redstone Division." Redstone Arsenal, Alabama.

HF5549.5.C6E351956, *Effective Communication on the Job*, M. Joseph Dooher, American Management Association, NY, 1956 // Front cover verso stamp, "Delmas C. Little, 1511 Cliff Drive, Newport Beach, California."

HF5550.W4431976, *Profit Planning and Control*, Glenn A. Welsch, Prentice-Hall Inc., Englewood Cliffs, NJ, 1976 // Title page stamp, "TUSLOG Det. 94, APO N.Y. 09324."

HF5386.H47

TUSLOG is a term with which I am intimately familiar. I was assigned for two years in Ankara, Turkey in the Joint United States Military Mission, Turkey (JUSMMAT). Part of my job was to monitor the TUSLOG designation. During the Cold War era the United States had scores of military units located in Turkey, comprised of all services. In order to disguise the missions of the units, because the military names often identified the mission, all U.S. units were assigned a detachment number as part of the cover designator, The United States Logistics Group TUSLOG. The detachment number was based on the arrival in the country, not on size or other criteria. During my time,

Ex Libris

Alexander A. Klieforth

Figure HE6226.S481946v1

1973-75, the highest number was just over 200. It is not certain whether the designation was for the purpose of hiding things from the Russians, or from the general Turkish population. Turkey was surrounded by countries that were not classified as friendly toward it, so the US/Turkish relationship was mutually beneficial.

HF5635.N561941, *Elementary Accounting*, George Hillis Newlove, D.C. Heath and Company, NY, 1941 // Front cover verso, "LeRoy O. Smith, Univ. of Tampa."

HF5635N741949, *Accounting Principles*, South-Western Publishing Company, Cincinnati, OH, 1949 // First free endpaper cursive, "LeRoy O. Smith" (same as above) and stamp, "School of Business, State College, Mississippi," and stamp, "Sample Copy."

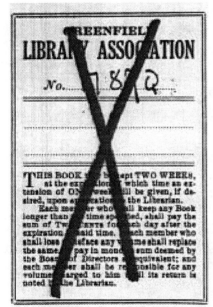

Figure HG4011.R51927

HF5635.T271938, *International Accounting*, Jacob B. Taylor, McGraw-Hill Book Company, NY, 1938 // Front cover verso cursive, "L.O. Smith, Accounting Department, University of Oklahoma." Seems as if LeRoy O. Smith did not last long at any one university.

HF5681.B2R28, *Segment Reporting for Managers and Investors*, Alfred Rappaport, National Association of Accountants, NY, 1972 // Front cover verso stamp, "Worcester Junior College."

HF5736.H81916, *Indexing and Filing*, E.R. Hudders, The Ronald Press, NY, 1916 // Title page oval stamp, "The Philadelphia Museums, Apr 25, 1916."

HG3755.M23, *Consumer Instalment (sic) Credit and Public Policy*, The University of Michigan, Ann Arbor, MI, 1965 // Title page oval stamp, "Library, Comptroller of the Currency, Nov. 4, 1976.

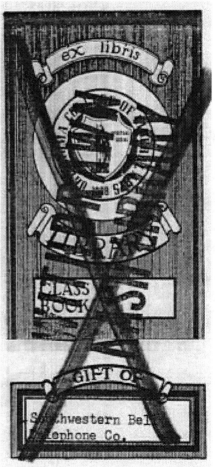

Figure HF5386.C58

HG3881.R7713, *Balance of Payments*, Jacques Rueff, The Macmillan Company, NY, 1967 // Front cover verso bookplate, "Dartmouth College Library." Figure HG3881.R7713.

HG4011.D56, *Corporate Finance*, Elvin F. Donaldson, The Ronald Press Company, NY, 1957 // First free endpaper stamp, "Property of Reference Center, AFIT/OSU School of Logistics." The OSU was blacked out, which stands for Ohio State University. AFIT is the Air Force Institute of Technology, which is at Wright-Patterson Air Force

Figure HG3881.R7713

Base in Dayton, Ohio. It appears that an early relationship between the two schools was terminated.

HG4011.R51927, *Main Street and Wall Street*, William Z. Ripley, Little, Brown, and Company, Boston, MA, 1927 // Front cover verso bookplate, "Greenfield Library Association." Figure HG4011.R51927. Notice that the late fine was 2 cents per day.

HJ1077.C6K4, *Jacques Cœur, Merchant Prince for the Middle Ages*, Albert Boardman Kerr, Charles Scribner's Sons, NY, 1927 // Front cover verso bookplate, "Francis Waring Robinson," Figure HJ1077.C6K4, and cursive, "Estelle M. Rose, August 1928." Francis Waring Robinson was the Curator of Art at the Detroit Institute of Art. In January, 1944 she gave a speech, "Books as Art," to the annual convention of the Special Libraries Association. The association is a grouping of libraries in southern Michigan at commercial companies and other organizations whose primary mission is not to run libraries.

HJ2051.S58, *The Budgetary Process of the United States*, Arthur Smithies, McGraw-Hill Book Company, NY, 1955 // Front cover verso stamp, "Library Center for International Affairs, Harvard University," and first free endpaper stamp, Harvard Defense Studies Program, 2 Divinity Avenue, Cambridge, 38, Mass."

HJ2377.G74, *Production, Jobs and Taxes*, Harold M. Groves, McGraw-Hill Book Company, NY, 1944 // First free endpaper cursive, "Dennis Chavez, July 5, 1944, U.S. Senate" and stamp, "Library, Senator Dennis Chavez, New Mexico." Chavez served as a U.S. Senator from 1935 until his death in November 1962.

Ex Libris
Francis Waring Robinson
Figure HJ1077.C6K4

HJ6619.G7, *The Smugglers*, Timothy Green, Walker and Company, NY, 1969 // Title page stamp, "NSB Library, King's Bay, GA." NSB is Naval Submarine Base at King's Bay, which in the extreme southeastern tip of Georgia, just across the St. Mary's River from Florida.

Library

EDUCATIONAL TESTING
SERVICE

OFFICERS   TURNBULL

Figure HK11.A671962

HK11.A671957, *American Psychological Association 1957 Directory*, American Psychological Association, Washington, D.C., 1957 // Front cover verso stamp, "Library, Larue D. Carter Memorial Hospital, 1315 W 10th Street, Indianapolis, Indiana."

HK11.A671962, *American Psychological Association 1962 Directory*, American Psychological Association, Washington, D.C., 1962 // Front cover verso bookplate, Library, Educational Testing Service." Figure HK11.A671962.

HK21.P871930, *Psychologies of 1930*, Carl Murchison, Clark University Press, Worcester, MA // Front cover verso cursive, "K.E. Coffield" and first free endpaper cursive, "Theodore E. Frank, Cairo, Nov. 20, 1920." There is a little town of Cairo in the southern most tip of Illinois, but we feel safe in placing this Cairo in Egypt, but based on absolutely no evidence.

HK131.M95, *Psychology for Nurses*, Maude B. Muse, W.B. Saunders Company, Philadelphia, PA, 1925 // Front cover verso stamp, "Health Department, City of Boston" and a sticker, "E.F. Mahady Co., Medical Books, Boston."

HK199.A8, *Motives in Fantasy, Action, and Society*, John W. Atkinson, D. Van Nostrand Company, Princeton, NJ, 1958 // Front cover verso and title page stamps, "Medical and General Reference Library, Veterans Administration, Washington, D.C."

HK203.K61947. *Gestalt Psychology*, Wolfgang Köhler, Liveright Publishing Company, NY, 1947 // Title page embossed stamp, "M. Paul Phillips Library, Birmingham Southern College, 1859."

Figure HK531.Y61943

HK319.H5 1940, *Conditioning and Learning*, D. Appleton-Century Company, Inc., NY, 1940 // First free endpaper cursive and stamp, "George E. Passey."

HK431.G628, *Measurement of Intelligence by Drawings*, World Book Company, Chicago, IL, 1926 // Front cover verso cursive, "J.B. Reynolds, 1411 Ellison Rd. Columbia, Tel 787-3935."

HK431.G78, *Measurements of Human Behavior*, Edward B. Greene, The Odessy Press, NY, 1941 // Front cover verso bookplate, "Geneseo Normal Library" and title page embossed stamp, "Geneseo N.Y. State Normal School Library." Figure HK431.G78. Geneseo is about 30 miles south of Rochester.

HK531.Y61943, *Emotion in Man and Animal*, Paul Thomas Young, John Wiley & Sons, Inc., NY, 1943 // Front cover verso bookplate, "Ruth N.

Figure HK431.G78

Kramer." Figure HK531.Y61943.

HK639.M3, *Peace, Power and Plenty*, Orison Swett Marden, Thomas Y. Crowell Company, NY, 1909 // First free endpaper cursive inscription by "Pauline Stripling Hedrice." Figure HK639.M3.

HK698.9.P47K4v1, *The Psychology of Personal Constructs*, George A. Kelly, W.W. Norton & Company, NY, 1955 // Front cover verso bookplate, "Phillip Miller Allen." Figure HK698.9.P47K4v1.

HK789.F4S551914, *The Great Fictions Which Are Ruining Mankind*, Charles Elihu Slocum, The Slocum Publishing Company, Toledo, OH, 1914 // Front cover verso bookplate, "Paul J. Stro??se," Figure HK789.F4S551914, and cursive, Bryan P. Saudle, Chittenden Hotel, Columbus, Ohio."

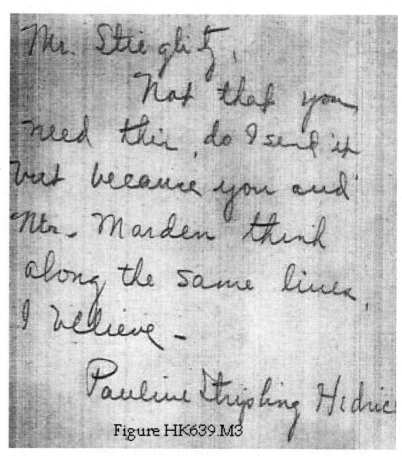

Figure HK639.M3

HK1073.P65D86, *Sleep Positions*, Samuel Dunkell, William Morrow and Company, Inc., NY 1977 // Title page stamp, "Library Naval Support Activity, Seattle, Washington 98115."

Figure HK698.9.P47K4v1

HL439.F6613, *Not Made of Wood*, Jan Foudraine, Macmillan Publishing Co., Inc., NY, 1971 // First free endpaper and last free endpaper stamps, "Station Library, Naval Air Station, Glynco, Georgia, 31520" and "Property of Library, Naval Weapons Station Charleston, S.C." Glynco is next to Brunswick, Georgia, in the southeastern part of the state and is also the home of the Federal Law Enforcement Training Center.

HL439.F85, *The Future Role of the State Hospital*, Jack Zusman, Lexington Books, Lexington, MA, 1975 // Title page stamp, National Institute of Mental Health Library, ??? Bldg. 5800 Fishers Lane, Rockville, Md

igure HK789.F4S551914

88

20852."

HL455.P731971, *Psychiatric Care of the Underprivileged*, Guido Belsaaao, Little, Brown, and Company, Boston, MA, 1971 // Front cover verso stamp, "Medical Library, Womack Army Hospital, Ft. Bragg, NC." I was stationed at Fort Bragg and visited the hospital, but not the medical library.

HL467.M61948, *The Psychology of Abnormal People*, John J.B. Morgan, Longman's, Green and Company, NY, 1948 // Front cover verso cursive, "Gewin W. Flowers, 4492 Hardee St. Chamblee, Ga."

HL480.5.F7131965, *The Doctor and the Soul*, Viktor E. Frankl, Alfred A. Knopf, NY, 1972 // First free endpaper stamp, "Commanding Officer, Naval Submarine Training Center Pacific, FPO San Francisco 96610."

HM66.B38, *Social Life*, John W. Bennett, Alfred A, Knopf, NY, 1948 // First free endpaper sticker, "William B. Baxter, Bard College, Annandale-on-Hudson, NY."

HM216.L5, *The Rediscovery of Morals*, Henry G. Link, E.P. Dutton & Company, NY, 1947 // Title page stamp, "Grand View College, Des Moines, Iowa."

Figure HN37.C3P7

HM261.C531967, *Voice of the People*, Reo M. Christenson, McGraw-Hill Company, NY, 1967 // Title page stamp, "Property of the Secretary of the Air Force, Office of Information, Professional Library."

HN29.L81942, *Social Research*, George A. Lundberg, Longmans, Green and Co., NY, 1946, // Front cover verso cursive, "Ruth N. Kramer, 1457 Worthington St. Col. O." [Columbus, Ohio] Refer back to Kramer's bookplate, HK531.Y61943. We now know where she lived.

HN31.M231945, *The Rise of the Tyrant*, Carl McIntire, Christian Beacon Press, Collingwood, NY, 1945 // First free endpaper, "Property of Quantico Library, FBI."

HN37.C3P7, *Creative Revolution*, J.F.T. Prince, The Bruce Publishing Company, Milwaukee, WI, 1937 // Front cover verso bookplate, "Rev. Robert E. Delaney," Figure HN37.C3P7 and cursive "1/15/38."

HN64.B91901, *The Social Unrest*, John Graham Brooks, The Macmillan Company, NY, 1901 // Title page stamps, "Property of Quantico Library, FBI," "Property of the Library, Metropolitan Life Ins. Co.," and "Property of Federal Bureau of Investigation, U.S. Department of Justice."

Figure HQ21.E471926

HN423.F5, *Les Salons*, Carlos Fischer, Editions Marcel Seheur, Paris, 1929 // Front cover verso sticker, "Librairie, Raymond Clavreuil, 37 Rue St Andre Des Arts, Paris, VI."

HQ21.E471926, *Man and Woman*, Havelock Ellis, A & C Black, Ltd., London, 1926 // front cover verso bookplate, "E.C. Jensen," with a sailing ship. Figure HQ21.E471926.

HQ766.D45, *Birth Control*, Lydia Allen DeVilbiss, Small, Maynard and Company, Boston, MA, 1923 // Title page sticker, "The Book League, 47 West 42nd Street, New York City.

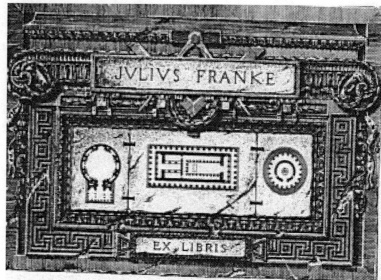

HS412.R3, *The Comacines*, W. Ravenscroft, Elliot Stock, London, 1910 // Front cover verso bookplate, "Julius Franke." Figure HS412.R3.

HV31.G41926, *Poverty and Dependency*, John Lewis Gilkin, The Century Co., NY, 1926 // First free endpaper cursive, "Sheila McCready, 322 College Ave., Ashland, Ohio," and a Morris G.

Figure HS412.R3

Caldwell stamp. Finding another person's name on one of Caldwell's stamped books was a rarity, as I'm sure I handled scores of his books in my search.

HV40.E251972, *Community Organizers and Social Planners*, Joan Levin Ecklein, John Wiley & Sons, Inc., NY, 1972 // First free endpaper stamp, "Property of General Library, Bldg ??, Naval Air Station, Lakehurst, N.J." Lakehurst is where the German dirigible, Hindenburg, burned on 6 May, 1937, killing 35 of 97 people on board and one Navy crewman on the ground.

HV43.W4, *A Rational Approach to Social Casework*, Harold D. Werner, Association Press, NY, 1965 // First free endpaper stamp, "Medical Library, VA Center, Dublin, Georgia."

HV91.K56, *From Philanthropy to Social Welfare*, Phillip Klein, Jossey-Bass Inc., San Francisco, CA, 1968 // Front cover verso sticker, "Ian Leeman Brooks, ACSW, P.O. Box 313, University, AL 35486." ACSW is the Academy of Certified Social Workers.

HV687.D8, *An Approach to Social Medicine*, Francis Lee Dunham, The Williams and Wilkins Company, Baltimore, MD, 1925 // Front cover verso stamp, "Northern Wisconsin Colony and Training School, Professional Library." This school is in Chippewa Falls, Wisconsin and serves as a facility for helping mongoloids.

Figure HV4088.L8M521950

HV4088.L8M521950, *London's Underworld*, Henry Mayhew, William Kimber, London, 1950 // Front cover verso bookplate, "Charles Woodard," which featured a Roman chariot with two men and two horses. Figure HV4088.L8M521950. Charles Woodard was a long-time resident of Huntsville and a developer of crossword puzzles for the *New York Times.*

HV6025.R561937, *The Criminals We Deserve*, Henry T.F. Rhodes, Oxford University Press, NY, 1937 // Front cover verso and title page stamps, "Library, U.S. Bureau of Prisons, Washington, D.C."

HV6700.K55, *Grand Deception*, Alexander Klein, J.B. Lippincott Company, NY, 1955 // First free endpaper cursive, "Bernard Geeliar(?), USA, Lt Col, Artillery, 1963."

HV6783.K3, *The Criminal and His Allies*, Marcus Kavanagh, The Boobs-Merrill Company, Indianapolis, IN, 1928 // Front cover verso bookplate, "Frederick C. Holliman." Figure HV6783.K3.

HV7419.5.E.251984, *Using Research*, John E. Eck, National Institute of Justice, U.S. Department of Justice, Washington, D.C., 1984 // Title page stamp, "National Institute of Justice Library."

HV9475.N78L28, *Invisible Stripes*, Lewis E. Lawes, Farrar & Rinehart, NY, 1938 // Front cover verso stamp, "Statewide Library Project, W.P.A. of ????, Indiana State Library."

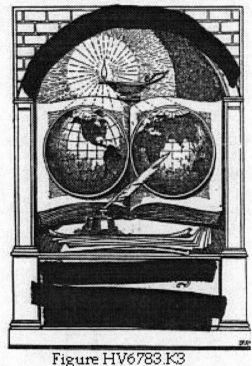

Figure HV6783.K3

JA81.D81905, *A History of Political Theories*, William A. Dunning, The Macmillan Company, NY, 1928 // Front cover verso cursive, "Virginia Cleve, 706 E. Buffalo St. Ithaca, New York."

JC491.A3, *The Theory of Social Revolutions*, Brooks Adams, The Macmillan Company, NY, 1913 // Front cover verso bookplate, "Mississippi A & M College Library." Mississippi A & M is now Mississippi State University. Brooks Adams was a well known historian of the early 20th Century and the youngest brother of the better known historian, Henry Adams. They were both great-grandsons of President John Adams and grandsons of President John Quincy Adams. Their father was Charles Francis Adams. They did not seek political office.

JC599.U5P36, *The Naked Society*, Vance Packard, David McKay Company, Inc., NY, 1964 // First free endpaper stamps, "Library, Naval Air Station Acana(?)" and "Naval Station Library Guam."

JF1351.G8, *Papers on the Science of Administration*, Luther Gulick, Institute of Public Administration, NY, 1937 // "Front cover verso bookplate (blued-out), New Orleans Branch, United States Department of Agriculture Branch."

JK268.C5, *Genesis and Birth of the Federal Constitution*, J.A.C. Chandler, The Macmillan Company, NY, 1924 // First free endpaper cursive, "Lister Hill, Montgomery, Ala, March 12th – 1925." Figure JK268.C5.

JK421.A311987-88, *Washington Information Directory*, Congressional Quarterly Inc., Washington, D.C., 1987 // Front cover verso bookplate (blacked out), "Evansville Campus, 1965, Indiana State University, Library Services."

JK421.R53, *Bureaucracy and Policy Implementation*, Randall B. Ripley, The Dorsey Press, Homewood, IL, 1982 // Title page stamp, "T.S.U. Library, Troy, AL." TSU is Troy State University.

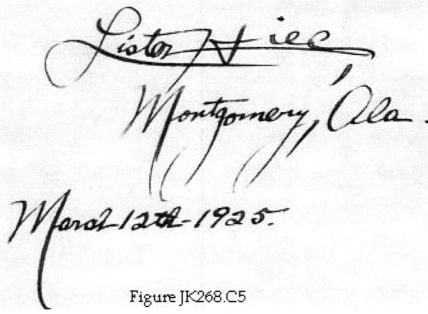

Figure JK268.C5

JK468.E7D68, *Ethics in Government*, Paul H. Douglas, Harvard University Press, Cambridge, MA, 1952 // First free endpaper and title page stamps, "State of Alabama, Public Library Service."

JK45311907, *Alabama Official and Statistical Register 1907*, Brown Printing Co., State Printers and Binders, Montgomery, AL, 1907 // Front cover verso stamp, "Hugh W. Cardon, Gift of Mrs. Marie Bankhead Owen, Nov. 11, 1929."

JN128.W51925, *The Making of the English Constitution*, Albert Beebe White, G.P. Putnam's Sons, NY, 1925 // Front cover verso cursive, "A.L. Verr??ee, 107 Calhoun Bldg., Vanderbilt University."

JN406.L3, *British Foreign Policy*, R. Victor Langford, American Council on Public Affairs, Washington, D.C., 1942 // Front cover verso bookplate (blacked out), "U.S. Tariff Commission, Library."

JN2413.P59v1, *Histoire des États Généraux*, Georges Picot, Librairie Hachette, Paris, 1872 // Fourth free endpaper cursive, "a???????? Monsieur Grisolet, ?????? affectueue (?), G.Picot." (author)

JQ96.B71963, *The New States of Asia*, Michael Brecher, Oxford University Press, London, 1963 // Front cover verso and first free endpaper stamps, "Prof. Carleton C. Chen, 98-05, 63rd Road, Rego Park, N.Y., 11374." Carleton Chen has reappeared, but I still find nothing about him on Google, but this citation shows that he was alive in 1963.

JQ1519.A5A61960, *Second Session of the Second National People's Congress of the People's Republic of China*, Foreign Language Press, Peking, China, 1960 // Front cover verso stamp, "Joe W. Hart, 7347 Eldorado Street, McLean, VA 22102, (703) 356-2879." Figure JQ1519.A5A61960.

Figure JQ1519.A5A61960

JQ16151932.Q5, *Japanese Government and Politics*, Harold S. Quigley, The Century Co., NY, 1932 // Front cover verso bookplate, "Library of the University of Michigan." Figure JQ16151932.Q5.

JS1234.A41978, *Pensions and New York City's Fiscal Crisis*, Damodar Gujarati, American Enterprise Institute for Public Policy Research, Washington, D.C., 1978 // First free endpaper stamp, "Pension Benefit Guaranty Corporation, Office of the General Counsel Library."

JS3025.P31v2pt1, *English Local Government*, Sidney and Beatrice Webb, Private Subscription by the Authors for Their friends and Supporters, March 1929 // Front cover verso bookplate, "Harvard College Library." Figure JS3025.P31v2pt1.

JX233.R8v1, *Foreign Relations of the United States 1918 Russia*, U.S. Government Printing Office,

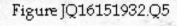

Figure JQ16151932.Q5

Washington, D.C., 1931 // First free endpaper stamp, University of North Carolina. Figure JX233.R8v1.

Figure JS3025.P32v2pt1

JX233.R8v4, *Foreign Relations of the United States 1918 Russia*, U.S. Government Printing Office, Washington, D.C.,

Figure JX233.R8v1

1931 // Front cover verso bookplate, "Honorable Barrett O'Hara" on horseback. Figure JX233.R8v4.

JX233.A31886, *Foreign Relations of the United States,*, U.S. Government Printing Office, Washington, D.C., 1887 // Second free endpaper verso cursive, unclear handwriting from "James L, Pugh."

JX233.A31918Suppl1v1, *Foreign Relations of the United States*, U.S. Government Printing Office, Washington, D.C., 1933 // Front cover verso bookplate, "Cushing-Martin Library, Stonehill College." Figure JX233.A31918Suppl1v1. Stonehill College is in Easton, Massachusetts.

JX233.R8A31937v5, *Foreign Relations of the United States*, U.S. Government Printing Office, Washington, D.C., 1954 // First free endpaper stamp, "Western Kentucky College Library." This college is in Bowling Green, KY.

Figure JX233.A31917Suppl2v2

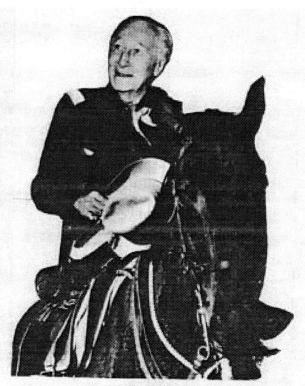

EX LIBRIS
Honorable Barratt O'Hara
Figure JX233.R8v4

JX233.A31917Suppl2vol2, *Foreign Relations of the United States*, U.S. Government Printing Office, Washington, D.C., 1932 // Front cover verso bookplate, "United States Department of the Interior, Law Library." Figure JX233.A31917Suppl2vol2. Also an embossed stamp from the same organization on the first free endpaper.

JX233.A31941v4, *Foreign Relations of the United States*, U.S. Government Printing Office, Washington, D.C., 1941 // Front cover verso stamp, "Office Of Alien Property Library," First free endpaper stamp, "From the Office of Senator Howard D. Cannon," and first free endpaper stamp,"??? Property of Idaho State University." Senator Cannon served four terms in the U.S. Senate for Nevada.

JX236A3v1, *Treaties, Conventions, International Acts, Protocols and Agreements*, Government Printing Office, Washington, D.C. // Front cover verso

Cushing-Martin Library
Stonehill College
North Easton, Mass.

Presented by

Rep. McCormick
Figure JX233.A31918Suppl1v1

94

stamp, "Confederate Library, Huntsville, Ala." Figure JX236A3v1.

JX236A3v4, *Treaties, Conventions, International Acts, Protocols and Agreements*, Government Printing Office, Washington, D.C. // Front cover verso bookplate, "Bureau of International Relations, University of California." Figure JX236A3v4.

JX237.W51886v2, *International Law Digest*, Government Printing Office, Washington, D.C., 1886 // First free endpaper cursive, "From the Dept. of the Interior, July – 1887," and front cover verso bookplate, "Hope College Library." Figure JX237.W51886v2. Hope College is in southwestern Michigan, close to the shore of Lake Michigan.

Figure JX236.A3v1

JX449.I5M3, *Immunity of State Ships*, N. Matsunami, Richard F. Flint & Co., London, 1924 // Author's bookplate. Figure JX449.I5M3.

Figure JX237.W51886v2

Figure JX236.A3v4

JX1395.M26, *Retrospect and Prospect*, A.T. Mahan, Little, Brown, and Company, Boston, 1902 // Front cover verso bookplate (blacked out), "Ship's Library, U.S.S. Brooklyn" and title page embossed stamp, "U.S. Navy Bureau of Equipment." There were two different USS Brooklyn's. The first was a heavy cruiser, CA-3, in service 1896-1921, and was active during the Spanish-American War. The second was a light cruiser (CL-40) during the period 1937-1951. It is surmised that the book was deployed on the first Brooklyn, since that was the era of Mahan's writings and more important to the Navy of that time.

With the Author's Compliments.

Would the gentlemen who wish to communicate with the Author please address as follows :—

Dr. N. Matsunami,
Tokyo Imperial University,
Tokyo.

Figure JX449.I5M3

JX1407.F51923, *American Diplomacy*, Carl Russell Fish, Henry Holt and Company, NY, 1923 // It appears as if this book was in the possession of George A. Bronson, Jr., judging by his name inscribed at least 20 times on the first 4 double pages which includes the inside of the front cover. Apparently he loved to see his name in print, even if it was his own printing. Maybe he thought he was going to be a famous diplomat someday, as he experimented with different signatures. Figures JX1407.F51923-1 & -2.

JX1412.C3, *The Controversy over Neutral Rights between the United States and France, 1789-1800*, James Brown Scott, Oxford University Press, NY, 1917 // First free endpaper stamp, "Carnegie Institution of Washington, Department of Historical Research" and also a Harry Truman Library embossed stamp previously cited.

JX1416.D78, *Can America Stay Neutral?*, Allen W. Dulles, Harper & Brothers Publishing, NY, 1939 // First free endpaper cursive, "Lister Hill, Oct 20, 1932." The UAH accession censor must have felt some pangs of conscience on this, because the date was blacked out, but Hill's signature was not.

JX1416.M3, *The Interest of America in International Conditions*, A.T. Mahan, Brown, Little, and Company, Boston, 1918 // Front cover bookplate, "War Service Library, This book is provided by the people of the United States through the American Library Association for the use of the soldiers and sailors," and the second free endpaper stamp, "Property of the U.S. Army, Technical Library, Army Chemical Center, Maryland." Alfred T. Mahan

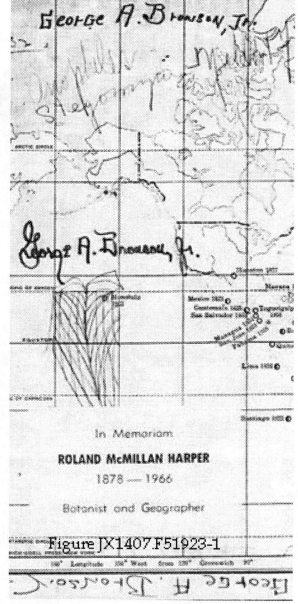

In Memoriam

ROLAND McMILLAN HARPER

1878 — 1966

Botanist and Geographer

Figure JX1407.F51923-1

Figure JX1416.M3

was a captain in the U.S. Navy and the 1890 author on the most influential book ever written about sea power, *The Influence of Sea Power on History, 1660-1783*. The words quoted above are in the blacked out right half of the bookplate.

JX1648.M61936, *Diplomacy and Peace*, R.B. Mowat, Robert M. McBride & Company, NY, 1936 // First free endpaper, "Chen Chu Pei, Graduate School, Georgetown University, Washington 7, D.C." This is Chen's second book by Mowat while at Georgetown (D217.M66).

JX1938.S35, *The Commonwealth of Man*, Frederick L. Schuman, Alfred A. Knopf, NY, 1952 // Front cover verso cursive, "James A. Robinson, William '59." Williams College is in Williamstown, the most northwestern town in Massachusetts.

JX1948.R3, *International Arbitration from Athens to Locarno*, Jackson H. Ralston, Stanford University Press, Stanford University, CA, 1929 // Front cover verso bookplate, "The General Services Schools Library" at Fort Leavenworth, Kansas. Figure JX1948.R3.

Figure JX1948.R3

JX1952.D351938, *The Problem of the Twentieth Century*, Lord Davies, Ernest Benn, Limited, London, 1938 // First free endpaper inscription to Senator Lister Hill by the author. Figure JX1948.R3.

JX1962.B 56V3519 83, *The Making of Peace: Jean De Bloch and the First Hague Peace Conferenc e*, Peter van den Dungen, Center for the Study of Armament and Disarmament, California State University, Los Angeles, CA, 1938 // Stamp on paper front cover, "U.S. Arms Control and Disarmament Library, Washington, D.C. 20451."

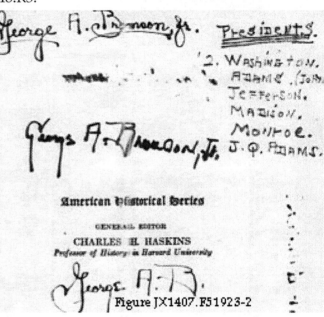

Figure JX1407.F51923-2

JX1975.R36, *Uniting Europe*, William E. Rappard, Yale University Press, New Haven, CT, 1930 // Front cover verso bookplate, "William Elder & Mary Chapin Marrus." Figure JX1975.R36.

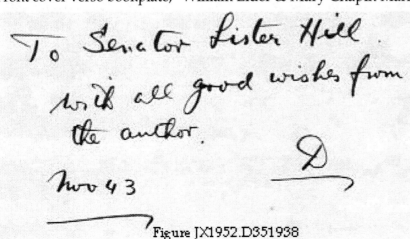

Figure JX1952.D351938

JX1975.W5427, *The Origins of the League Covenant*, Florence Wilson, The Hogarth Press, London, 1928 // First free endpaper cursive inscription by the author. Figure JX1975.W5427.

JX5211.D25, *Maritime International Law*, John A. Dahlgren, B.B. Russell, Boston, 1877 // Front cover verso bookplate, "Library of the Navy Department." Figure JX5211.D25.

K26.G3411925, *Derecho Privado Positivo*, Francisco Geny, Editorial Reus, Madrid, Spain, 1925 // Second free endpaper and dedication page stamps, "Juan R. Gerala, 123 N. Cortez Street, New Orleans 19, LA." Juan Gerala is an active member of the Osher Lifelong Learning Institute at UAH. Note that the name of this group changed slightly in 2005, but I still call it the Academy.

KD20.B541836v2, *Commentaries on the Laws of England*, Sir William Blackstone, W.E. Dean, NY, 1840 // Front cover verso cursive. Figure KD20.B541836v2.

KF361.P6, The Formative Era of American Law, Roscoe Pound, Little, Brown and Company, Boston, 1938 // Front cover verso and first free endpaper stamps, "Univ of Kentucky, Law Library."

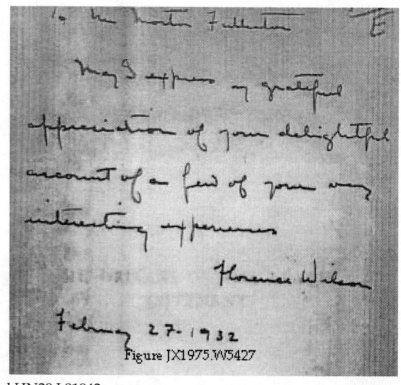

Figure JX1975.R36

KF373.D35T53, *Darrow*, Kevin Tierney, Thomas Y. Crowell, Publishers, 1079 // Front cover verso stamp, "This Book Provided by North Alabama Cooperative Library System." The North Alabama Cooperative Library System was a group of public libraries in Dekalb, Marshall, Madison and Jackson Counties, which Huntsville Public Library joined in 1978. The coordinator was in Huntsville, but the cooperative fell apart several years later.

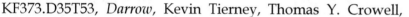

Figure JX1975.W5427

LB1051.P68, *Casebook of Research in Educational Psychology*, Sidney L. Pressey, Harper & Brothers Publishers, NY, 19378 // Front cover verso bookplate, "Zavelle Book Stores." Figure LB1051.P68. First free endpaper cursive, "Ruth Kramer, 1457 Worthington St." We met Ruth Kramer previously at HK531.Y61943 and HN29.L81942.

LB2321.N5471953, *University Sketches*, John Henry Newman, The Newman Press, Westminster, MD, 1953 // First free endpaper bookplate, "Huntsville Council #4080, Knights of Columbus." Figure LB2321.N5471953.

LC2851.H32T3, *Samuel Armstrong Talbot*, Doubleday, Page and Company, NY, 1904 // Title page embossed stamp, "Brooklyn Institute of Arts and Science, Children's Museum Library, Founded 1924." Figure LC2851.H32T3.

LD1436.T8, *My Generation*, William Jewett Tucker, Houghton, Mifflin Company, Boston, MA, 1919 // Front cover verso bookplate, "William Carroll Hill." Figure LD1436.T8.

ML390.H265, *Minute Sketches of Great Composers*, Eva vB. Hansl, Grosset & Dunlap, NY, 1932 // Title page stamp, "Army Service Library, Tilton General Hospital, Fort Dix, New Jersey."

N5310.W45, *The Origins of Art*, Gene Weltfish, The Boobs-Merrill Company, NY, 1953 // Front cover verso bookplate, "Dr. Joseph Caldwell," Figure N5310.W45, and first free endpaper stamp, "Dept. of Anthropology, Baldwin Hall, University of Georgia, Athens, Georgia 30602."

ND497.H7D6, *William Hogarth*, Austin Dobson, The McClure Company, NY, 1907 // Front cover verso bookplate, "William Hogarth." This is the bookplate of the book's subject, so the bookplate is part of the printing of the front cover verso. Perhaps it should not count, but it has a nice design. Figure ND497.H7D6.

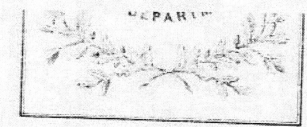

Figure JX5211.D25

ND533.P5D77, *Goodbye Picasso*, author, publisher and date could not be determined // Front cover verso cursive, "Kithy Currington, 5 October 1977, Riyadh, Saudi Arabia."

NK4085.B51911, *Nineteenth Century English Ceramic Art*, J.F. Blacker, Little, Brown and Company, Boston, 1911 // First free endpaper inscription. Figure NK4085.B51911.

PA367.W6, *Elementary Lessons in Greek Syntax*, S.R. Mitchell, D. Appleton and Company, NY, 1896 // Front cover verso sticker, "C.N. Caspar's Book Store, 437 East Water St. Milwaukee, Wis."

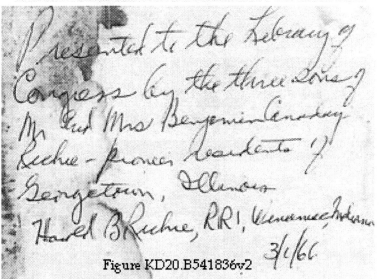

Figure KD20.B541836v2

PA459.F3, *An Aid to Greek at Sight*, John C. Buckbee and Company, Chicago 1890 // First free endpaper and title page cursive, "Jacob Hammer, Columbia University, New York."

PA445.E5C61951, *Greek Dictionary*, Follett Publishing Company, Chicago, 1951 // Front cover verso sticker, "Hampels' Bookshop, Milwaukee."

PA2087.H531945, *Latin Grammer*, Robert J. Henle, Loyola University Press, Chicago, 1945 // First free endpaper cursive, "Adolphine Brumgardt, freshman, 1956-57 at Ursuline Academy, New Orleans."

Figure LB2321.N5471953

PA3016.A1 M31931, *Character-Portraiture*, John S. McDonald, The University Press of Sewanee Tennessee, 1931 // First free endpaper stamp, "Jacob Hammer, Hunter College, New York City" and Bellarmine College, Joques Library, Plattsburg, N.Y." Note that Jacob Hammer was also at PA459.F3.

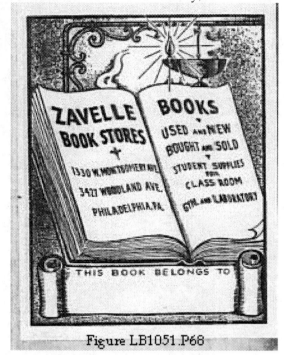

Figure LB1051.P68

Figure LD1436.T8

PA4037.B791871, *Homerische Kosmographie und Geographie*, Dr. E. Buchholz, Verlag von Wilhelm Engelmann, Leipzig, 1871 // Front cover verso bookplate, "Denison University" and title page punch-through stamp, "Denison University, Granville, Ohio." Figure PA4037.B791871.

PA4037.W4, *Weissenborn's Homeric Life*, Gilbert Campbell Scoggin, American Book Company, NY, 1903 // First free endpaper cursive, "W. Harry Allen, '08, Columbia University, New York, April 6, 1905."

Figure N5310.W45

PA4081.V6,   *Über*

Figure ND497.H7D6

Homericifche Geographie und Weltfunde, Dr. R.S.M. Bolder, Im Berlage ver Hahn'fchen Hohbuchhandlung, Hannover, Deutschland, 1830 // First free endpaper inscription, "Gift for Mr. Dr. Meinecke, Rector des Fachhochschule Gymnasiums on 19 September 1831. Gottlieb Röger." Figure PA4081.V6.

PA4241.A31892, *Ten Selected Orations of Lysias*, George P. Bristol, Allyn and Bacon, Boston, 1892 // First free endpaper bookplate, "Charles D. Perry" ▮ (name blacked out) Figure PA4241.A31892.

PA6111.S8P631926, ▮ *The Menaechmi of Plautus*, Harold North Fowler, Benj. H. Sanborn & Co., NY, 1926 // First free endpaper bookplate, light pencil writing did not copy, "Joanne Duffield, Lincoln Hall, Gettysburg College." Figure PA6111.S8P631926.

PA8122.W31933, *Mediaeval Latin Lyrics*, Helen Waddell, Henry Holt and Company, NY, 1933 // Front cover verso bookplate, "Hester Ann Corner." Figure PA8122.W31933.

PC1625.M351926, *Il Nuouissimo Melzi Dizionario Completo*, Ant, Vallardi, Milano // Front cover verso cursive, "A.E. Terry, Roma, 10 VIII 26."

EX LIBRIS
HESTER ANN CORNER

.. It may be we shall touch the Happy Isles....

Figure PA8122.W31933

PC2111.F883, *Standard French Grammar*, W.H. Fraser, D.C. Heath and Company, NY, 1931 // Front cover verso stamp, "University Extension Division, Madison, Wisconsin."

PC2111.H33, *Si Nous, Écrivions*, Paul K. Hartsall, D.C. Heath and Company, NY, 1937 // Front cover verso bookplate (partially obscured), "John Lee Johnson, 44 N. Salisbury, West Lafayette, Indiana."

PC2111.S62, *Introduction to French*, E.H. Sirich, Henry Holt and Company, NY, 1952 // First free endpaper stamp, "This book sold to University of Tennessee Book Store, Date, 7-5-55, Signature, Bobby McClay."

Figure PA4081.V6

PC53 27.L5 1942, *Peque no dicion ario brasil eiro da*

Figure PA4037.B791871

lingua portuguesa, Editora Civilizacao Brasileira S/N, Rio De Janiero, 1942 " First Free endpaper stamps, "Ministério da Educaçao E Saude, Institututo Nacional Do Livro, End.Avenida Rio Branco no.

219/39, Edifico da Biblioteca Nacional, Rio de Janeiro" and "Property of University of Georgia, The Romance Language Department."

PE1135.K41946, *American Pronunciation*, John Samuel Kenyon, George Wahn, Publisher, Ann Arbor, MI, 1946 // First free endpaper bookplate, "Stuart E. Wilcox." Figure PE1135.K41946.

Figure PE1135.K41946

PF3680.P71930, *Etymologisches Wörtenbuch Der Deutschen Sprache*, A. Pinlocxhe, Libraire La Rousse, Paris, 1930 // Front cover verso bookplate, "A.E. Terry." Figure PF3680.P71930.

PG3365.V61957v1/2, Russian title and author in Russian make the typing of the words too difficult to put into Cyrillic although the word processor has that capability, Moscow, 1957 // Front cover verso UAH Gift bookplate, Eugenia Ashworth, and first free endpaper inscription. Figure PG3365.V61957v1/2.

Figure PA4241.A31892

PG3463.N2I7, *The Lower Depths*, Maxim Gorky, Duffield & Company, NY, 1912 // Front cover verso bookplate, "William Wedge." Figure PG3463.N2I7.

PG3467.M4M131927, *Akhnaton*, author and publisher not identified // Front cover verso cursive, "Harold H. Punke, Valdosta, Georgia, 12/10/34."

Figure PF3680.P71930

PH355.W3D31953, *The Dark Angel*, Mika Waltari, G.P. Putnam's Sons, NY, 1953 // Front cover verso stamp, "United States Air Force, AFL 4418, Base Library, Charleston, S.C."

Figure PG3365.V61957v1-2

PN47.S71924, *What Can Literature Do For Me?*, C. Alphonso Smith, Doubleday, Doran & Company, Garden City, NY, 1930 // Front cover verso cursive, "James T. Brown, 1932, 694 East 2nd St. Brooklyn, NY."

PN59.B351925, *Talks on the Study of Literature*, Arlo Bates, Houghton Mifflin Company, NY, 1925 // Front cover verso cursive, "Grace E. Mueller, 626 Sheridan Rd., Evanston, ILL, Northwestern University, Jan. 1930," and first free endpaper stamp, "Property of Fenwick High School Library, Oak Park, Illinois. There was also a UAH gift bookplate, "Dr. Benjamin Graves," who was the first president of UAH.

PN511.B6, *Studies from Ten Literatures*, Ernest Boyd, Charles Scribner's Sons, NY, 1925 // Front cover verso bookplate, "Dean Charles Heyward Barnwell," Figure PN511.B6, and first free endpaper sticker, "The Studio Book Shop, Birmingham, Alabama, 408 N. 20 Street, Main 7903."

Dean Barnwell's biographical bookplate is the first such item discovered.

Figure PN511.B6

PN751.F7, *Romanticism Reconsidered*, Northrop Frye, Columbia University Press, NY, 1963 // Front cover verso bookplate, "Henry Edward Jacobs." Figure PN751.F7. The scene in the bookplate is an approximation of the common depiction of Johann Gutenberg's first print shop, circa 1454, when Guttenberg printed the Bible with the first movable printing press. This event was selected as the most important

Figure PN751.F7

activity of the Second Millennium because it allowed books and papers to be produced in volume in a relatively short time. Prior to Guttenberg's invention, monk scribes might take one year to copy an existing Bible by hand, thus manuscript. Woodcuts of scenes and letters could not be changed. At the right rear of the bookplate scene is a typesetter with his collection of individual and common collective words in little compartments. He was always working on the next page after the one in the press at center. Letters could be melted down and reformed in molds as needed. The man on the left is the inker. He holds in each hand a handle with a hemisphere on the end. The hemisphere is made of dog skin with horse hair stuffed inside. Dog skin was determined to provide the best combination of holding ink, yet not smearing the edges of the metal letters. The paper was flat on the table and the letters in their form were lowered onto the paper by the wooden press, which had a long handle to maximize the pressure on the paper. The papers were printed in perhaps 20 copies, depending on the order, and then hung on the rafters to dry.

PN771.D7, *Contemporary European Writers*, William A. Drake, The John Day Company, NY, 1928 // Front cover verso cursive, "J.R. Thaxton, May 30, 1934."

PN1035.C5, *Rhetoric and Poetry in the Renaissance*, Donald L. Clark, Columbia University Press, NY, 1922 // First free endpaper and title page stamps, "College Library, St. Gregory's Seminary, 6616 Beechmont Avenue, Cincinnati 30, Ohio."

PN2251.W61855, *Personal Recollections of the Stage*, William B. Wood, Henry Carey Baird, Philadelphia, PA, 1855 // First free endpaper bookplate, "Daniel B. Lloyd," Figure PN2251.W61855. Second free endpaper cursive, "Maj Gen W.F. Wood, U.S.A. from his father, Wm. B. Wood. Major General Wood died in 1859 in Texas."

PN2638.G8A34, *If Memory Serves*, Sacha Guitry, Doubleday, Doran & Co., Garden City, NY, 1936 // Front cover verso cursive, "Guitry is now under arrest by the F.F.I. as an active collaborationist with the Nazis. However, this is one of the most charming and entertaining autobiography I've ever read. <u>A</u>." There was no indication who "A" might be. Guitry was a French playwright and film actor, director, and screen writer born in Russia in 1885 according to a Wikipedia entry. After spending sixty days in prison following World War II, he was cleared of all charges

> THIS BOOK IS A GIFT
>
> FROM THE LIBRARY OF
>
> DANIEL B. LLOYD
>
> BUENA VISTA FARM
>
> PRINCE GEORGES COUNTY, MD.
>
> *Official Reporter of*
>
> THE UNITED STATES SENATE
>
> From 1877 to 1943

Figure PN2251.W61895

PN3355.U91962, *Narrative Technique*, Thomas H. Uzzell, Harcourt, Brace and Company, NY, 1934 // Front cover verso cursive, "Property of Jeanie Baker, 69 Stecher St., Newark, N.J."

PN3503.L7, *Preface to Fiction*, Robert Morss Levett, Thomas S. Rockwell Company, Chicago, 1931 // First free endpaper embossed stamp, "John C. Kunstmann, University of Chicago."

PN6014.N641940v1-5, *New Writing*, John Lehmann, Allen Lane Penguin Books, NY, 1940 // First free endpaper stamp, "David Clay Jenkins, Post Office Box 81, Auburn, Alabama" and cursive, "M.R. Sharpe, 24 May 1953, Auburn, Ala."

PN6151.I6, *The Humor of France*, Elizabeth Lee, Charles Scribner's Sons, NY, 1893 // Simple title page stamp, "Loggins Library, Winona, Miss," also a UAH gift bookplate from Dr. John C. White.

PQ119.C5, *French Literature in Outline*, Philip H. Churchman, The Century Co., NY, 1928 // Front cover verso stamp, "War Relief Services, National Catholic Welfare Conference, Aid to Prisoners of War."

Figure PQ231.E661896

PQ119.R8, *French Authors*, Mildred Lewis Rutherford, The Franklin Printing and Publishing Company, Atlanta, GA, 1906 // Second free endpaper cursive, "Lucy Bryan, Lucy Cobb Institute, Senior, '07." The book's author was the niece of the Institute's founder, T.R.R. Cobb, taught at the school between 1880 and 1928, and was principal of the secondary school for women for 22 years. The school, in Athens, GA, closed in 1931, but the two buildings now house the University of Georgia's Carl Vinson Institute of Government.

Figure PQ1997.G6E51896v1

PQ231.E861896, *Poésie Française*, Sainte-Beuve, Bibliothèque-Charpentier, Paris, 1893 // Front cover verso bookplate, "Amida Stanton" (blacked out). Figure PQ231.E861896.

PQ1997.G6E51896v1, *The Adventures of Gil Blas of Santillana*, Lesage, Gibbings & Company, London, 1896 // Last free endpaper recto cursive by George F. Scannell, February 27, 1932. Read through it, as it gives a gloomy perspective of that era, poor fellow. Figure PQ1997.G6E51896v1.

Figure PQ2039.A54v1

PQ2039.A54v1, *Julie ober Die neue Heloise*, Drud und Berlag von Phillip Reclam, Leipzig // Front cover verso bookplate, "William Eugene Mosher." Figure PQ2039.A54v1.

Figure PQ2161.C59v2-1

PQ2161.C59v2, *The Comedy of Human Life*, H. de Balzac, Hardy, Pratt & Co., Boston, MA, 1896 // Front cover verso bookplate, "E.P. Williams," Figure PQ2161.C59v2-1 and a bookplate on the first free endpaper, "Edward Mason Williams," Figure PQ2161.C59v2-2. The bookplates facing each other are just wonderful, but I favor E.P.'s because a man is reading in a rocking chair with his feet on a hassock and may be

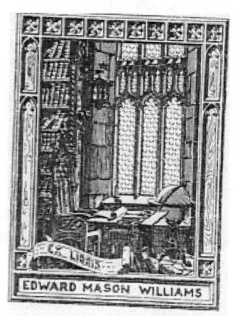

Figure PQ2161.C59v2-2

holding a pipe in his right hand close to his mouth. I believe we should assume that Edward Mason was E.P.'s son since E.P.'s bookplate was on the cover verso in the most frequent position.

PQ2191.Z5S81958, *Baudelaire*, Enid Starkie, A New Directions Book, NY, 1958 // Front cover verso bookplate, "Charles W. Dean, Jr." Figure PQ2191.Z5S81958. This is a clever bookplate, starting with the squirrel reading, using the word "Hoard"

Figure PQ2273.A631910

Figure PQ2191.Z4S81958

instead of library and ending with three firm admonitions: Read Thoughtfully, Handle Carefully, and Return Promptly. Wonderful!

PQ2199.I31903, *Une Idylle Tragique*, Paul Bourget, Librairie Plon, Paris, ? // Second free endpaper stamp, "Libreria Moderna, Durango – Mex., J. Villarreal de la Constitucion."

PQ2205.Z5M32, *Chateaubriand*, André Malirois, Harper & Brothers, NY, 1938 // Front cover verso stamp, "Converse College Library, 1890, Spartanburg, S.C."

PQ2273.A631910, *The Abbé Constantin*, Ludovic Halévy, Current Literature Publishing Company, NY, 1910 // First free endpaper bookplate, "Frederick Merrill Webster." Figure PQ2273.A631910.

PQ2283.C61901v3, *The History of a Crime*, Victor Hugo, Peter Fenelon Collier & Son, NY, 1901 // Front cover verso stamps, "The Birmingham News, The Birmingham Age-Herald, Library Exchange," "Bradford School Library," and "Private Library of Dr. and Mrs. W.P. McAdory, Please Return."

PQ2362.Z5D4, *Prosper Mérimée*, G.H. Johnstone, George Routledge & Sons, Ltd., London, 1926 // Front cover verso bookplate, "R.G. Clark." Figure PQ2362.Z5D4.

Figure PQ2362.Z5D4

PQ2603.E36I531954, *She Came to Stay*, Simone de Beauvoir, The World Publishing Company, NY, 1954 // Front cover verso bookplate, "Yale University Library." Figure PQ2603.E36I531954.

Figure PQ2603.E362I531954

PQ2603.E88G81926a, *Gueule D'Amour*, Andre Beucler, Gallimard, Paris, 1926 // First free endpaper sticker. "Mme. Paul Terraillion, 6816 Criner Road, Huntsville, Alabama 35802, U.S.A."

PQ2603.L37V4, *Verdun*, Georges Blond, Presses de la Cité, Ottawa, Canada, 1961 // Front cover verso bookplate with a candle, open book and name blacked out. Figure 03.L37V4.

Figure PQ2603.L37V4

PQ2605.L2S61929, *Le Soulier de Satin*, Paul Claudel, Librairie Gallimard, Paris, 1929 // Title page embossed stamp, "Canisius College, Students Library." Canisius College is located in Buffalo, New York.

PQ2607.E834Z9, *Celine: The Novel as Delirium*, Allen Thiher, Rutgers University Press, New Brunswick, NJ, 1972 // Simple title page embossed stamp, "Library of Kevin P. Begos."

PQ2613.R3Z5, *Memories of Happy Days*, Julian Green, Harper & Brothers, NY, 1942 // Front cover verso bookplate, "Anna Goldman Collection." Figure PQ2613.R3Z5.

PQ2635.O5J4131914, *Jean-Christophe Journey's End*, Romain Rolland, Henry Holt and Company, NY, 1914 // Front cover verso bookplate, "Louis Banigan." Figure PQ2635.O5J4131914.

Figure PQ2613.R3Z5

Figure PQ2635.O5J4131914

PQ2643.E48T51948, *Tides of Mont St. Michel*, Roger Vercel, Random House, NY, 1938 // Front cover verso cursive, "Mrs. Anna Koenig, Hubbard Rd. Madison, Ohio, RFD #2."

PQ4335.C6, *Dante and Other Essays*, R.W. Church, Macmillan and Co., Ltd., London, 1906 // Front cover verso bookplate, "Reverend Richard Davidson, Emmanuel College." Figure PQ4335.C6. There are several Emmanuel colleges, but this one is presumed to be in Boston, MA.

PQ4801.L35T851936, *Two Years*, Alberto Albertini, The Viking Press, NY, 1936 // Front cover verso

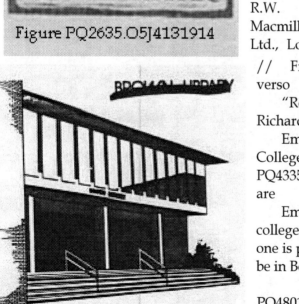

Figure PQ4801.L35T851936

Figure PQ4335.C6

bookplate, "Brown Library, Virginia Western Community College, Roanoke, Virginia." Figure PQ4801.L35T851936.

PQ6039.Z6, *De Garcilaso a Rodó*, Clara Ines Zolési, Editorial "Fides," Montevideo, Uruguay, 1927 // Title page stamp, "Donacion de la Biblioteca Nacional, Montevideo."

PQ6449.A2, *Lope de Vega*, Clasuos Castell Y Moreton, Barcelona, Spain, no date // Simple title page embossed stamp, "Library of Juan Bautista Gerala."

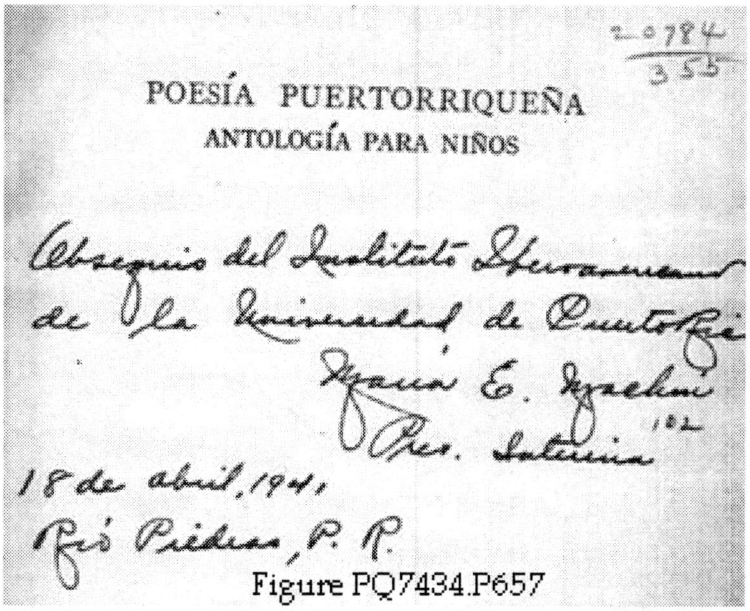

PQ6603.E69P3,v2, *El Pasajero*, José Bergamín, En La Editorial Seneca, Cuidad de Mexico, 1943 // Front cover verso stamp, "The Hispanic Foundation … From the Archer M. Huntington Purchasing Fund."

PQ6603.L2S61912, *Sonnica*, V. Blasco Ibanez, Duffield & Company, NY, 1918 // Front cover verso bookplate, ""The Library of Georgetown College." This college is presumed to be the one in Georgetown, Kentucky, rather than the college that is part of Georgetown University in Washington, D.C.

Figure PQ7434.P657

PQ6609.S5C31923, *El Cáliz Rojo*, Concha Espina, Renacimiento, Madrid, Spain, 1923 // Front cover verso sticker, "Liberia General de Victoriano Suarez, Precianos 19, Apartado 32, Telefono 11334, Madrid."

PQ7434.P657, *Poesía Puertorriqueña*, Juan Ramón Jiménez, Edición, La Habana, Cuba, 1938 // Simple title page cursive. Figure PQ7434.P657.

Figure PQ7499.H3S4-1

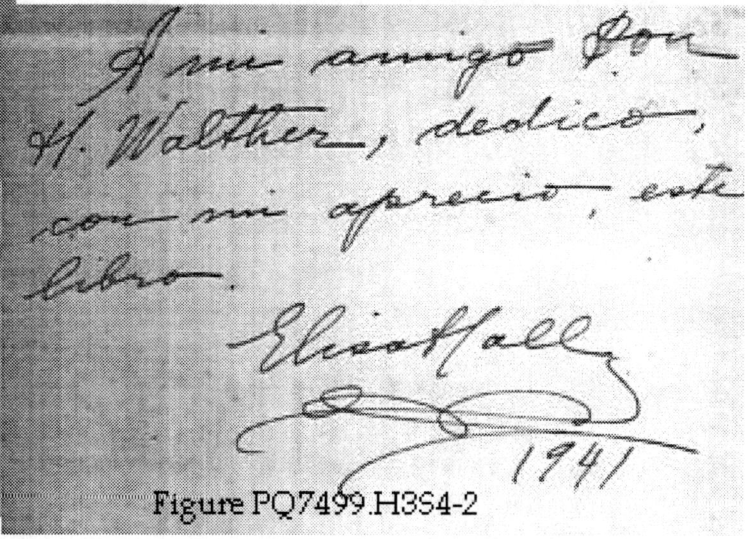

Figure PQ7499.H3S4-2

PQ7499.H3S4, *Senilla de Mostaza*, Elisa Hall, Impreso en la Tipografia Nacional, Guatemala Centro-America, 1938 // Front cover verso stamp, "Taller de Oncuaderacion, Guatemala, Yilescas Hno," Figure PQ7434.P657-1, and first free endpaper inscription by the author, Figure PQ7434.P657-2.

PR191.B7, *The History of Early English Literature*, Stopford A. Brooke, The Macmillan and Co., NY, 1892 // Title page stamp, "Gloucester, N.J. Catholic High School." This school is in Gloucester City, just across the Delaware River from Philadelphia.

PR447.E5v1, *Survey of English Literature 1780-1830*, Oliver Elton, Edward Arnold, London, 1912 // Front cover verso bookplate, "Carnegie Library, Rock Hill, S.C." Note the full name of the college around the circumference of the medallion. That was the name of the institution in 1920, it became Winthrop College in 1974 and Winthrop University in 1992. Figure PR447.E5v1. Andrew Carnegie, born in Scotland, was an American steel magnate in the late 19th and early 20th centuries. He was the first of the super-rich to give his money to worthy causes, and wrote a treatise on the subject. He gave grants, $56,136,430.97 total, to build 1,681 libraries in the United States and another 826 in countries from England to Tasmania. Huntsville received $12,500 in 1914, and the Carnegie Library was located at the

Figure PR447.E5v1

corner of Madison Street and Gates Avenue (now parking garage) from 1916 until 1966 when it was demolished.

PR471.W261940. *Twentieth Century Literature*, A.C. Ward, Longmans, Green and Co., NY, 1940 // Front cover verso bookplate, "Rev de Jacob Sedlet," (blacked out). Figure PR471.W261940.

PR826.L31897, *The English Novel*, Sidney Lanier, Charles Scribner's Sons, NY, 1900 // Front cover verso bookplate, Figure PR826.L31897, with the name blacked out, but was in color with men rowing a boat toward the larger ship in the background.

PR1175.H633, *The Leading English Poets*, Lucius H. Holt, Houghton Mifflin Company, NY, 1915 // First free endpaper cursive, "Irene M. O'Neill, Sargent School, Cambridge, Mass." The Sargent School of Physical Training was founded in 1882 by Dr. Dudley Allen Sargent. It is now a college under Boston University.

Figure PR471.W261940

Figure PR826.L31897

PR1175.S8, *From Milton to Tennyson*, L.D. Syle, Allyn and Bacon, Boston, 1894 // Title page stamp, "St. Joseph College, Portland, Maine."

PR1301.R4, *Masters of Nineteenth Century Prose*, Joseph J. Reilly, Ginn and Company, NY, 1930 // First free endpaper cursive, "Edward W. Sine, Buffalo, 1932."

PR1905.W31880, *Chaucer*, Adolphus W. Ward, Harper & Brothers, NY, 1880 // Front cover verso bookplate, "C. Wells Moulton." Figure PR1905.W31880.

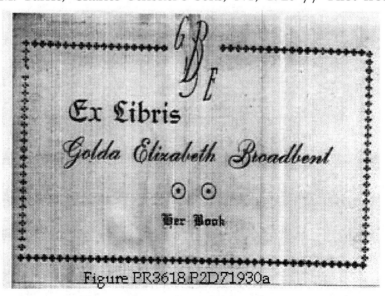

Figure PR1905.W31880

Figure PR2894.A31923a

PR2894.A31923a, *A Life of William Shakespeare*, Joseph Quincy Adams, Houghton Mifflin Company, NY, 1922 // Front cover verso bookplate, "George W. Corner IV." Figure PR2894.A31923a.

PR3618.P2D71930a, *Pepys*, John Drinkwater, Doubleday Doran & Company, Garden City, NY, 1933 // Front cover verso bookplate, "Golda Elizabeth Broadbent." Figure PR3618.P2D71930a.

PR3692.A1S45v1, *Smollett's Novels*, Roderick Random, Houghton Mifflin, NY, 1926 // Front cover verso bookplate (blacked out), "Anderson Memorial Library, Emporia, Kansas."

PR4074.A21926, *Representative Plays*, J.M. Barrie, Charles Scribner's Sons, NY, 1926 // First free endpaper cursive, "Charles Patterson, Emory, 1932." Presumably that is Emory University in Atlanta, GA.

PR4770.A2, *Collected Works of William Hazlitt*, 12 volumes and an Index, J.M. Dent, London, 1904 // Bookplate "Albemarle Club". The Albemarle Club was a well-known social club in London in the late nineteenth century. The famous and witty Irish writer, Oscar Wilde, 1854-1900, was a member of the club when he was involved in a trial in 1895. Two of his most famous plays were "The Importance of Being Earnest" and

Figure PR3618.P2D71930a

"The Picture of Dorian Gray." Now that I am retired, my favorite quote from Oscar Wilde is, "Work is only for those people who have nothing else to do."

PR4872.I251883.v4, *Imaginary Conversations*, Walter S. Landor, J.C. Nimmo and Bain, London, 1883 // Front cover verso bookplate (blacked out), "Philip F. Kelly, Jr., Philadelphia."

Figure PR5177.M61908

PR4905.A11900, *The Caxtons*, Edward Bulwer Lytton, A.L. Burt Company, NY, 1849 //

The Woodside Library.
San Carlos, North of Fourth
Carmel-by-the-Sea
California
Figure PR5042.C641924a

First free endpaper cursive, "Ruth B. Joly, 1/7/30, Private Library Sale at Putnam's."

PR5042.C641924a, *Conversations in Edbury Street*, George Moore, Boni and Liveright, NY, 1924 // First free endpaper bookplate, "The Woodside Library." Figure PR3618.P2D71930a.

PR5177.M61908, *The Mother of the Man*, Eden Phillpotts, Dodd, Mead & Company, NY, 1908 // Front cover verso bookplate, "John G. McCullough Free Library." Figure PR3618.P2D71930a.

PR5189.P5T431845b, *Thaddeus of Warsaw*, Jane Porter, H.M. Caldwell Company, NY, no date // Front cover verso bookplate printed by the publisher, but no one put in his/her name. Figure PR5189.P5T431845b.

PR5317.A221893, *The Abbot*, Sir Walter Scott, American Book Company, NY, 1893 // First free endpaper stamp, "Memorial Library of Washington and Jefferson College, Withdrawn." Washington and Jefferson College is in Washington, PA about 20 miles southwest of Pittsburgh.

PR5506.L31876, *Laus Veneris*, Algernon C. Swinburne, Carleton, Publisher, NYU, 1877 // First and second free endpapers, "Sime E. Parsons, Feb 28th 1877, Rockford, Ala." Rockford is about 40 miles north of Montgomery.

Figure PR5189.P5T431854b

PR5523.A31903a, *John Addington Symonds*, H.F. Brown, Smith, Elder & Co., London, 1903 // Front cover verso bookplate, "Harold Hulme." Figure PR5523.A31903a. This bookplate was described at DA32.H9 because it was blacked out there.

Figure PR5523.A31903a

Figure PR5795.W7Z53

PR5714.L31910, *Lady Merton Colonist*, Mrs. Humphry Ward, Doubleday, Page & Company, NY, 1910 // Forward page stamp, "Lenox Hill Hospital, 111 East 76th St., New York, N.Y."

PR5795.W7Z53, *Letter to Three Friends*, William Hale White, Oxford University Press, London, 1924 // Front cover verso bookplate, "James McCoy." Figure PR5523.A31903a.

PR5837.T31858, *Lights and Shadows of Scottish Life*, Professor Wilson, William Blanchard and Sons, Edinburgh, Scotland, 1823 // Front cover verso bookplate, "Belfast Free Library" (blacked out), with a building that represents a library. Figure PR5837.T31858. The Belfast Library is presumed to be in Belfast, Ireland.

PR5900.A1v1, *W.B. Yeats Collected Works*, Shakespeare Head Press, Stratford-on-Avon, England, 1908 // Front cover verso bookplate, "Blyth Webster." Figure PR5900.A1v1.

PR6001.M6L81968, *Lucky Jim*, Kingsley Amis, Victor Gollancy, Ltd., London, 1968 // First free endpaper bookplate, "Mt. Desert Island High School Library." Figure PR6001.M6L81968. Mount Desert Island is better known as the island off the central coast of Maine that has Acadia National Park on it.

Figure PR5837.T31858

Figure PR5900.A11908v1

PR6003.E45S41929, *Shadowed*, Hilaire Belloc, Harper & Brothers, Publishers, NY, 1929 // Front cover verso bookplate and title page punch-through stamp, "Brooklyn Public Library." Figure PR6003.E45S41929.

PR6003.L3K31918, *Karma*, Algernon Blackwood, E.P. Dutton & Company, NY, 1918 // Front cover verso bookplate (color) of a jester writing, with a woman looking through the window, "Harry Barlie Smith." Figure PR6003.L3K31918.

Figure PR6001.M6L81968

Figure PR6003.E45S41929

PR6007.E7J61908, *Joseph Vance*, William De Morgan, Henry Holt and Company, NY, 1908 // First free endpaper cursive, "Universalist Parish Library, North Salem, N.Y." North Salem is in southeastern New York State next to the Connecticut border and has a population of about 1,000.

PR6011.O56C351939v1, *Captain Horatio Hornblower*, C.S. Forester, Little, Brown and Company, Boston, 1939 // front cover verso bookplate, "William Donaldson." Figure PR6011.O56C35 1939v1.

PR6013.A5D331 913, *The Dark Flower*, John Galsworthy, Charles Scribner's Sons, NY, 1913 // Second free endpaper cursive, "M.L. Thiebaud, 625 North Limestone St., Springfield, Ohio."

PR6013.A5J8191 4 // *Justice*, John Galsworthy, Charles Scribner's Sons, NY, 1914 // Front

Figure PR6011.O56C351939v1

Figure PR6003.L3K31918

cover verso bookplate, "Book of Mine" with the name blacked out.

PR6013.O74G7, *Green Dolphin Street*, Elizabeth Goudge, Coward-McCann, Inc., NY, 1944 // Front cover verso bookplate, "Marscha Florsheim" partially covered by a UAH sticker of the early days of the university.

Figure PR6013.O74G7

PR6013.R2S31930, *St. Vitus Day*, Stephen Graham, Ernest Benn Limited, London, 1930 // Front cover verso sticker of a swan. Figure PR6011.O56C351939v1. The letters on the sticker might be Greek or Russian, but my Microsoft symbols failed to help me to make certain.

PR6013.U2Z51937, *Angry Dust*, Nikolai Gubsky, Oxford University Press, NY, 1937 // Front cover verso stamp, "Bertrand Smiths Agres of Books, 104 Pacific Avenue, Long Beach, Calif."

PR6015.A578B41917, *The Beloved Captain*, Donald Hankey, E.P. Dutton & Co., NY, 1917 // Front cover verso bookplate, "Bertha Hathaway." I could not determine why it was important to black out the sides of the plate, but leave the name intact.

Figure PR6013.A5J81914

Figure PR6013.R2S31930

PR6015.E58H6, *Holy Deadlock*, A.P. Herbert, Doubleday, Doran & Company, Inc., Garden City, NY, 1934 // First free endpaper inscription, "This book helped in the campaign resulting in changing the marriage & divorce laws in Scotland, 1937." Herbert became M.P. & sponsored the bill. Figure PR6015.E58H6. "M.P." is Member of Parliament.

PR6021.A8T7, *The Tramping Methodist*, Sheila Kaye-Smith, E.P. Dutton & Company, NY, 1922 // Front cover verso bookplate, "Charlotte Hunnerwell Martin." Figure PR6021.A8T7.

PR6023.E42B31945b, *The Ballad and the Source*, Rosamond Lehmann, Reynal & Hitchcock, NY, 1945 // First free endpaper cursive, "Given to me by Aceo(?) ???, July 14, 1945, Majorie Rezjo(?) ???, Cold Spring on Hudson, New York." Cold Spring is across the Hudson River from Highland Falls and the U.S. Military Academy at West Point.

Figure PR6015.A578B41917

Bertha Hathaway

PR6025.A2526R61927, *Rogues and Vagabonds*, Compton Mackenzie, George H. Doran Company, NY, 1927 // Title page verso stamp, "St. Louis Mercantile Library." The Mercantile Library is the oldest library west of the Mississippi River and was established in 1846. It is now on the campus of the University of Missouri St. Louis.

PR6025.A86D6, *Don Fernando*, W. Somerset Maugham, Doubleday, Doran & Company, Garden City, NY, 1935 // Front cover verso bookplate, "Helen R. Swartz," with Pegasus the winged horse. Figure PR6025.A86D6.

PR6025.I65I81929, *The Ivory Door*, A.A. Milne, Chatto & Windus, London, 1929 // Front cover verso stamp, "The Kate Emil-Behnke Stage School."

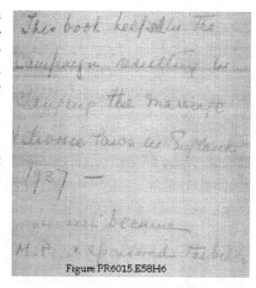
Figure PR6015.E58H6

Figure PR6025.O79S6361927

PR6025.O79S6361927, *The Spanish Farm Trilogy*, R.H. Mottram, Chatto & Windus, London, 1924 // Front cover verso bookplate, "Samuel Heiman" (blacked out), Figure PR6025.O79S6361927-1, and author's inscription on first free endpaper, Figure PR6025.O79S6361927-2, "Signed for Mr. Samuel Heiman, who knew how to be generous as well as just – by the author, Ralph H. Mottram (blacked out), 14 Sep 1928."

Figure PR6021.A8T7

PR6029.B65 W5, *Without My Cloak*, Kate O'Brien, Doubleday, Doran & Company, Garden City, NY, 1933 // Front cover verso bookplate, "Orlena J. Quilling." Figure PR6025.O79S6361927.

PR6031.O867W61929, *Wolf Solent*, John Cooper Powys, Simon and Schuster, NY, 1929 // Front cover verso bookplate, "Carola M. Bibo." Figure PR6031.O867W61929.

PR6037.M42P61937, *Portrait of a Lady*, Eleanor Smith, Doubleday, Doran & Company, Garden City, NY, 1937 // First free endpaper stamp, "American Red Cross, Motor Service, Bronxville Unit, Westchester County, New York."

EX LIBRIS
Helen R. Swartz
Figure PR6025.A86D6

PR9368.K6C61943, *The Covenant*, Brigid Knight, Thomas Y.

Crowell Company, NY, 1943 // Front cover verso bookplate, "Rosalie P. Pisek." Figure PR9368.K6C61943.

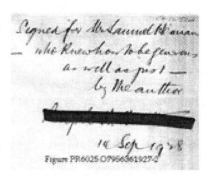

Figure PR6029.B65W5

PR9369.2S3D741924, *Dreams*, Olive Schreiner, Little, Brown and Company, Boston, 1924 // Front cover verso bookplate, "Paul Sophie." Figure PR9369.2S3D741924.

PS261.S55rv2, *Southern Writers*, M.E. Church, South, Nashville, TN, 1903 // Front cover verso bookplate, "Sondley Reference Library," Figure PR9369.2S3D741924, and title page embossed stamp, "Sondley Library, Ashville."

PS371.V359, *Contemporary American Novelists*, 1900-1920, Carl Van Doren, The Macmillan Company, NY, 1923 // First free endpaper cursive, "Albert S. Borgman, May, 1925."

PS536.S41948, *Cross Section 1948*, Edwin Seaver, Simon and Schuster, NY, 1948 // First free endpaper stamp, "From the Rhode Island State Library Book Pool for the Armed Forces."

PS551.P26, *Segments of Southern Thought*, Edd Winfield Parks, The University of Georgia Press, Athens, GA, 1938 // First free endpaper author's inscription, "For John Wade, Without whose help through the years this book could never have been written. Affectionately, Edd Parks, Nov. 29, 1938."

PS645.G7, *Great American Short Stories, 1919-1934*, Blanche Colton Williams, Doubleday, Doran & Company, Garden City, NY, 1930 // First free endpaper cursive, "L.H. Duke, Strasburg, VA, 1935."

Figure PR6029.B65W5

PS648.S3A5511964, *Analog II*, John W. Campbell, Doubleday, & Company, NY, 1964 // Front cover verso stamp, "Library, NWS, Fallbrook, California." NWS is Naval Weapons Station, a facility immediately adjacent to Camp Pendleton Marine Corps Base.

Figure PS261.S55rv2

PS648.S3C281964v2, *New Writings in SF2*, John Carnell, Bantam Books, NY, 1964 // Front cover verso bookplate, "Heterick Memorial Library, Ohio Northern University, Ada, Ohio, Presented by Charles Collett." Figure PS648.S3C281964v2.

PS648.S3K54vol.9, *Orbit 9,* Damon Knight, G.P. Putnam's Sons, NY, 1971 // Front cover verso stamps, "Property U.S. Army, Special Services Library #12, 20th SG, ASCOM, APO, Btry B1 2D ADA, APO 96220." The collection of military letters is sorted out as follows: SG=Support Group; ASCOM=Area Support Command; Btry B1 2D ADA=Battery B, 1st

Figure PR9369.S37D741924

Battalion, 2nd Regiment, Air Defense Artillery. There was also a stamp, "Recreation Services Library # 63."

PS648.S3K54vol.12, *Orbit 12,* Damon Knight, G.P. Putnam's Sons, NY, 1973 // Front cover verso sticker, "Capt & Mrs, B.W. Lane, USMC Retired, 4658 East Yale Avenue, Fresno, CA 93703."

PS688.M3, *A Book of Modern Essays*, Bruce W. McCullough, Charles Scribner's Sons, NY, 1926 // First free endpaper cursive, "Irving J. Brokaw, New York Military Academy." This academy, for grades 7-12, is located in Cornwall on Hudson, about five miles north of the U.S. Military Academy at West Point.

PS688.P4, *Essays by Present Day Writers*, Raymond Woodbury Pence, The Macmillan Company, NY, 1924 // First free endpaper cursive, "Tom(?) Lenaye(?) Lee ?????, Rich Hall 311, DePauw University, Greencastle Indiana, March 6, 1926,

Figure PS1031.C491897

Figure PS648.S3C281964v2

Wabash, Indiana."

PS1031.C491897, *The Choir Invisible*, James Lane Allen, The Macmillan Company, NY, 1897 // Front cover verso bookplate, "Edgar A. Buzzell." Figure PS1031.C491897.

PS1042B51923, *Black Oxen*, Gertrude Atherton, A.L. Burt Company, NY, 1923 // First free endpaper stamp, "Whitey's Furniture New – Use – Antique, 3708 Gallia St., New Boston, Ohio." New Boston is a town of some 3,000 folks on the Ohio River in south-central Ohio.

PS1042.R8561904, *Rulers of Kings*, Gertrude Atherton, Macmillan Company, Limited, London, 1904 // First free endpaper embossed stamp, "W.H. Smith & Son, London."

PS1064.B3M51895, *Mr. Bonaparte of Corsica*, John Kendrick Jones, Harper & Brothers, NY, 1902 // Front cover verso bookplate, "John Harold Knapp." Figure PS1064.B3M51895.

Figure PS1064.B3M51895

PS1120.B5S61903, *The Southerners*, Cyrus Townsend Brady, Charles Scribner's Sons, NY, 1903 // Front cover verso and first free endpaper stamps, "Schrager the Druggist, 215 Ridgewood Ave. Con Hale Ave., Brooklyn, NY" and Front cover verso cursive, "Jas Le Kemp, # 80 Etria St. Brooklyn."

PS11301987, *Alcuin*, Stephen Calvert, Kent State University Press, (Kent, Ohio) 1987 // Front cover verso bookplate, "in memory of Henry E. Jacobs, 1946-1986." This is the same wood cut picture at PN751.F7 that belonged to Jacobs, but it now has words honoring Jacobs.

PS1244.C3, *The Cavalier*, George W. Cable, Charles Scribner's Sons, NY, 1901 // First free endpaper cursive, "Catherine McLain New, Indianapolis, Washington, D.C., April 1902."

PS1297.M51927, *Mr. Crewe's Career*, Winston Churchill, The Macmillan Company, NY, 1927 // First free endpaper stamp, "St. Elizabeth Convent, Purcell, Okla."

PS1313.D821899v1, *Joan of Arc*, Jean François Alden, Harper & Brothers, NY, 1899 // Front cover verso cursive, "Property of W.H. Mackin, 3504 Norwood Blvd., Birmingham, Ala."

Figure PS1667.L71889

119

R. Bliss Edgar

Old friends are best
For their ties are the strongest
            you see.
They like you most firmly
For liking you longest
            Like me.

William T. Gay
Figure PS2112.R523

Figure PS2436.A3v1

E.M. Evoy." Figure PS2142.H31913.

PS1331.A21924v2, *Mark Twain's Autobiography*, Harper & Brothers, NY, 1924 // First free endpaper and title page stamps, "Orange County Community College."

PS1400.E91v1, *Cooper's Works*, James Fenimore Cooper, P.F. Collier, NY, 1891 // First free endpaper cursive, "M. Katharine Besore, Charlotte, North Carolina, 1891."

PS1649.P5S751910b, *Strictly Business*, O. Henry, Doubleday, Page and Company, NY, 1910 // Second free endpaper cursive, "A Merry Christmas to my dear old room-mate, Harry, Dec 25, '11, Morris ? Houser."

PS1667.L71889, *A Little Book of Western Verse*, Eugene Field, Charles Scribner's Sons, NY, 1901 // Front cover verso bookplate, "Hal Marchbanks." Figure PS1667.L71889.

PS1667.W51892a, *With Trumpet and Drum*, Eugene Field, Charles Scribner's Sons, NY, 1897 // Front cover verso and first free endpaper cursive, "To Darling Fred, This little Book your grandfather bought ??? seven years ago. I have marked ??? over. I hope you will read and learn some day soon. Always remember your Grandfather & Grandmother. John Barnett, Centreville, New York, Aug 12, 1897, to Fayal Barnett, Evanston, Ill. Dec 25, 1944."

Figure PS2142.H31913

PS2112.R523, *Henry James*, Lyon N. Richardson, American Book Company, NY, 1941 // First free endpaper printing. Figure PS2112.R523.

PS2142.H31913, *Hagar*, Mary Johnston, Houghton Mifflin Company, NY, 1913 // Front cover verso bookplate, "Richard

PS2436.A3v1, *Motley's Works*, George William Curtis, Society of English and French Literature, NY, 1889 // Front cover verso bookplate, "Lee W. Parke." Figure PS2436.A3v1.

PS2514.T851916, *Two Little Confederates*, Thomas Nelson Page, Charles Scribner's Sons, NY, 1940 // Front cover verso sticker, "Duttonhofer's Book Treasures, Rare, Old and Hard, 214 W. McMillan Street, Cincinnati, Ohio 45219, (513) 381-1340."

PS2864.C61891c, *Colonel Carter of Cartersville*, Houghton Mifflin, NY, 1891 // Title page stamp, "Jersey City, People's Palace, To Be Taken From The Library."

PS2954.W361915, *We and Our Neighbors*, Harriet Beecher Stowe, Houghton Mifflin Company, NY, 1873 // Front cover verso stamp, "Property of Washington Twp. Public Library" and First free endpaper stamp, "Rules." Centerville, Ohio

Figure PS2954.W361915

PS3089.T65K551909, *King Alfred's Jewel*, Katrina Trask, John Lane Company, NY, 1909 // First free endpaper cursive, "To Mrs. F. Martin from Elizabeth, Christmas 1909."

PS3089.T65W51919, *Without the Walls*, Katrina Trask, The Macmillan Company, NY, 1919 // Front cover verso bookplate, "Elizabeth Jordan." Figure PS3089.T65W51919.

PS3158.W7Z53, *Barrett Wendell and His Letters*, M.A. De Wolfe Howe, The Atlantic Monthly Press, Boston, MA, 1924 // Front cover verso bookplate, "James Hazen Hyde." Figure PS3158.W7Z53.

PS3312.M31892, *Maurine and Other Poems*, Ella Wheeler (Wilcox), Morrill Higgins & Co., Chicago, 1892 // Front cover verso bookplate (blacked out), Figure PS3312.M31892, and second free endpaper cursive by the author, "Ella Wheeler Wilcox, New York, 1892." The author used the name Ella Wheeler for the book, and dropped off Wilcox.

Figure PS3089.T65W51919

Figure PS3158.W7Z53

PS3503.A9233S4, *Secret Sentence*, Vicki Baum, Doubleday, Doran & Company, Garden City, NY, 1932 // Front cover verso bookplate, "Arthur N. Field." Figure PS3503.A9233S4.

PS3503.E18L31922, *The Ladies*, E. Barrington, The Atlantic Monthly Press, Boston, MA, 1922 // Front cover verso stamp, "New York Orthopedic Dispensary & Hospital."

Figure PS3503.A9233S4

PS3503.U198P61945a, *Portrait of a Marriage*, Pearl S. Buck, Peoples Book Club, Chicago, 1941 // Front cover verso bookplate, "Mrs. Hubert Clepper." Figure PS3503.U198P61945a.

PS3505.A153C61920, *The Cords of Vanity*, James Branch Cabell, Robert M. McBride & Co., NY, 1921 // First free endpaper cursive, "Mariana F. N. Kraus, 141 West 75 Street, New York, NY, Jan 21, 1922."

PS3505.A322T73, *Tragic Ground*, Erskine Caldwell, Duell, Sloan and Pearce, NY, 1944 // Front cover verso sticker, "M. Lincoln Schuster, 11 East 73rd Street, New York City, Butterfield 8-2978."

PS3505.A7265G41941, *Genesee Fever*, Carl Carmer, Farrar & Rinehart, Inc., NY, 1941 // First free endpaper cursive, "Marie Short, 634 E. 4th St., Alton, Ill, Jan 21, 42."

Figure PS3312.M31892

Figure PS3503.U198P61945a

PS3505.A858T51920, *The Simian World*, Clarence Day, Jr., Alfred A. Knopf, NY, 1921 // Front cover verso bookplate, "Library of Western College, Oxford, Ohio, Gift of Dr. & Mrs Edgar Stillman Kelley." Figure PS3505.A858T51920. Western College is part of Miami University.

PS3507.O77T51943, *Tidewater*, Clifford Dowdey, Little, Brown

& Company, Boston, 1943 // Front cover verso cursive, Evelyn L. Wendt, Ohio Ave., Massapequa, NY." This wonderfully named town is in southern Long Island.

PS3507.R8H51895b, *The Heart of Old Hickory*, Will Allen Dromgoole, Dana Estes & Co., Boston, 1895 // Front cover verso sticker, "Books of all Publishers, Cole Book Co., 69 Whitehall St., Atlanta, GA."

PS3509.R6)6, *One Fight More*, Susan Ertz, D. Appleton Century Company, NY, 1939 // Last free endpaper, "Green Door Book Shop, A.I. Manville, North Woodbury, Connecticut."

PS3511.A87D761923, *Druida*, John T. Frederick, Alfred A. Knopf, NY, 1923 // Front cover verso bookplate, "J. George Frederick." Figure PS3511.A87D761923.

Figure PS3507.A858T51920

PS4511.L449Z521959, *Pay, Pack, and Follow*, Inglis Fletcher, Henry Holt and Company, NY, 1959 // Front cover verso sticker, "Jane Ann Woody, 1306 Governors Dr. Huntsville, Ala 35801."

Figure PS3511.A87D761923

PS3513.L34A5, *The Ancient Law*, Ellen Glasgow, Doubleday, Page & Company, NY, 1908 // Front cover verso bookplate,

"D.H. Tuholske." Figure PS3513.L34A5.

Figure PS3513.L34A5

PS3515.E98M31928r, *Mamba's Daughters*, DuBose Heyward, Doubleday, Doran and Company, Garden City, NY, 1929 // Front cover verso bookplate, "Ruth Hopper." Figure PS3515.E98M31928r.

PS3519.E27B41941, *Be Angry at the Sun*, Robinson Jeffers, Random House, NY, 1941 // Front cover verso stamp, "Base Library, Army Air Base, Richmond, Va." I could not exactly locate this base, but it was probably active only during World War II

Figure PS3523.E94A67

and the immediate aftermath. The establishment of the U.S. Air Force as a separate branch and the improvement of aircraft capabilities would have a small runway obsolete, as happen to dozens of WWII airfields across the country.

PS3523.E94A67, *Ann Vickers*, Sinclair Lewis, Doubleday, Doran and Company, Garden City, NY, 1933 // Front cover verso bookplate, "Yonkers Public Library" and title page punched-through "Public Library, Yonkers." Figure PS3523.E94A67.

PS3523.O46Z7, *John Barleycorn*, Jack London, Grosset & Dunlap, NY, 1913 // First free endpaper cursive, "Frances G. Wright." Figure PS3523.O46Z7.

PS3525.A187C3, *Castle Craneycrow*, George Barr McCutcheon, Grosset & Dunlap, NY, 1893 // Front cover verso bookplate, sailing ship, in color, with name blacked out.

Figure PS3515.E98M31928r

PS3525.A83D61920, *Domesday Book*, Edgar Lee Masters, The Macmillan Company, NY, 1920 // Front cover verso bookplate, "Eugene Edmund Murphey." Figure PS3525.A83D61920.

Figure PS3525.A187C3

PS3525.A9464F61945, *The Folded Leaf*, William Maxwell, Book Find Club, NY, 1945, First free endpaper bookplate, "Esther & Bib Brown." Figure PS3525.A9464F61945. The scribe's cloak and continuation over his arm to the floor was red.

PS3525.O71S51918, *Shandygaff*, Christopher Morley, Garden City Publishing Co., Garden City, NY, 1918 // Front cover verso bookplate, "From the Books of Etheleen Altwig." Figure PS3525.O71S51918. Opposite was the name "Pat" Altwig. Pat is not the mouthful that Etheleen is.

PS3525.O71T481942c, *Thorofare*, Christopher Morley, Harcourt, Brace and Company, NY, 1942 // Title page circular embossed stamp, "Ames Senior High School Library, Ames, Iowa."

PS3527.O437H51945, *The High Barbaree*, Charles Nordhoff, Little, Brown and Company, Boston, 1945 // Front cover verso stamp, "NAS Library, Ault Field, Whidbey Island, Washington." NAS = Naval Air Station and Ault Field is the name of a town on the northern part of Whidbey Island, a rambling long island in the northern part of Puget Sound north of Seattle.

PS3529.N5Z573, *The Case of the Misbegotten*, Croswell Bowen, McGraw-Hill Book Company, NY, 1959 // Simple title page stamp, "Base Library, 615th ACWRON, APO 132, USAF" and title page verso stamp, "Base Library, FL 5537, APO 09194." ACWRON =

Figure PS3525.O71S51918

Aircraft Control and Warning Squadron and the 615th was located in Prüm, Germany, about 15 miles east of the intersection of the borders of Luxembourg, Belgium and Germany.

PS3529.O58mo, *Mourning Becomes Electra*, Eugene O'Neill, Horace Liveright, NY, 1931 // First free endpaper bookplate, "??? Harbour" with the owl and candle. Figure PS3529.O58mo.

Figure PS3525.A83D61920

PS3531.76426T5, *The Title Market*, Emily Post, Dodd, Mead and Company, NY, 1909 // Front cover verso bookplate (blacked out), "This book is the property of Frank L. Chipman, Please return."

PS3535.I73A4, *The Amazing Interlude*, Mary Roberts, Rinehart, Grosset & Dunlap, NY, 1918 // First free endpaper address label bookplate (blacked out), "Ann Watkins, Inc., 210 Madison Avenue, New York City."

PS3535.O1253W31946, *Wake of the Red Witch*, Garland Roark, Little, Brown and Company, Boston, 1946 // Simple title page bookplate, "Noel Collison." Figure PS3535.O1253W31946.

PS3535.O183R51962, *The River and the Wilderness*, Don Robertson, Doubleday & Company, NY, 1962 // Front cover verso stamp, "St. Vincent Ferrer Priory, New York City."

PS3535.R9F61909, *For the Soul of Rafael*, Marsh Ellis Ryan, A.C. McClure & Co., Chicago, 1909 // Front cover verso bookplate, "Finch College." Figure PS3535.R9F61909.

Esther and Bib Brown
Figure PS3525.A9464F61945

PS3537.C4D2, *David the King*, Dial Press, NY, 1946 // First free endpaper stamp, "Conrad Library." Figure PS3537.C4D2.

Figure PS3529.O58mo

PS3537.C5253E41965, *Electra*, Gladys Schmitt, Harcourt, Brace & World Inc., NY, 1965 // Front cover verso stamp, "Depot Library, Parris Island, S.C." This is a Marine Corps base.

PS3537.C89B741, *Breathe Upon These Slain*, Evelyn Scott, Harrison-Smith and Robert Haas, NY, 1934 // First free endpaper bookplate, "george and beulah schochet." Figure PS3537.C89B741.

PS3537.H384T7, *The Troubled Air*, Irwin Shaw, Sears Readers Club, Chicago, 1951 // First free endpaper cursive, "Pearl Koppel, 88-11 Elmhurst Ave., Elmhurst, N.Y., 12/23/51."

John S. Millard

Figure PS3537.M2895T61948

Figure PS3535.O1253W31946

PS3537.H825T451940a, *There Shall Be No Night*, Robert E. Sherwood, Charles Scribner's Sons, NY, 1940 // Front cover verso cursive, "To Charles S, Mother and Dad, Chicago-Oct-24, 1940, In Memory."

PS3537.I85R481953, *The Return of Lanny Budd*, Upton Sinclair, The Viking Press, NY, 1953 // Title page verso stamp, "Property of U.S.A.F., Base Library, Wurtsmith Air Force Base." Wurtsmith AFB was in Oscoda, Michigan, along the shore of Lake Huron just north of Saginaw Bay. The base was the home of B-52 bombers and closed in 1993.

THIS BOOK IS A GIFT FROM THE

CONRAD LIBRARY

OPEN DAILY INCLUDING

SUNDAYS & HOLIDAYS

Seamen's Church Institute of N. Y.

25 SOUTH STREET, NEW YORK CITY

Figure PS3537.C4D2

Figure PS3535.R9F61909

PS3537.M2895T61948, *Tomorrow Will Be Better*, Betty Smith, Harper & Brothers, NY, 1948 // Front cover verso bookplate, "John S. Millard." Figure PS3537.M2895T61948.

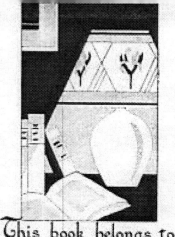

This book belongs to
george and beulah schochet
Figure PS3537.C89B741

PS3537.M4655W31960, *Waikiki Beachnik*, H. Allen Smith, Little, Brown and Company, Boston, 1960 // First free endpaper stamp, "Clarksville Base Library, Clarksville Base, Clarksville, Tennessee." Clarksville Base was located within the confines of Fort Campbell, on the Kentucky – Tennessee border. It was used for the storage of special weapons, which translates into nuclear weapons.

PS3537.M473K31932, *Kamongo*, Hower W. Smith, The Viking Press, NY, 1932 // Front cover verso bookplate, "John R. Winterbotham." Figure PS3537.M473K31932.

PS3537.T4753Z93, *Introduction to Wallace Stevens*, Henry W. Wells, Indiana University Press, Bloomington, IN, 1964 // Front cover verso stamp, "Indiana – Purdue Library, Fort Wayne."

PS3537.T4854S75, *Storm*, George R. Stewart, Random House, NY, 1941 // First free endpaper bookplate, Alpha Phi." Figure PS3537.T4854S75. Alpha Phi is an international fraternity for women founded in 1872.

PS3537.T5377R51940, *River of Earth*, James Still, The Viking Press, NYU, 1940 // First free endpaper stamp, "Nellie Spiller, Brownfield, Maine." Brownfield is a small town in the upper part of the state.

PS3537.T8278G31945, *The Gauntlet*, James Street, Doubleday, Doran & Co., Garden City, NY, 1945 // Front cover verso bookplate, "Harry Nadler." (blacked out) Figure PS3537.T8278G31945.

JOHN R. WINTERBOTHAM
Figure PS3537.M473K31932

Figure PS3537.T48545S75

PS3545.A55F7, *From Every Mountain Side*, Lillie Toney Wallace, Carlton Press, Inc., NY, 1972 // Front cover verso stamp, "Afro-American Book Dist., 2537 Prospect, Houston, Texas 77004."

PS3545.H16B71938, *The Buccaneers*, Edith Wharton, D. Appleton-Century

Figure PS3537.T8278G31945

Company, NY, 1938 // Front cover verso stamp, "Officers' Service Club, Newfoundland Base, U.S. Army." This base was located at Fort Pepperrell, see E814.1.T7.

Figure PS3545.H16B71938-2

PS3545.H16D41904, *The Descent of Man*, Edith Wharton, Charles Scribner's Sons, NY, 1904 // Front cover verso bookplate, "Tabard Inn Library." Figure PS3545.H16D41904-1. As a bibliophile, I got excited when I researched Tabard on the Internet. The site www.libraryhistorybuff.org/tabard-inn.htm provided the following item and pictures.

The Tabard Inn Library was founded in 1902 by Seymour Eaton, It was administered by the Booklovers Library, another Eaton enterprise. Eaton was a remarkable entrepreneur and promoter who was also an author, journalist, and educator. He was the author of the "Teddy Bear Books." The Tabard Inn Library was a membership library with stations in the form of revolving bookcases, Figure PS3545.H16D41904-2, located in drug stores and other commercial establishments throughout the United States. In an initial advertisement for the library, Eaton indicated that 10,000 of these bookcases would be manufactured at a rate of 25 and then 50 a day. Photographs of a Tabard Inn Library Bookcase are located in the Elisha D. Smith Public Library in Menasha, WI. The bookcases held 120 books which were to be changed from a central location every week. A member deposited five cents in a compartment in

THE
· Tabard · Inn ·
· Library ·

RULES GOVERNING TABARD INN SERVICE

1. This book may be exchanged at any TABARD INN Station on payment of the fee of five cents.

2. A Tabard Inn book can be obtained from a Tabard Inn Library or Exchange Station only on presentation of another Tabard Inn book or book check. No other identification is necessary.

3. If a book or its equivalent book check is lost, the service may be resumed by purchasing another exchangeable book.

4. To temporarily discontinue the service, a book check should be secured when the book is returned and the five-cent exchange fee paid. To resume service this book check should be presented but no exchange fee need be paid.

No. _____

The Tabard Inn Library

Main Office: 1611 Chestnut St., Philadelphia

Figure PS3545.H16D41904-1

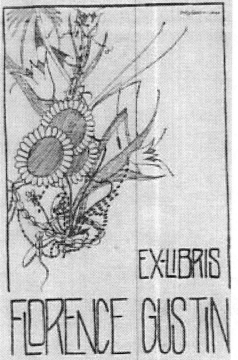

EX-LIBRIS
FLORENCE GUSTIN

Figure PS3545.H16D41914

128

the bookcase to exchange a book. A carved message around the top of the bookcase read "The Best Reading Rooms In the United States Are the Homes of the American People." Initially a lifetime membership cost $3.00 and was good anywhere in the United States. The cost was later reduced to $1.50. Eaton used this procedure to develop a mailing list containing the names of a million men and women to promote other ventures, including the Tabard Inn Food Company. Eaton's conglomerate of enterprises came to an end in March, 1905 when he declared bankruptcy.

PS3545.H16D41914, *Madame De Treymes*, Edith Wharton, Charles Scribner's Sons, NY, 1914 // Front cover verso bookplate, "Florence Gustin." Figure PS3545.H16D41914.

PS3545.H61913, *Gold*, Stewart Edward White, Doubleday Page & Co., Garden City, NY, 1913 // Third free endpaper cursive, "Clifford C. Newell from Bertha, December 25, 1913" and front cover verso bookplate, "C.C. Newell." Figure PS3545.H6G61913.

PS3545.I5365Z871983, *Tennessee Williams*, Dakin Williams, Arbor House, NY, 1983 // First free endpaper stamp, "Presented To The Henry Edward Jacobs Collection." Figure PS3545.I5365Z871983. Refer to PN751.F7 and PS11301987.

Figure PS3545.H6G61913

PS3547.E65G21961, *The Garfield Honor*, Frank Yerby, The Dial Press, NY, 1961 // First free endpaper stamp, "Nimitz Hill Library" and "US Naval Hospital Crew's Library." The Nimitz Hill Library is on the island of Guam.

PS3551.N378F51974, *Fire Time*, Poul Anderson, Doubleday & Company, Inc., Garden City, NY, 1974 // Front cover verso stamp, "Recreation Services Library # 50, 69 Trans Bn, Cp Eiler, APO96483," first free endpaper stamp, "Rec Svcs Lib # 80, Btry C, 1/2D ADA, APO S.F. 96301, and fourth leaf cursive, "8-81, Trans from USARSOK" and title page verso stamp, "Gunter Base Library, Gunter Air Force Station, AL 36115." The translation of the military abbreviations follows. The book started at the 69th Transportation Battalion at Camp Eiler, near Kimpo Airport, the primary airport serving Seoul, Korea in the middle of the 20th century. The next owner was Battery C, 1st Battalion, 2nd Regiment, Air Defense Artillery. The US Army South Korea, the

Presented To The Henry
Edward Jacobs Collection
In English And American Literature
By O.B. Emerson
In Memory Of
Henry E. Jacobs
Beloved Colleague And Friend

Figure PS3545.I5385Z871983

major command, took charge of the book when the previous units were phased out of Korea. The US Air Force at Gunter Air Station, Montgomery, Alabama was the next recipient of the book.

PS3551.O37E61926, *The Enemy*, Channing Polleck, Grosset & Dunlap, NY, 1926 // Front cover verso cursive, "Mrs. Trevor Ferguson, Frankfort, N.Y., 8/19/36." Frankfort is a small town near Utica in upstate New York.

PS3552.O84O851968, *Out of the Sun*, Ben Bova, Holt, Rinehart and Winston, NY 1968 // Top and bottom edges stamp, "Hoover High School Library." This high school undoubtedly is in Hoover, Alabama, a suburb of Birmingham, although there are other Hoover High Schools across the country.

PS3554.O469O51982, *The One Tree*, Stephen R. Donaldson, Ballantine Books, NY, 1982 // Title page stamp, "Valley Station Branch – B, Bookmobile H 28." There is a Valley Station near Louisville, Kentucky, but an association with our book could not be confirmed.

PS3555.Y7C471959, *The Chinese Box*, Katherine Wigmore Eyre, Appleton – Century – Crofts, Inc., NY, 1959 // First free endpaper and title page stamps, "East Rockaway free Library, East Rockaway, N.Y." This town is just east of J.F. Kennedy Airport in southwest Long Island.

PS3537.O75T51969, *A Time of Predators*, Joe Gores, Random House, NY, 1969 // First free endpaper stamp, "Library, USS Iwo Jima." The USS Iwo Jima was an assault landing ship supporting US Marine Corps operations. The first ship, LPH-2, was commissioned in 1963 and decommissioned in 1993. A second Iwo Jima, LDH-7, was commissioned in 1997 and is still in service.

PS3558A8289V6, *Voyage*, Sterling Hayden, G.P. Putnam's Sons, NY, 1976 // First free endpaper stamp, "Ship's Library, USS Wainwright (DLG-28)." This ship the third ship named after four Navy personnel of a much earlier era. The first two were destroyers. This ship, DLG-28, was a guided missile cruiser commissioned in 1966 and decommissioned in 1993. It was sunk in 2002 as part of target practice.

PS3561.E667S61964, *Sometimes a Great Notion*, Ken Kesey, The Viking Press, NY, 1964 // First free endpaper stamp, "Property of Library, Naval Support Activity, New Orleans, LA."

PS3563.E73R34, *Rachel Cade*, Charles Mercer, G.P. Putnam's Sons, NY, 1956 // First free endpaper stamp, "Shop of the Seven Seas, 2 Eastchester Road, New Rochelle, N.Y."

PS3568.O224C31961, *The Carpetbaggers*, Harold Robbins, Trident Press, NY, 1961 // First free endpaper stamp, "Field Library, 32 FTR Intcp Sq, APO New York 09292." The 32nd Fighter Interceptor Squadron, Slobberin' Wolfhounds, had a long lineage starting in 1939 with different types of aircraft in different locations. It was deactivated in November 2005.

PS3569.T673P7, *Presidential Emergency*, Walter Stovall, E. P. Dutton, NY, 1978 // First free endpaper stamp, "Surveyed, Subic Library." Subic Bay was a U.S. Naval Base on Luzon in the Philippine Islands. It was the next large bay northwest of Manila Bay. "Surveyed" is a military short term for Report of Survey, which means the loss of an item, even a book, was officially investigated to determine if the loss was the fault of an individual, in which case the individual might pay for the item, or the loss was acknowledged as on official loss with no further action taken. This allows property books to account for all material.

Figure PT85.V71934v2

PT285.V71934v.2, *Geschichte der Deutschen Literatur*, Prof Dr. Friedrich Bogt, Bibliographisches Institut, Leipzig, Germany, 1934 // Front cover verso bookplate, "A.E. Terry," of a monk in his scriptorium. Figure PT285.V71934v.2.

PT134.I5C5, *Deutsche Innerlichkeit*, Ulrich Christoffel, R. Biper & Co., Verlag, München, Germany, 1940 // First free endpaper stamp, "Nationalsoz. Deutsche Arbeiterpartei, Reichschule der NSDAP. Feldafing." NSDAP is National Socialist German Workers Party Empire School.

PT1155.E451936, *Der Barde*, Walther Eggert-Windegg, C. H. Berfsche Verlagsbuchhandlung, München, Germany, 1936 // First free endpaper bookplate, "Gabe des Deutschen Reichs." Figure PT1155.E451936.

Nationalsoz. Deutsche Arbeiterpartei
Reichsschule der NSDAP. Feldafing

Figure PT134.I5C5

PT1155.E841949, *Ewige Melodie*, Arbeitsgemeinschaft Thüringisher Verlagen, Gebr. Richters Verlagsanstalt, Erfurt, Germany, 1949 // Title page stamp, "Dr. Karl J. Pschera, 7909 Seville Drive, S.E., Huntsville, Alabama."

PT1338.P61946, *Moderne Deutsche Erzähler*, Robert O. Röseler, W.W. Norton & Company, Inc., NY, 1946 // First free endpaper cursive, "Jean Michel Perreault, Rockhurst College." Rockhurst College, a university since 1999, is a private, co-educational Jesuit school in Kansas City, Missouri. Perreault received his Bachelor of Arts degree in English and philosophy from Rockhurst College.

PT1828.B7A81905, *Aprilwetter*, Hans Arnold, D.C. Heath & Co., Boston, MA, 1910 // Front cover verso cursive, "Margaret Hall, Evanston, Illinois, 1142 Maple Ave." and a UAH gift plate from Hertha Heller.

PT1891.C01v1, *Goethes Werke*, Bibliographsches Institut, Leipzig, Germany, // First free endpaper verso bookplate, "Siebel" and a UAH gift plate from Nathias Seibel. Figure PT1891.C01v1.

Figure PT1895.C01v1

PT2295.A55H4, *In Paris*, Friedrich Hebbel, Südverlag // First free endpaper cursive by Hannes Luehrsen. Hannes

Gabe des
Deutschen
Reichs

Figure PT1155.E451936

Luehrsen was an architect and part of the Wernher von Braun rocket team that came from Germany after World War II and ended up in Huntsville after a stay in El Paso, Texas. Hannes' son, Thomas, donated this book with a UAH gift plate and many others to the UAH library. Hannes was a disputed contributor to the design of Memorial Parkway in Huntsville in the early 1950s.

PT2328B7, *That Man Heine*, Lewis Browne, The Macmillan Company, NY, 1927 // First free endpaper cursive, "Love and congratulations to dear Esther, from Aunt Jennie, January 26/28."

PT2374.G7, *Der grüne Heinrich*, Gottfried Keller, Hesse & Beder Verlag, Leipzig, Germany // Front cover verso bookplate, "A.E. Terry." Stamp on first free endpaper and title page, "Stanford University, Germanic Languages Department Library, No. 2815, Sold by German Dept., Stanford University."

PT2398.M3P7, *Minna von Barnhelm*, Gotthold Ephjraim Lessing, D.C. Heath & Co., NY, 1889 // First free endpaper cursive, "H. Donald Settle, 404 Seventh St., Huntington, Pa."

PT2468.T3P31900, *Wilhelm Tell*, Friedrich Schiller, Henry Holt and Company, NY, 1900 // Front cover verso cursive, "Kate L. Mitchell, 1023 Maple Ave., Evanston." This address is only one block away from the address in PT1828.B7A81905.

PT2603.R397Z893, *The Art of Bertolt Brecht*, Walter Weideli, New York University Press, NY, 1963 // First free endpaper stamp, "Henry E. Jacobs, Dept. of English, Ballatine Hall, Indiana University, Bloomington, Indiana 47401." Henry Jacobs was discovered several times earlier, but this was the first time with his location.

Figure PT2295.A55H4

PT2603.R658A11941, *Die auf den Morgen Warten…!*, Paul Brock, Verlag Franz Eher rachs, Gmbh., München, Germany, 1941 // Front cover verso sticker, "Deutsche Buchhandlung, Anton Goss, Dresden [Germany] A. Morigstr. 16."

PT2607.I6W4, *Wer einmal aus dem Blechnap frist*, Rowohet, Berlin, 1934 // Front cover verso sticker, "W. Beyer, Books & Art, 259 Fifth Ave., New York."

PT2611.U72J81898, *Jugenfreude*, Ludwig Fulda, Verlag der H.G. Gotta'schen Buchhandlung, Stuttgart, Germany, 1898 // Front cover verso bookplate, "Bibliotek der Deutschen Gesellschaft von Pennsylvanien." Figure PT2611.U72J81898. Front cover verso sticker, "Schaefer & Koradi, Buchhandlung, Philadelphia, Pa." Title page stamp, "Library of the German Society, Philadelphia." Notice the mixture of English and German. This was typical of the German communities in the

United States until the beginning of the First World War, when it was stopped because of the anti-German sentiment.

PT2621.A23E61945, *Emil and die Detektive*, Erich Kästner, Henry Holt and Company, NY, 1945 // First free endpaper sticker, "Tulane Book Store, New Orleans, 9/26/47, $.20."

PT2625.A44J6331944, *Joseph the Provider*, Thomas Mann, Alfred A. Knopf, NY, 1944 // First free endpaper bookplate, "Martha Sheffry(?)" Figure PT2625.A44J6331944.

Figure PT2625.A44J6331944

PT2625.A848S 381890, *Der Schwarze Mustang*, Karl May, Union Deutsche Verlagsgesellschaft, Berlin, 1890 // Front cover verso cursive on a publisher's fill-in bookplate, "Liese und Grete Polaczak." Figure PT2625.A848S 381890. Front cover verso sticker,"Schwedler's Buchhandlung u. Antiquariat, Reichenberg, Schükengasse 16." I have refrained from commenting on the many famous authors whose works are cited. Karl May is now an exception, because his works have an unusual twist. He was German, 1842-1912, who wrote novels about American Indians, which were immensely popular in Germany. Adolf Hitler was one of May's loyal readers and used May's noble Red Indian chief, Winnetou, as a leadership model. May's second protagonist was Old Shatterhand, an American pioneer of German descent, but May did not visit the United States until 1908, four years before he died and 30 years after he wrote about Winnetou.

Figure PT2611.U72J81898

PT2625.O64G31922, *Galgenlieder*, Christian Morgenstern, Verlag von Bruno Cassirer, Berlin, 1922 // Front cover verso cursive, ""für Hannes, nach Texas, Weihnacht 1946." This book was apparently sent from Germany to Hannes Luehrsen, one of the Operation Paper Clip German rocket scientists brought to the United States in 1946. This would have been his first Christmas in America. *Galgenlieder*

Figure PT2625.A848S381890

translates to gallows' songs, which some may thought was a possibility in the post-World War II environment. Refer to PT2295.A55H4.

PT2635.E68A73, *Arch of Triumph*, Erich Maria Remarque, D. Appleton-Century Company, NY, 1945 // Front cover verso stamp, "Bridgewater Home Library." This library is probably the one now named Bridgewater Public Library in Massachusetts.

PT2635.I45W31940, *Die Weise von Liebe und Tod des Cornets Christoph Rilke*, Rainer Maria Rilke, Im Insel Verlag zu Leipzig, Germany, 1940 // Front cover verso UAH gift plate from Thomas Luehrsen and a sticker, "J. Greven, Buch & Kunsthandlung, Krefeld, Hochstrasse 52, Tel 23285."

PT2635.I65S71928, *Das Stunden Buch*, Rainer Maria Rilke, Insel-Verlag, Leipzig, Germany, 1928 // First free endpaper stamp, "Deutsches Heim, Schloss Cöpenick." Figure PT2635.I65S71928.

Figure PT2635.I65S71928

PTPT2640.F61900, *Frau Sorge*, Hermann Sudermann, Philadelphia Demokrat Publishing Co., 612 und 614 Chestnut Str., Philadelphia, Pa // Front cover verso sticker, "Koelling & Klappenbach, Booksellers, Chicago" and UAH gift plate from Hertha Heller, a long-time language professor at UAH. Note the mixture of German and English words in the publisher's description.

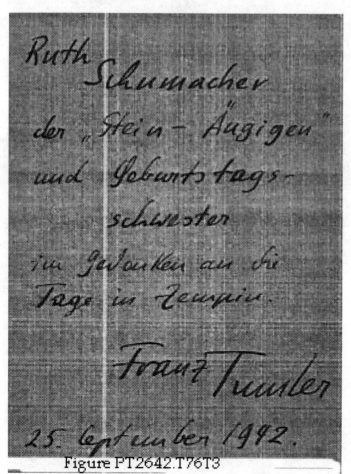

Figure PT2642.T76T3

PT2640.Z3K31898, *Regina or The Sins of the Fathers*, Hermann Sudermann, John Lane, The Bodley head, London, 1898 // Front cover verso bookplate and stamp, Figure PT2640.Z3K31898.

Figure PT2640.Z3K31898

PT2642.T76T3, *Das Tal von Lausa und Duron*, Franz Tumler, Albert Langen/Georg Müller, Muünchen, 1935 // Front cover verso UAH gift plate of Thomas Luehrsen and first free

134

endpaper cursive by the author. Figure PT2640.Z3K31898.

PT2647.A3W28, *Wagrainer Geschichtenbuch*, Karl Heinrich Waggerl, Otto Müller Verlag, Salzberg, Austria, 1950 // Title page stamp, "Spande der Martin Behaim Gesellschaft, Darmstadt" and UAH gift plate from Hertha Heller.

PT2647.E77Z31940, *Embezzled Heaven*, Franz Werfel, The Viking Press, NY, 1940 // Front cover verso bookplate, "The Village Book Shop." Figure PT2640.Z3K31898.

PT2647.I25T6731940z, *Der Totenwald*, Ernst Wiechert, Verlag Kurt Desch, München, Germany // Front cover verso sticker, "Adler's Foreign Books, 114 4ᵗʰ Ave., New York" and Willy Ley UAH gift plate.

PT2653.W42J41923, *Jeremias*, Stefan Zweig, Insel-Verlaf zu Leipzig, 1923 // front cover verso sticker, "Peabody Book Shop, Baltimore."

PT2668.O3S813, *The Deputy*, Rolf Hochhuth, Grove Press Inc., NY, 1964 // First free endpaper stamp, "Property of United States Air Force, Camp New Amsterdam Base Library." This base was located at Soesterberg, in central The Netherlands, until deactivation in 1995.

CIRCULATING LIBRARY

THE VILLAGE BOOK SHOP

8027 AGNES AVENUE · DETROIT

FITZROY 4887

Figure PT2647.E77Z3E51940

PT7269.N4E531911r, *The Story of Burnt Njal*, Sir George Webbe Dasent, J. M. Dent & Sons, Ltd., London, 1960 // Title page sticker, "Odin Lives! Write to: Gambanreide Statement, P.O. Box 616, Springville, AL 35146-0616." Springville is on Interstate 59 just northeast of Birmingham.

PT8852.G4P31890v1-4, *Henrik Ibsen*, Gesammelte Werfe, Verlag von Philipp Reclam, Leipzig, Germany, 1980 // First free endpaper script, "C.K. Barry, Barry, Leipzig, 15 may, [18]93."

PT8865.A51925, *Gengangere*, Henrik Ibsen, Norsk Forlag, Oslo, Norway, 1925 // Front cover verso cursive, "A.E. Terry, Oslo, 3 IX 26." This is the fifth book identified with A.E. Terry. The first one, PC1625.M351926, placed him in Rome on 10 August 1926 and this one puts him in Oslo on 3 September 1926. He was apparently having a fine trip around Europe visiting bookstores, among other things.

PZ3.B7715Do, *Don't Go Near the Water*, William Brinkley, Random House, NY, 1956 // First free endpaper stamp, "The Book Shop, Russel Erskine Hotel Building, Phone JE2-5752, Huntsville, Alabama."

PZ3.L829A4, *Alice McDonald*, James the Less (J.B. Logan, D.D.), C.P. Publishing House, Nashville, TN, 1900 // First free endpaper cursive, "E.M. Neill, Pune'y, Pa, Aug 23, 1901." The abbreviated town named might be Punxsutawney, now known as the home of the spring-predicting ground hog.

Q1.A05W921950, *World List of Scientific Periodicals, 1900-1950*, William Allan Smith, Academic Press Inc., Publishers, 1952 // Title page stamps, "Property of US Army, Guided Missile Library, Technical Library, Redstone Arsenal, Alabama."

Q125.W851951, *The Growth of Scientific Ideas*, William P.P. Wightman, Yale University Press, New Haven, Ct, 1953 //Front cover verso stamp, "J. Ralph Thaxton." Figure Q125.W851951.

Q127.R9S69, *Soviet Science and Technology*, John R. Thomas, The George Washington, Washington, D.C., 1977 // Front cover verso stamp, "Foreign Science and Technology Center (FSTC) Library." FSTC is in Charlottesville, VA.

QA3.N48v2, *The World of Mathematics*, James R. Newman, Simon & Schuster, NY, 1956 // Front cover verso stamp, "Delmas C. Little, 1511 Cliff Drive, Newport Beach, California" and UAH gift plate, "HSV Campus Lib, D.C. Little." Delmas C. Little also lived at 1910 Hixon Drive, Las Cruces, NM. After discovering several of his books, I finally noticed that he placed a written number in the upper left corner of the front cover verso. Each book had a different number so it is assumed that was his inventory number. The highest noticed was in the 160s.

QA3.Y7, *Monographs of Modern Mathematics*, J.W.A. Young, Longmans, Green and Co., NY, 1915 // First free endpaper cursive, "Albert Allen, University of Chicago, June 21, 1916" and UAH gift plate from Lloyd S. Johnson.

Figure Q125.W851951

QA552.S72, *Theorie der Kegelschnitte*, Dr. C.F. Geiser, Druck und Verlag von B.G. Teubner, Leipzig, Germany, 1887 // Front cover verso bookplate of road through forest and blacked out name. Figure QA552.S72

QA911.T52, *Applied Hydro-and-Aero-Mechanics*, O.G. Tietjens, McGraw-Hill Book Company, Inc., NY, 1934 // Inside front and back cover stamps. Figure QA911.T52.

Figure QA552.S72

GOVERNMENT PROPERTY
NOT TO BE APPROPRIATED TO PRIVATE USE.
REVISED STATUTES SEC. 5439, March 4, 190
UNIVERSITY OF MICHIGAN
NAVAL TRAINING UNIT

Figure QA911.T52

QA931.T54, *Theory of Elastic Stability*, S. Timosenko, McGraw-Hill Book Company, Inc., NY, 1936 // Front cover verso stamp, Technical Library, R.&D. S, ,SO(Rocket), Fort Bliss, Texas, U.S. Property" and stamp, "Redstone Scientific Information Center."

QB43.H38, *Splendor in the Sky*, Gerald S. Hawkins, Harper & Brothjers, Publishers, NY, 1961 // First free endpaper verso bookplate, "Goddard Space Flight Center." Figure QB43.H38.

QB54.M28, *Intelligence in the Universe*, Roger A. Mac Gowan, Prentice-Hall, Inc., Englewood Cliffs, NJ, 1966 // Top, bottom and fore edge stamps, "IBM Huntsville Library."

QB991.P31934a, *Creations Doom*, Desiderius Papp, D. Appleton-Century Company, NY, 1934 // First free endpaper stamp, "Reference Copy, Not to be taken from the Library, D. Appleton-Century Co., Inc." and Willy Ley UAH gift plate. The evidence above makes the case that Willy Ley used his fame to charm the publisher into giving him its reference copy.

Figure QB43.H38

Figure QC174.B8

QC7.E5, *The Evolution of Physics*, Albert Einstein, Simon and Schuster, NY, 1938 // Front cover verso bookplate, "Norman F. Williams Collection" and first free endpaper cursive, "Norman F. Williams."

QC39.E331950, *Industrial Instrumentation*, Donald P. Eckmanm, John Wiley & Sons, NY, 1950 // Front cover verso sticker, Delmas C. Little, M.D.F.R.L., Fort Knox, Kentucky." I have no idea what those five letters stand for.

QC173.T431947, *The Atom*, Sir George Thomson, Oxford University Press // Front cover verso stamp, "Property United States Air Force, Cambridge Research Center, Electronics Research Center." This location is at Hanscomb Air Force Base in Bedford, MA, just west of Boston.

QC174.B5, *The Quantum Theory of the Atom*, George Birtwistle, Cambridge University Press, London, 1926 // Front cover verso bookplate, "Joseph Denison Elder." Figure174.B8.

QH3072.B561970, *Biology and the Future of Man*, Philip Handler, Oxford University Press, NY, 1910 // Title page stamp, "Smithsonian Tropical Research Institute Library."

QL45.B781879v1, *Brehm's Illustrirtes Thierleben*, Verlag des Bibliographischen Institute Leipzig, Germany, 1879 // Front cover verso bookplate, "Theodor Berger." Figure QL45.B781879v1.

RAI3.P72dsuppl1893, *Poole's Index to Periodic Literature*, William I. Fletcher, The Riverside Press, Cambridge, MA, 1893 // Front cover verso bookplate, "Ex-Libris, Bibliothecæ Coll Hobart." Figure RAI3.P72dsuppl1893.

RCT100.C81943, *Current Biography 1943*, Maxine Block, H.W. Wilson Company, NY, 1944 // Front cover verso bookplate, "Los Angeles Public Library." Figure RCT100.C81943.

Figure RCT100.C81943

Figure RAI3.P72dsuppl.1893

T66.B471926a, *History of Manual and Industrial Education Up to 1870*, Charles A. Bennett, Chas. A. Bennett Co., Inc., Peoria, IL, 1926 // First free endpaper embossed stamp, "From the Library of Brent B. Goodwin, Ph.D., BBG."

TA12.H6, *Black Engineers in the United States*, James K.K. Ho, Howard University Press, Washington, D.C., 1974 // Front cover verso bookplate, "Department of the Navy, Sea Systems Command, Technical Library." Figure TA12.H6.

Figure RCT100.C81943

TA139.H3, *The Great Engineers*, Ivor B. Hart, Methuen & Co., London, 1928 // Front cover verso sticker, "Books & Careers, 485 Oxford Street, London, W.I., GROsvenor 0654."

TA151.E81952a, *Handbook of Engineering Fundamentals*, Ovid W. Eshbach, John Wiley & Sons, Ltd., NY, 1954 First free endpaper cursive, "Jerry Guinn, Lambda Chi, Auburn, Ala."

Figure TA12.H6

TA157.M5, *The Engineer in Society*, John Mills, D. Van Nostrand Co., Inc., NY, 1946 // Front cover verso bookplate, name blacked out, but figure includes a lamp and surveyor's transit. Figure TA157.M5.

TA174.O87, *Design, Planning, and Development Methodology*, Benjamin Ostrofsky, Prentice-Hall Book Company, Englewood Cliffs, NJ, 1977 // Title page stamp, "Property of NFPCA, National Fire Reference Service, U.S. Department of Commerce, Washington, D.C., 20230."

Figure TA157.M5

Figure TC774.P14

TC774.P14, *The Panama Canal in Peace and War*, Norman J. Padelford, The Macmillan Company, NY, 1942 // Front cover verso bookplate, "Library, Air Corps, Technical School." Figure TC774.P14.

TF147.H451943, *This Fascinating Railroad Business*, Robert S. Henry, The Bobbs-Merrill Company, NY, 1953 // Title page stamp, "Property of Baltimore & Ohio R.R. Employees Library." Item HE2741.v3 was from the B&O *Research* Library.

TJ151.M371941, *Mechanical Engineers Handbook*, Lionel S. Marks, McGraw-Hill Book Company, NY, 1941 // Index page stamp, "Property of Burke Aircraft Corp." There was also a Willy Ley UAH gift plate.

TJ1975.K511939, *Mechanism*, Robert M. Keown, McGraw-Hill Book Company, NY, 1939 // Front cover verso cursive, "Richard L. Phares, W. Va. University, Sept 20, 1949."

TJ275.C771937, *Steam Power and Internal Combustion Engines*, Dudley P. Craig, McGraw-Hill Book Company, BT, 1937 // Front cover verso sticker, "Harry F. Vincent, P.O. Box 88, Washington University, Saint Louis, Missouri."

TK140.E3J75, *Edison*, Mathew Josephson, McGraw-Hill Book Company, NY, 1959 // First free endpaper stamp, "Bob Nicholosi, 294 Richland Pike, Marion, Ohio," and cursive, "January 23, 1960."

TK147.R61940. *Electrical Engineering Laboratory Experiments*, C.W. Ricker, McGraw-Hill Book Company, NY, 1940 // Front cover verso bookplate, "W.L. Shippey, Vanderbilt University, Box 434." Figure TK147.R61940.

TK1425.M8L53, *TVA*, David Lilienthal, Harper & Brothers, NY, 1944 // First free endpaper cursive, "Pathé News, 625 Madison, New York City, 1944."

TK147.R61940

TK3226.G83v11931, *Communication Networks*, Ernst Guillemin, John Wiley & Sons, NY, 1931 // First free endpaper stamp, "Return to Penn State, War Training, GI Room, ASTP ADV." ASTP = Army Specialized Training Program, which sent many World War II soldiers to universities to gain specialized training that was not available in the Army. The US Army of the 1930s was really not ready for much action of any kind because there were no perceived threats, despite Hitler being on the move in Europe for four years prior to 1941.

Figure TP155.F81942v1

TK6015.C3, *The History of the Telephone*, Herbert N. Casson, A.C. McClung & Co., Chicago, IL, 1910 // Front cover verso stamp, "R.R. Dept. Library, No. 729, Portland, ME, Y.M.C.A."

TP155.F81942v1, *Rogers Manual of Industrial Chemistry*, C.C. Furnas, D. Van Nostrand Company, NY, 1942 // Front cover verso bookplate, "I enjoy sharing ... safely home." It is a shame that the owner's name was covered by the UAH accessionist.

TP986.A2N35, *The Chemistry and Technology of Plastics*, Raymond Nauth, Reinhold Publishing Corp. NY, 1947 // Front cover verso sticker, "Harry D. Thurlow, Books and Magazines, 304 S. Collins Ave., Balto 29 MD."

UA23.P64, *A Guide to National Defense*, Patrick W. Powers, Frederick A. Praeger, NY, 1964 // Title page stamp, "Property of U.S. Army, Post Library, Carlisle Barracks, PA."

VF313.G4, *Accuracy and Probability of Fire*, James H. Glennon, Press of Isaac Friedenwald, Baltimore, MD, 1888 // First free endpaper cursive, "Nov. 2, 1892, H.A. Pearson, USNA, Annapolis, Md." USNA = United States Naval Academy.

Z992.T17, My original work on this book is below, untouched from the original.
Carrousel of Bibliophiles, by William Targ
Provenance,
By Paul A. Hays, September 2004

    Carrousel of Bibliophiles, A Treasury of Tales, Epigrams and Sundry Curious Studies Relating to a Noble Theme, ISBN: 0-84864-617-7, Edited, with an Introduction by William Targ, was in the M. Louis Salmon Library, University of Alabama in Huntsville, Alabama, Z 992.T17, in August 2004. The book was published in 1947 by Philip C. Duschnes, New York. It contains 415 pages, divided into the normal numbering of 400, plus an additional 15 pages at the end for lists of books. The book has red cloth boards, and the spine is faded.

    I checked the book out of the Salmon Library in August 2004.

    On the free endpaper is a hand written inscription, "For Ben Graves in the fellowship of good books. Warmest regards and esteem. From Bill Targ, 2/21/48" This book qualifies as a "presentation copy."

    I called Dr. Graves at his home address in the telephone book. He answered and I introduced myself that I'd taken his course at the Academy in 1994. I asked about the inscription. He thought that Bill Targ had been in his class at LSU, where Dr. Graves had his first teaching job. I do not know the circumstances of Dr. Graves first job, but William Targ was born in 1907, so he would have been 41 years old when he inscribed the book in 1947. Dr. Graves did not know James D. Ramer, whose bookplate was inside the front cover and opposite the inscription. The bookplate qualifies the book as an "association copy."

Graves opined that Salmon got the book from his personal papers, which he had donated to Salmon when he cleaned out his office in Administrative Science Building in the spring of 2004. This could not be because I'd spotted it in Salmon Library long many months before as a book I eventually wanted to read.

I called Anne Coleman, Special Collections, as two of her books were analyzed in my *Harem of Books*. She said that she and Gary Glover had cleaned out the Graves accumulation several months ago and it was being processed. She would like to add this book to the collection when I'm finished, and not return it to the normal shelves. Salmon does not have accession data before 1990, so they are no help to establish the possession of the book.

The verso of the front cover has a bookplate, *Ex Libris* with the name, James D. Ramer. I checked Google and discovered James D. Ramer, who founded the University of Alabama Graduate School of Library and Information Science and was the first Dean in 1971. Dr. Ramer received the Eminent Librarian Award from the Alabama Library Association in 1988.

On the inside the back cover is the Library's barcode label. On the top left of the inside of the cover are the words in pencil, "Et Dono Edition (?) 2/48."

Z1001.F77, *Modern Documentation and Information Practices*, O. Frank, International Federation for Documentation, The Hague, Netherlands, 1961 // Title page stamp, National Science Foundation Library, Date: Apr 16, 1962."

Z1002.B595, *Bibliographic Index, 1953-1954*, Marga Franck, H.W. Wilson Company, NY, 1944 // Front cover verso bookplate, "The Johns Hopkins University, Baltimore, 1876."

The remainder of the items is from Special Collections (SC), therefore the cataloguing system will not followed.

Harvie P. Jones, E483.5A5H84, *History of the Alabama Division, United Daughters of the Confederacy*, Mattie M. Huey, The Post Publishing Company, Opelika, AL, 1937 // First free endpaper stamp, "Merrimack Mfg. Co., Joe Bradley School Library, Huntsville, Ala," and title page stamp, "Westlawn Junior High School Library, Given to Harvie P. Jones, Dec. 1988."

Frances Roberts SC, *Territorial Papers of the United States*, Clarence E. Carter, U.S. Government Printing Office, Washington, D.C., 1940 // Front cover verso cursive, "Rae Venable, Tulane University, New Orleans 18, La, 27 McAlister."

Frances Roberts SC, *Grace Church, Kirkwood, Missouri, Its Story*, Shirley & Adele Seifert, Messenger Printing and Publishing Co., Kirkwood, MO, 1959 // First free endpaper cursive, "With all our love to Father on his 92 Christmas! Mary Lyon & George, Christmas 1961."

Figure
FRSC, Banking in Alabama

Frances Roberts SC, *Hell's Branch Office*, Horace Ridaught, 1937 // First free endpaper cursive, ""To my winged friend, Bob Johnson, with good wishes, Horace Ridaught, Chief, Florida's Choctaws, 16 January 1958."

Frances Roberts SC, *Banking in Alabama, 1816-1860*, William H. Brantley, Oxmoor Press, Birmingham, AL, 1967 // Front cover bookplate, "Frances Roberts." Figure Frances Roberts SC.

Frances Roberts SC, *Old Petersburg and Broad River Valley of Georgia*, Ellis Merton Coulter, University of Georgia Press, Athens, GA, 1965 // Front cover verso cursive, inscription to Alice McCrary Thomas. Figure Alice McCrary Thomas.

From the Library of
ARTHUR D. ANDERSON

Figure SpacePR6005.L36S261952

Figure SpaceQ123.U461960

SpacePR6005.L36 S261952, *Sands of Mars*, Arthur C. Clarke, Gnome Press Inc., NY, 1952 // Front cover verso bookplate, "Arthur D. Anderson." Figure SpacePR6005.L36S2 61952.

SpacePS3503.U687P 7151925, *Eine Mars Prinzessin*, Edgar Rice Burroughs, Died T Coin, Stuttgart, Germany, 1925 // First free endpaper inscription by the author, who was the creator of the Tarzan, the well-known fictional character. Note that Burroughs lived on Tarzan Ranch. Figure SpacePS3503.U687P7151925. This book was written in German, as Tarzan had a wide following.

SpaceQ123.U46Jan1960, *Soviet-Russian Scientific and Technical Terms*, Library of Congress, 1960 // Front cover verso bookplate, "Frederick Ordway III." Figure SpaceQ123.U46Jan1960. Frederick Ordway was the principal author collaborator with the German rocket scientist, Wernher von Braun, as well as writing his own books about the space program.

Figure FRSC, Old Petersburg

SpaceQ125.B32131967B, *The Hunt for German Scientists*, Michel Bar-Zohan, hawthorn Books, Inc., NY, 1967 // Title page stamp, "Washington Memorial Library, Macon, Georgia."

SpaceQ162.B62P61919, *Populäre Schriften*, Ludwig Bollzmann, Johan Ambrosius Barth, Leipzig, Germany, 1919 // Front cover verso bookplate, "Edmund Neusser." Figure SpaceQ162.B62P61919.

SpaceQA911.T51957, *Fundamentals of Hydro- and Aeromechanics*, L. Prandtl, McGraw-Hill Book Company, NY, 1934 // First free endpaper and title page cursive, "Dr. Rudolf Hermann."

Figure Space162.B62(61919

SpaceQB43A71v1, *Astronomic populaire*, Francois Arago, Gide, Editeur, Paris, 1857 // Front cover verso sticker, "1ere DIV, Bibl. Cath., Poitiers."

Figure SpaceTL793.C621960b

SpaceQB44.D561904, *Diesterweg's populäre Himmelskunde*, Dr. M. Wilhelm Meyer, Verlag von Henri Grand, Bamburg, Germany, 1904 // Title page stamp, "Library Workmen's Educational Association, New York." This book is in German, as the German language was widely used in the United States until the beginning of World War I.

SpaceQB88.P4, *Men, Mirrors, and Stars*, G. Edward Pendray, Funk & Wagnalls Company, NY, 1935 // First free endpaper inscription, "To Willy Ley, with the compliments of the Author! G. Edward Pendray, March 30, 1935."

SpaceTL545.H641907, *Die Luftschiffahrt*, Alfred Hildebrandt, Druck und Verlag von R. Oldenbourg, München, Germany, 1907 // First free endpaper stamp, "Th. Hagnauer, Amsterdam."

SpaceTL586.W41938, *Air Navigation*, Philip Van Horn Weems, McGraw Book Company, NY, 1938 // Title page punch-through stamp, "New York Public Library."

SpaceTL782.Z5, *Rockets and Jets*, Herbert S. Zim, Harcourt, Brace and Company, NY, 1945 // Front cover verso and title page stamps, "Saint Andrews School Library." There are a number of schools with this name and no clues were available to determine where this book originally resided.

SpaceTL793.C621960b, *Interplanetary Flight*, Arthur C. Clarke, L. Harper & Brothers, NY, 1960 // Front cover verso bookplate, Figure SpaceTL793.C621960b.

ArchivesM2060.D28, *Church Anthem Book* // Front cover verso stamp, "Property of Christ Church, Grosse Pointe, Choir."

ArchivesM2060.P23v1, *The Parish Choir, Volume First, 1874-1877*, Rev. Charles L. Hutchins, Medford, MA, 1877 // Front cover verso stamp, "DeLancey Divinity School, 1908." DeLancey is part of Hobart College in Geneva, New York.

ArchivesM2117.R6V51925b, *Victorious Service Songs*, Homer Rodeheaver, The Rodeheaver Company, Chicago, 1925 // First free endpaper cursive, "Presented by Mrs. Mary Studebaker Hinshaw, 637-B-N.E., Washington, D.C., to the Byler Family."

ArchivesM2117.S653N27, *The New Church Hymnal*, H. Augustine Smith, D. Appleton-Century Company, NY, 1937 // First free endpaper inscription by the author, Figure ArchivesM2117.S653N27. The cited Camp Mack is probably Camp Alexander Mack, a church camp on Lake Waubee, near Milford in northeast Indiana.

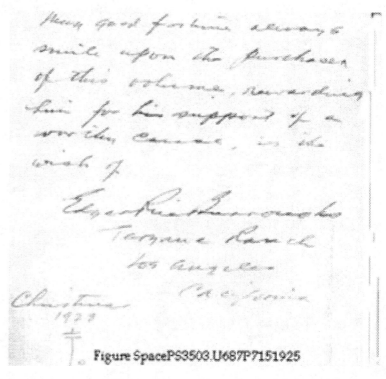

Figure SpacePS3503.U687P7151925

ArchivesM2126.L965H91941, *The Lutheran Hymnal*, Conodia Publishing House, St. Louis, MO, 1941 // Front cover verso stamp, "Grace Lutheran Church, "The Church of the Lutheran Hour," P.O. Box 695, St. Cloud, Fla 32769."

RT40.S541901, *Text Book of Nursing*, Clara S. Weeks, D. Appleton and Company, NY, 1901 // Front cover verso bookplate, "St. Louis Medical Library Association." Figure RT40.S541901.

Figure ArchivesM2117.S653N27

Rare, *A Letter to Martin Folkes, Esq.,* Jacob Ilive, York, England, 1746 // Front cover verso bookplate, "Philip Earl Stanhope." This bookplate probably belonged to the 5th Earl of Stanhope, 1805-1875, an English historian later known as Lord Mahon. He is credited with the statement, "Whatever is worth doing at all is worth doing well."

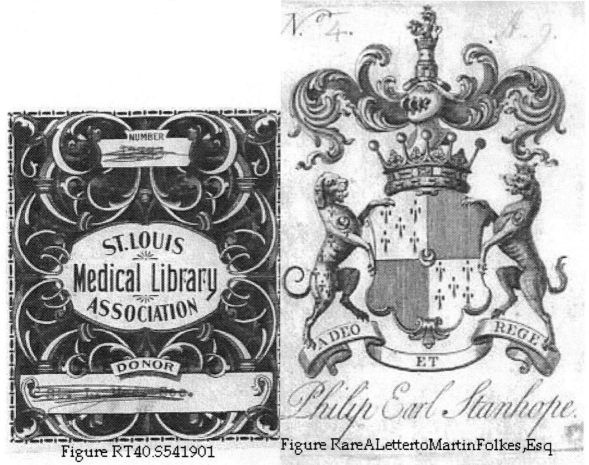

Figure RT40.S541901   Figure RareALettertoMartinFolkes,Esq